Judaism, Human Values, and the Jewish State

YESHAYAHU LEIBOWITZ

JUDAISM, HUMAN VALUES, AND THE JEWISH STATE

EDITED BY ELIEZER GOLDMAN

Translated by Eliezer Goldman and Yoram Navon, and by
Zvi Jacobson, Gershon Levi, and Raphael Levy

HARVARD UNIVERSITY PRESS
Cambridge, Massachusetts
London, England
1992

Portions of this work have been translated from *Yahadut, 'am Yehudi,
u-medinat Yisra'el* by Yeshayahu Leibowitz, copyright © 1975 by
Schocken Publishing House Ltd., Tel-Aviv, Israel, and from *Emunah,
Historyah, va-'arakhim,* by Yeshayahu Leibowitz, copyright © 1982
by Academon, The Hebrew University Students' Printing and
Publishing House (tr. by Yoram Navon). See pp. 280–282 for
specific sources.

This book is printed on acid-free paper, and its binding materials have
been chosen for strength and durability.

Library of Congress Cataloging-in-Publication Data

Leibowitz, Yeshayahu, 1903–
  [Essays. English. Selections]
  Judaism, human values, and the Jewish state / Yeshayahu Leibowitz ;
  edited by Eliezer Goldman ; translated by Eliezer Goldman, Yoram
  Navon, Zvi Jacobson, Gershon Levi, and Raphael Levy.
      p.   cm.
  Translations from Hebrew.
  Includes index.
  ISBN 0-674-48775-3
  1. Judaism.   2. Jewish law—Philosophy.   3. Judaism—Israel.
4. Religion and state—Israel.   5. Israel—Politics and government.
6. Jewish-Arab relations—Religious aspects—Judaism.   I. Goldman,
Eliezer.   II. Title
BM45.L378   1992
296—dc20   91-28563
                                                                CIP

Contents

INTRODUCTION

Eliezer Goldman

(1991)

Aptly characterized as the "conscience of Israel," Yeshayahu Leibowitz has been, since the early 1940s, perhaps the most incisive and controversial critic of Israeli culture and politics. His stance has been characteristically polemical, his criticism trenchant and caustic: government policies, the religious establishment, shibboleths of Israeli society, dominant conceptions have all been derided by him in turn. He is hard-hitting, persistent in argument, and still indefatigable in pressing his views. (At the age of 86 he thought nothing of flying to Germany to participate in a television panel on an issue close to his heart and returning the following day to Israel to meet several appointments.) Because of his highly individual views and uncompromising adherence to principles, he has never remained attached for long to a political party—although he was, at least on one occasion, instrumental in founding one. On specific issues he has small groups of ardent supporters, whom he has succeeded in goading into effective action. Quite often they disagree with him on other issues; they may even fail to follow his line of thought. Because his conclusions are often grounded in idiosyncratic considerations, he is often admired for the wrong reasons. His views on political questions meet with angry dissent and often provoke vehement reactions from the general public, but he seems to enjoy the Socratic role of the gadfly and remains undaunted by an unfavorable reception of his message.

In a tribute to Leibowitz on the occasion of his eightieth birthday, Sir Isaiah Berlin remarked: "It is not so much his intellectual attainments and achievements as a thinker and teacher that have made so profound an impression on me . . . as the unshakable moral and political stand which he took up for so many years in the face of so much pressure to be sensible, to be realistic, not to let down the side, not to give comfort to the enemy, not to fight against conventional current wisdom . . . Professor Leibowitz has never betrayed the ideals and beliefs which brought him to this country [Israel]. He was, and is, a Zionist. He holds, so I believe, that it is possible and right to create a free, democratic, tolerant, socially harmonious sovereign Jewish state, a self-governing and independent community of socially and politically equal citizens enjoying full civil liberties, free from exploitation of one body of men by another, and, above all, free from that kind of political control by the majority over minorities which we [Jews] have suffered so long and so cruelly as defenceless strangers in every land . . . Of him, I believe, it can be said more truly than of anyone else that he is the conscience of Israel: the clearest and most honorable champion of those principles which justify the creation of a movement and of a sovereign state achieved at so high a human cost both to the Jewish nation and to its neighbors."[1]

This is a just characterization of Leibowitz, the political and moral critic. Leibowitz himself does not accept this assessment. He does not deny his public activity and moral and political positions, but disclaims the motives attributed to him. Sir Isaiah considers him a humanist, but while his political stand may be consistent with the humanist position, his own reasons are entirely different. In a published letter that was both an expression of gratitude and a rejoinder to Sir Isaiah, Leibowitz wrote: "As far as I understand, humanism, in the spirit of Kant, envisages the human person as the supreme value and end within any reality which man is capable of knowing. It follows that all thought and action are to be judged and evaluated in terms of their relation to this end. From the stand-point of Judaism . . . man as a natural creature, like all of natural reality, is of neutral value. His existence can be meaningfully evaluated only in terms of his position before God as expressed in his mode of life. Judaism recognizes no expression of such a position other than the "acceptance of the yoke of the Kingdom of Heaven and the yoke of Torah and its *Mitzvoth*."[2] Leibowitz expresses his indefatigable opposition to the Israeli occupation of the territories conquered in 1967 in terms of political and religious considerations, not humanistic ones. Politically, the occupation is corrupting the state of Israel.

All its mental and physical resources are squandered on dominating the recalcitrant population of the territories. It has none left for dealing with what ought to be at the center of attention of a Jewish state. The exigencies of political and military domination are converting it into a police state with its attendant evils. Power interests of the state tend to become ends in themselves, thus giving rise to the most insidious form of idolatry in the modern world.

Leibowitz is especially concerned with the impact of this situation upon religious circles. As he sees it, the very essence of Judaism is the denial of inherent sanctity to any natural phenomenon. Only God is holy, and any sanctity in the human sphere is bound up with the divine commandments. The conquest of the territories has fanned the ever-smoldering embers of idolatrous tendencies, the overcoming of which is a constant religious challenge. One instance of idolatry, prevalent among religious Zionists today, is to ascribe inherent holiness to the land and even to the state. For Leibowitz, himself a pious Jew, this is one of the most fearful consequences of the occupation.

Biographical Note

Yeshayahu Leibowitz was born in Riga in 1903 and brought up in a home which belonged, in his words, to "a Jewish world in which Judaism and European culture were interwoven." He received his elementary education at home, where he continued his Jewish studies after entering secondary school. During the civil war in Russia in 1919, the family fled to Berlin, where Leibowitz studied chemistry and philosophy at the University of Berlin, then one of the great centers of scientific research. After receiving his doctorate in 1924, he spent several years at the Kaiser Wilhelm Institute and went on to study medicine at Köln and Heidelberg. Because of anti-Semitic discrimination in the German universities after the Nazis came to power, he took his M.D. in Basel.

In 1934 he arrived in Palestine, where he began teaching chemistry at the Hebrew University in Jerusalem. Very soon he came to be regarded as a brilliant teacher. Hundreds of students used to flock to his lectures on the physiological bases of the mental processes. His teaching extended beyond the campus to teachers' enrichment courses, adult education programs, and even youth groups. The subjects on which he lectured reflected the encyclopedic breadth of his interests. His appearances on television and radio as teacher, lecturer, and commentator on the weekly reading of the Torah have brought him to wider audiences. Many Jerusalemites recall the small study-groups that gathered regularly to study some classic text of Jewish thought under his direction. The discussion of one such group on Maimonides' introduction to his commentary on the mishnaic Tractate *Aboth* has been published. It is a sample of the give-and-take of ideas which took place at such sessions.[3] With these groups he has completed several cycles of study of the text of Maimonides' *Guide of the Perplexed*. After retirement from his academic post, he continues lecturing and conducting seminars at the university on the philosophy and history of science.

The years of intensive teaching and research did not prevent him from constant engagement with public issues. His views were rarely popular with the general public and almost never met with the approval of the relevant establishments. This never daunted him. At times he even seemed to enjoy outraging his audiences. In retrospect, he can claim much greater foresight than his antagonists. Early in the 1940s, speaking at one of the kibbutzim in the Valley of Yizra'el, then considered the exemplar of Jewish settlement in Palestine, he called the entire valley a huge cemetery—referring thereby to the extremely low birth-rate in the region at the time. His listeners considered him a crank. Today, few people would deny the critical significance of the demographic factor for the future of the Jewish state.

During the late 1930s and the 1940s Leibowitz was preoccupied with the inability of the rabbinical establishment to appreciate the halakhic implications of the Zionist effort. Political and social Jewish autonomy was bound to raise religious dilemmas.[4] Leibowitz had been active in organizing a company of religiously observant people within the Hagganah, the Jewish self-defense organization which eventually became the nucleus of the Israel Defense Force (IDF). At the time, observant Jews found it difficult to integrate directly into the Hagganah organization because their insistence on observing the Sabbath brought them into conflict with the command. However, it soon became evident that military activity, even within the ranks of the observant, raised difficult halakhic problems resulting from unprecedented situations. Rabbinic authorities tended to shy away from taking a stand. They seemed to hint that religious Jews might keep away from such matters, which could be better-handled by the nonobservant. This brought Leibowitz up against what he considered to be a parasitic tendency that boded ill for the future of the Jewish religion in a future Jewish state. For millennia, religious authorities had not been confronted with the functions of a sovereign authority. These had been in the hands of the foreign governments. It was therefore necessary to deal with questions of internal and external security and the economic needs of an all-encompassing society, as distinct from those of individuals. Much of Leibowitz's writing during this period was devoted to pointing out the need for a novel approach to halakhic decision under conditions of independent statehood. With the emergence of the state of Israel, such questions became acute.

In the 1950s and early 1960s Leibowitz took up cudgels in a variety of causes. He was active in a committee of scientists and public figures which agitated against the introduction of nuclear weaponry to the Israeli arsenal. His detestation of parasitism in any form led him to join a heterodox group fighting for a change in the economic order. During the mandatory period, political parties in Israel engaged in agricultural settlement and a variety of economic enterprises. This was especially true of the Labor party, which, through its control of the Histadruth, the general association of Jewish workers in Palestine, also directed its extensive business operations.[5] The economic effort was funded largely by the Jewish Agency. These moneys were funnelled to their destinations through the channels of the political parties. After the establishment of the state, many regarded this system as distorting the structure of the economy. But it continued, with the government as a primary source of funding. Enterprise, public and private, became increasingly dependent in this respect upon government. Political pressures could be brought to bear upon governmental departments to come to the aid of firms which were not economically viable. Appropriations which should have gone toward development of the infrastructure were doled out directly to various private and cooperative entrepreneurs, who lost any sense for the genuine profitability of their operations. Leibowitz and members of the group in question were convinced that this must lead to political corruption and foster an economy which was unable to stand on its own legs. Instead of utilizing the contributions of world Jewry and the aid of foreign governments for developing its productive resources on a firm economic basis,

Israel was squandering them on maintaining a standard of living which was beyond its own capacity. Much of the agitation of this group was conducted on the pages of the periodical *Beterem,* which published many of Leibowitz's articles on a variety of subjects. The group was successful in disclosing and ending some particular cases of corruption. It did not succeed in putting across its message and eventually disbanded. Its prognoses were only too well confirmed by recent developments of the Israeli economy. Pressure of political parties for support of favored projects has made a travesty of budgetary policy.

The Kibiyeh incident of 1953 directed Leibowitz's attention to a question which to him seemed ever more pressing.[6] The Zionist armed forces in the period antedating the state and the Israel Defense Force (IDF) in its early years had always avoided killing outside the direct context of warfare or self-defense. What change of attitude made possible the wanton killing of civilians in Kibiyeh? The motive was clear, retaliation for a series of murders by Palestinian terrorists. But what was it that removed the inhibitions to the murder of innocent civilians? Leibowitz's answer was that secular motifs and institutions had been endowed with a sanctity which is valid only within a religious context. Leibowitz finds no fault with secular Zionism as such. In fact he considers Zionism, including his own variety, as being essentially secular, with the clear limitations of secularity. Imputation of holiness to the secular, however, is religiously a form of idolatry and morally pernicious. The nation and its state acquire supreme value, and their interests are considered capable of justifying any action which promotes them.

In their time these causes seemed to interest a rather narrow public. It has been quite otherwise with the question of the occupied territories, which has divided Israeli opinion ever since 1967. For many it is an issue loaded with emotions that make clear and unbiased thinking very difficult. Leibowitz's foresight in predicting the consequences of the Israeli occupation of the West Bank and the Gaza Strip is all the more remarkable. In an article which, in slightly different versions, was published in several periodicals as early as 1968, he attempted to point out the likely effects of the occupation on Israeli society and government, as well as on its security and international status.[7] To almost all readers he seemed at the time to exaggerate matters beyond all proportion, and even today some of his contentions seem too far-fetched.

Yet from year to year more of his predictions appear to be confirmed. To ignore them requires one to be oblivious to the facts. Unfortunately, too many Israelis prefer not to have unpleasant realities brought to their attention. One consequence of the politics of occupation—which Leibowitz failed to foresee—is an unwillingness to be confronted with information which runs counter to widespread prejudices. The more reliable the coverage of the communications media, the more convinced are many people of their intention to distort.

During the Lebanese campaign of 1982–83, Leibowitz was not only active in demanding the withdrawal of troops from Lebanon, but lent his moral backing to members of the reserves who refused to serve in Lebanon and officers who resigned their posts. At the time, this refusal gathered momentum and gained considerable popular support owing to widespread public opinion favoring withdrawal from Lebanon. He still continues his support, now in the face of public opinion, for the conscientious objectors who refuse to serve in the occupied territories, especially after the Palestinian uprising of 1987. In this, his position has not met with sympathy. Even among those who share his criticism of Israel's policy in the territories, many feel that conscientious objection is unjustified. The public at large supports the official policy and favors a strong arm in dealing with the uprising. Nevertheless he continues, in private conversation and public lecture, to justify refusal to serve in the territories.

His statements rarely discuss the casuistics of conscientious objection, which seems to occupy the attention of those who deal with this issue. The concept he constantly reiterates is that no matter how important political obedience may be, the state and its politics have only instrumental functions. Their value is not absolute and their demands not always overriding. The religious person, for religious reasons, and the humanist, for moral reasons, may have decisive grounds for disobedience.

Religious-Philosophical Premises

The brief retort to Sir Isaiah Berlin's tribute should serve as a warning against abstracting Leibowitz's views on current political issues from the broader context of his thought. Theological considerations entered even into his opinions on so distinctly political an issue as that of the occupied territories. His enduring importance as a contemporary Jewish thinker is associated with his radical theological conceptions and their implications for Judaism and Jewish nationhood. These, in turn, must be understood against a background of philosophic premises.

Human knowledge. Two distinct traditions affect Leibowitz's conception of the nature and limitations of knowledge. The first is the theology of Maimonides, with its emphasis on the absolute transcendence of God, who cannot be conceived by the human mind. He can be known only through his works, that is to say, through the natural order of things. The second tradition stems from the Kantian critique of theoretical reason and supplies an epistemological underpinning for this agnostic type of theology, but also radicalizes it. The domain of knowledge is restricted to that which can be a datum for experience. Not only must the transcendent remain unknown, but even its existence cannot be demonstrated. Critics of Leibowitz have taken this theological agnosticism for atheism without realizing that it is but a working out of the implications of a theology which, like that of Maimonides, insists on the total transcendence of the divine.

Knowledge, in the proper sense of the word, is the result of the application of the scientific method. This is the only way we have of obtaining reliable information about natural reality. But if reality is understood in terms of a system of functional relations, as it is by those utilizing this method, and not as a system of ends and materials, as it was in ancient and medieval times, the natural world is religiously indifferent. Hence it is absurd to regard revelation as a surrogate or supplement for natural knowledge. Whatever relation may exist between man and God must be of a normative character.

Radical decision. Leibowitz accepts Kant's dichotomy of factual and normative, but his interpretation of this dichotomy is more along positivistic lines. His discussion of the subject calls to mind Max Weber's. Ultimately, all normative obligations and value-imputations are dependent upon personal decision. A valuation may, of course, be justified in terms of already recognized values, but one's ultimate values cannot be validated by anything beyond them. They cannot be the subject of rational argument. Their validity for a person results from decision, not from recognition. Since Leibowitz regards religion as an exclusively normative domain and denies that Scripture was intended to be a body of information, this is as true of religious commitment as it is of all other basic life-values. Factual knowledge may be forced upon us by experience. There is nothing to compel one into acceptance of any ultimate value-commitments, including that of religious faith.

This leads to a curious dialectic of autonomy and heteronomy. The religious value of an act consists in its being performed because it is a divine command. Yet the very idea of a divine commandment and acceptance of any specific system of norms as a body of divine prescriptions can only follow from an autonomous decision. The very ascription of normative force to a divine command is a matter for decision. Like many other weighty decisions, this one may be tacit rather than explicit. In the typical case, one is committed to halakhic practice as a result of socialization. Only in situations in which it cannot be taken for granted need the decision enter one's awareness. The tradition presents the decision to accept the Halakhah as a unique historical event which committed the future generations of Israel. However, if we follow out the logic of Leibowitz's position, it would appear that recognition of the validity of this commitment requires constant renewal of the basic decision. The heteronomous force of the Torah and its Mitzvoth is dependent upon continued autonomous commitment (either explicit or tacit) on both communal and personal level.

Decision is not merely a condition for entertaining value; it is constitutive of value. Only what is freely chosen—a goal to which one aspires or a property one seeks to embody in reality—is, properly speaking, a value. In Leibowitz's opinion, a need cannot possibly be a value since it is given, not chosen. Freedom of choice is not a value in its own right, but a condition of all valuation. It is something imposed, part of the human condition, not an end in itself. Autonomy does not commit one to any specified norms, not even to "the Moral Law." Hence there is nothing contradictory about the idea of autonomous commitment to a heteronomous system of rules.[8]

Religion and morality. Few of the author's contentions have been as confusing to his readers and audiences as the often reiterated statement that morality is an atheistic category. If so, how to account for the moral criticism to which much of his writings is devoted? To a certain extent, such statements may be attributed to his penchant for shocking formulations. It may reflect Leibowitz's failure to organize his ethical theorizing systematically. However, careful study of the contexts in which morality and religion are presented as conflicting should make

Leibowitz's position more plausible. He is not claiming that a religious person cannot be a moral agent. At no point does he maintain that religious demands upon the person or the community are total in the sense of all-inclusive. On many matters the Halakhah is silent. At such points, moral considerations may very well come into play and ought to govern one's actions. The immorality of a religious person under such circumstances may even reflect upon his religiosity and constitute what is called *Hillul Hashem,* desecration of God's name.

Leibowitz does insist that a person acting as a moral agent cannot be acting as a religious agent and that a religious action cannot be simultaneously a moral action. This is a corollary of his view that human actions, as contrasted with natural events, can only be identified in terms of the agent's intention. The morality of an action is determined not by its consequences (though these enter into moral deliberation) but by the agent's intention to perform his duty. The religious character of an action is determined by the motive of worshipful service of God. The same external act may on one occasion be moral and on another religious, depending upon the agent's motivation. The idea of a religious duty to act morally when this seems to be required would not be a contradiction of Leibowitz's basic position, even if it may not be consonant with some of his formulations. A moral act done out of respect for religious duty would be a religious act. The person's proximate motive would be moral, but his ultimate motive religious. The intrinsic ultimacy of the religious motive is the point Leibowitz is trying to bring out.

Ends and means. Leibowitz makes a sharp distinction, drawn by Maimonides and reflecting Aristotelian influence, between ends-in-themselves and secondary ends, which are ends for us only because they subserve some further end. The original context of this distinction was a teleological concept of nature according to which things had their natural ends. As used by Leibowitz, without any reference to such a context, the distinction is rather similar to the familiar classification of values as intrinsic and instrumental. Yet there is a difference. Though there is no natural hierarchy of ends, some ends, once recognized, must be taken as ultimate. They are incapable of being validated by reference to further ends. But Leibowitz goes further. He adopts two crucial doctrines of Maimonides on this matter: first, the religious end is not only an end-in-itself but is *the* ultimate end; second, an ultimate end is desecrated when it is made to serve as a means to some other end.

What is the religious end? For Leibowitz it is worshipful service of God, or halakhic praxis. It could not affect God, and bears no comparison with ordinary human values. The religious practitioner will divorce his religious action from any hope for reward or fear of punishment other than the status before God achieved in living the life of Halakhah. This is a religious contention, not a sociological one. One need not deny the functionality of religious practices for social solidarity or their role in preserving the national identity of Jews. But these are empirical questions that are religiously irrelevant. To attempt to justify adherence to Mitzvoth by its consequences, whether for society, nation, or individual, is to take up a secular point of view which does not recognize the primacy and ultimacy of the worshipful service of God. Religiously, this is an inversion of the scale of values.

Jewish Faith

The thesis that Jewish faith is basically the commitment to observance of the Halakhah as worshipful service of God has a polemical thrust. Among others, it is directed against Reform Judaism, which regards the Halakhah as a husk hiding the essential core of religion. Some take it to be morality, others a set of metaphysical beliefs, or even the inner religious experience of the individual. On Leibowitz's premises, none of these would be of distinctly religious significance. However, one cannot argue effectively with people who reject these premises. Leibowitz, therefore, conducts his argument at the historical level.

Given the long history of the Jewish religion, the varying circumstances in which its adherents lived, the movements of Jewish thought in the course of Jewish history, and the diverse life styles of Jews in different epochs, what is it that fixed the identity of Judaism over the ages? Leibowitz's answer is: the religious practice determined by the Halakhah. No other facet of Jewish religion had its continuity and relative invariance. Jewish theologies were so diverse and so dependent upon the variant philosophic assumptions of different schools and different ages that they can hardly be said to present a significant unity. Inner religious experience varies from individual to individual. Leibowitz seems to feel that it cannot be communicated.[9] One cannot ignore the fact that the Jewish religion was practiced by a collective, and that this practice had a highly institutionalized structure. Systems of belief and personal religious experience can hardly account for the unity of the institutions of Jewish religion. Furthermore, at any given point in time, it is the life of Halakhah that distinguishes the Jewish religion from others. Even its monotheism cannot be said to constitute its identity *vis-à-vis* Islam or Christianity. Islamic monotheism does not differ from that of Judaism. As for Christian Trinitarianism, one need only recall that Kabbalists were accused by their opponents of belief in a decimalian deity. Historically, what definitively severed Christianity from Judaism was its rejection of "the Law."

To understand the meaning of the halakhic way of life is to understand Jewish religion. It is a method of orienting one's day-by-day existence by the sense of one's standing before God, which can be expressed only in worshipful action. To live with such an orientation involves a normatively significant decision. This is the basis act of faith: "Acceptance of the yoke of the Kingdom of Heaven and the yoke of the Mitzvoth," in the idiom of the rabbinic Sages.

To what end?

The very question reflects a misunderstanding of the religious attitude best summed up in the words of the psalmist: "Whom have I in heaven (but you) and there is none upon earth I desire but You . . . But for me to draw near to God is good" (Ps. 73:25, 28). To stand before God is the ultimate good, which is to be pursued only for its own sake. But how does one draw near the absolutely transcendent? By observing His Mitzvoth for the sole reason that in so doing we are worshipping Him. The rabbis denote such motivation by the word *lishmah* (for its own sake) and distinguish him who serves God lishmah from him who serves not-lishmah, that is, for some ulterior good. One who serves God lishmah sets aside all consideration of advantages which may accrue from so doing or of loss from failing to do so. In the talmudic literature this is a distinction of rank, of different levels of religiosity.

Two men of faith are paradigmatic for Leibowitz. The first was Abraham, who was ready to sacrifice what was humanly most valuable for the sake of God. The other is Maimonides, for whom being motivated *lishmah* was of the essence of religiosity. This follows from his view that an ultimate end is desecrated by being utilized as a means. It is no mere theoretical opinion. It is applied halakhically in his strict prohibition of studying Torah at the public expense or receiving remuneration for teaching it. Expectations of reward and punishment trivialize the religious act, which is the highest attainment of which man is capable. Halakhah is religious practice in the present; the religion of man in his natural condition. Religion does not bring about a radical change in the human condition. This is a denial of the concept of salvation as it is understood by Christians. The religious condition of man, as contrasted with his technological or cognitive attainment, remains constant. Although any individual, or the community as a whole, may advance their level of adherence to the norms of religious observance, their basic religious status does not change. A recurrent simile for the religious condition is the figure of the housewife, persisting in her work which begins ever anew. There is no further goal beyond that of living a halakhic life geared to the service of God. The religious life is a ceaseless cyclical process. Messianic expectations have no genuinely religious significance. At best, the messianic idea represents an ever receding goal. At worst, as anticipation of a nearby redemption, it disrupts the religious life of the community. In historically typical instances, it has led to apostasy.

What then can be meant by "Jewish faith" if it is neither a set of beliefs nor a body of expectations? Leibowitz's answer probably sounds more plausible in Hebrew than in English, since the word *Emunah,* by which the equivalents of the Greek *pistis* are usually translated, means, in its biblical usage and in most of its talmudic occurrences, "steadfastness," "dependability," or "righteousness." Jewish faith consists in the steadfast commitment to the life of religious observance, to the halakhic service of God. Since the inner religious experience, according to Leibowitz, varies from person to person, the inner awareness accompanying such commitment will also vary, and, as a matter of fact, always was differently perceived by different individuals and different groups. For a life of halakhic practice to be religiously meaningful, it must be motivated by the intention to worship God. It may have no ulterior motive. This does not mean that every halakhic act at the moment of performance must be accompanied by a subjective intention. It does imply that one's life of halakhic observance as a whole be intentionally directed to the service of God. It involves some awareness, however vague, of living in the presence of the wholly transcendent God, an evaluation of this as of the utmost importance, and acceptance of the Torah as the divinely ordained, though humanly interpreted, way of living "before" God.

Purity of faith is most likely to come to those who recognize the natural world as governed by functional relations which are indifferent to man's hopes and aspirations, and who do not interpret the religious idea of Providence as a kind of divine interference with the order of nature. In our religious observance, our intentions transcend any natural interest. This great conception means that the concern of the truly religious person is not with the relation of God to man but with the relation of man to God.

Jewish Peoplehood

For centuries the Jews existed as a people apart without any of the attributes which nineteenth-century nationalist ideology regarded as the marks of nationhood: language, territory, state, and so on. Yet they themselves, as well as the peoples among whom they lived, never doubted their identity as a nation. That this national identity was determined by their religion was never questioned. Only late in the eighteenth century, in the emerging European nation-states and with the urge of emancipation, did the nature of this identity become problematic for those Jews who rejected the alternative of complete assimilation. Those who wanted to keep their religion and at the same time merge with their host-nations attempted to separate religion from nationality and retain their religious identity in some form, while relinquishing their Jewish nationality. The wave of secularization, which spread even to Jews who wished to retain their Jewish identity, raised new questions and new programs for Jewish existence. Zionism has proved to be the most viable of these.

Mainstream Zionism set itself the goal of achieving "normalization" of Jewish national existence, by acquiring for it the features which nineteenth-century theory considered characteristic of nationality. Return to the historic land of Israel, revival of Hebrew as a spoken language, and creation of the state of Israel were realizations of this program. Since a common culture was considered to be an important aspect of national life, an attempt was made to reinterpret the literary sources and the traditional symbols so as to make them appear elements of a national culture which were not essentially religious. The Halakhah was represented as a product of life in Exile. Jewish religion was accorded an historic function as having preserved Jewish life under conditions of exile. With the reconstitution of normal Jewish life in the homeland, it became otiose.

Leibowitz strongly derides the idea of a secular Jewish identity. As a matter of empirical fact, the identity of the Jewish people over the ages has consisted in adherence to the religion of Halakhah. Moreover, the very idea of "normalization" is questionable. No particular set of properties is definitive of nationality. Different factors have determined the nationhood of different peoples. Whatever, in fact, makes for the national solidarity of a people may be taken as the essential constituent of its nationhood. In every instance, this will be a matter of subjective consciousness. As Leibowitz puts it, a nation is a being of the mind. A group's self-perception as a nation makes it a nation, and the attributes it perceives as identifying its nationality are what constitutes its nationhood. In the case of Israel that attribute has been its religious praxis. Given Leibowitz's conception of the supremacy of religious commitment over all over values, it follows that evaluating the Jewish religion in terms of its contribution to Jewish survival is an egregious distortion of the value-scale. Such a contribution may be a historic fact, but that does not make Jewish survival the end of Halakhah. Commitment to Halakhah is the *constitutive* factor in Jewish nationality; it confers the special significance upon the existence of the Jewish people. To impute the value of halakhic religion to its function in providing for the national survival is sheer idolatry—worship of the nation.

The creed of secularized Jewish nationalism is not the only current form of idolatry. A type of religious nationalism which has gained popularity in recent years fosters a more insidious idolatry: imputing an immanent sanctity to Israel, to the land of Israel, and to the state. In one sense, it is true, holiness may be predicated of things human or mundane, namely, as being assigned a special halakhic status or as heightening the religious commitment. To attribute holiness to a people because of a hereditary strain of which they are (absurdly) considered the carriers, to a state because it is the state of that people, or to a piece of land because it is their land, independently of any halakhic norms applying to it, is mere fetishism. People, land, or state may, of course, be held precious and valuable. But in attributing to them, as intrinsic, the specifically religious value of holiness, one is setting up a false God. The consequences of such attribution are likely to be morally vicious; even more so than those of the secular idolatry. Such religious nationalism leads to the overriding of moral considerations by political interest, subordination of regard for humanity to irredentist aspirations, and complete disregard for the claims of others when they conflict with those of the sacred people.

Leibowitz is critical of the attempts to base Jewish nationalism on a specific Jewish culture which is severed from Jewish religion. In divorcing elements of Jewish culture from their religious matrix, we deprive them of any significance. Compared to parallel cultural contributions of others, their value is negligible. This is not to deny that some elements of culture are distinctively Jewish. However, insofar as they are authentically Jewish, they derive their meanings from the religious context in which they originated. Apart from this context, the cultural achievements of Jews have been either universal in import, or contributions to the culture of the societies within which they were active. The antecedents of such cultural creativity are non-Jewish, even when the Jewish writers and artists draw on their personal experience as Jews.

Religion, State, and Society

Many believe that Leibowitz's views on the relation of religion, state, and society have undergone great changes. Some go so far as to refer to the early Leibowitz and the later Leibowitz. They find a serious discrepancy between the earlier emphasis on adapting the Halakhah to conditions of political independence and the later call for separation of state and religion; between the initial concern with the religious significance of the state and the eventual insistence upon the secular character of the state. This assessment neglects some conceptual distinctions as well as the implications which developments in Israeli society and polity have had for Leibowitz.

In maintaining that the state, by its very nature, is a secular institution, he is applying his criterion of motivation. Has it been instituted, and does it continue to be maintained, as worshipful service of God or does it have another end in view? The very functions of the state indicate its secular nature. This does not preclude the possibility that the Halakhah is intended to govern the political life no less than that of the individual: many halakhic prescriptions appear to be intended for regulation of the polity. In the 1920s and 1930s many religious settlers considered the Torah as practiced in exile to be a truncated Torah, because it could not be applied to the political life of the community of Israel. Realization of the Torah in its full scope became a major goal of their Zionism. The state was still a dream. The tightly knit and well-disciplined quasi-political organization of the Yishuv (pre-state Jewish community) was conducted on a voluntary basis. The social as well as geographical space was sufficiently wide to permit each of various sectors of the Yishuv to try to realize its own utopia. The society was to be built up from scratch. In this situation religious pioneers established tightly organized model communities, guided by the Halakhah in conducting modern economic and social activities, even in providing for their defense against marauders. These they considered pilot plants to test and develop ways of application of Halakhah to the life of a politically independent Jewish society. Their experiment paralleled the project of the Labor wing of the Zionist movement to create nuclei of a socialist society. Leibowitz's positions on the public issues of the time were oriented to this voluntaristic configuration.

One question of both theoretical and practical significance was how the Halakhah would be applied in an autarchic religious community, all members of which were Torah-observant. Leibowitz and like-minded people insisted that any responsible halakhic instruction had to cover all citizens. Yet nation-wide observance of the Halakhah as it has come down through the ages could be disastrous. For instance, exemption of religious personnel engaged in police or security activities involving desecration of the Sabbath might be feasible, but total abstention from all such activity on the Sabbath could well be calamitous. The dilemma for the religious leadership was whether to continue in religious isolation or to work out new halakhic solutions to these and other problems of statehood.

The official rabbinate in the late thirties did not meet this challenge. It failed to come to grips with the problems; there was a good deal of evasion. At times, the implication seemed to be that the observant should avoid problematic situations and leave them to the nonobservant. Most rabbis avoided taking a stand on Sabbath observance as it conflicted with defense activity, and hinted that these matters might be left to others who were not troubled by questions of Sabbath observance. In answer to farmers confronted with difficult problems of halakhic observance, some rabbis suggested they might avoid such problems if they were to engage in commerce rather than agriculture. Leibowitz felt that this was to make halakhic observance by religious Jews parasitic upon the nonobservance of the secular. On such a basis, halakhic observance by the totality of the community was impossible. This conflicted with the conception of Halakhah as intended for realization by the whole Jewish community.

With his penchant for defining issues in the sharpest form, Leibowitz posed the question: Was the Halakhah capable of prescribing forms of life for a politically independent community of Jews committed to its observance? His own answer was that, because halakhic life had been conducted for so long under conditions of political subservience and depended upon socioeconomic structures over which Jews had no control, such dependence had become a basic assumption of halakhic observance. The potentially applicable principles of the Halakhah required restatement. However, the mentality of the halakhic authorities was so conditioned by the context of life in exile that they were unable to adjust their thinking to the demands of new circumstances. The required shape of halakhic observance would have to be developed by the practice of the general community of those faithful to the Torah.

Another kind of question seemed no less pressing: was religion relevant to the solution of the grave social problems of the time? In the 1920s and 1930s this question was troubling young religious Jews the world over, in Palestine, Poland, Germany, even in the United States, just as it was troubling Christian thinkers such as Paul Tillich in Germany, Leonhardt Ragaz in Switzerland, and Reinhold Niebuhr in the United States. In the Jewish formulation, if the Torah is truly an encompassing way of life for the people of Israel, surely it must offer some guidance with respect to the social and political order.

In the Diaspora individual Jews could voice opinions, participate actively in political movements, and be politically committed in their literary and artistic activities. In a Jewish commonwealth, however, they would have to participate actively in shaping the social and political order of a Jewish polity. What did halakhic Judaism have to say as to the nature of the sociopolitical system? One might have expected the religious leadership of rabbis and scholars to address this issue. For the most part, however, this community tended to oppose Zionism to the point of regarding it as religiously illegitimate. Even those who were sympathetic to the project of reconstituting Jewish national independence were not too well versed in the issues of the time and hardly understood what was wanted of them. The matter was taken up by the religious workers and by members of the religious youth movements.

The typical apologetic response was that, after all, a body of Jewish civil law operated for hundreds of years in the Diaspora wherever, as was usually the case, the Jewish community possessed legal autonomy. Principles of administration and political structure might be culled from talmudic sources, which Maimonides codified as late as the twelfth century. Leibowitz was not alone in pointing out that this could not answer the need of the hour. A civil code does not institute a social order; it regulates transactions within it. The supposedly relevant Halakhah was adapted to a technological and social milieu quite different from ours.

Another common suggestion was to have recourse to general principles of justice and equity. This idea was justified by various authoritative rabbinic pronouncements to the effect that the formality of halakhic law required supplementation by ethical guidance. Leibowitz pointed out, however, that the ethical guidelines were applicable to a variety of social orders. Even in a system based on slavery, relations between master and slave could reflect higher or lower standards of justice. What is called for is halakhic legislation. Again, free decision is unavoidable. We could only try to surmise what kind of sociopolitical order, given the circumstances of our time, would be most consonant with what appears to us to be the intention of the Torah. In view of the relative alienation of the community of rabbinic scholars from the contemporary world, this must be undertaken by the general community of Torah observers on the basis of their understanding of the implications of the broad aims of Halakhah for our times.

The foundation of the state of Israel brought about complex changes, with implications that were barely perceived by the intellectual and political leadership of religious Jewry in Israel. Within the Zionist Organization and the administrative and political institutions of the Yishuv under the mandatory regime, a *modus vivendi* had been attained in religious matters. This resulted partly from the need for voluntary cooperation between the religious and secular sectors in the Zionist Organization, but more considerably from the mandatory power's having taken over many of the provisions governing religious minorities under Ottoman rule. The local Jewish communities, all of them composed of voluntary participants, were empowered to tax members for the maintenance of schools. Such community-supported schools might be religious or affiliated with one of the existing secular educational systems. The local communities were united in an overall organization called Knesseth Israel, which *de facto* constituted the political organization of the Yishuv. All members of Knesseth Israel were subject to the rabbinic courts, which had jurisdiction in matters of personal status and were supported by the local communities who were empowered to levy taxes for this purpose.[10] The Chief Rabbinate was established as the highest rabbinic instance, and the Great Rabbinic Court was a rabbinic court of appeals. The *modus vivendi* in question also included a modicum of religious observance to be maintained in the public sphere and by enterprises conducted by the Zionist Organization. The Sabbath was the recognized day of rest. In Jewish townships such as Tel-Aviv places of business were closed down on the Sabbath, and public transportation suspended.

The transformations under the state of Israel did not so much change the substantive nature of the *modus vivendi* as modify the institutional structure of the religious establishment. The rabbinic courts, which had previously functioned within the framework of a voluntarily organized community, became official judicial organs of the state. Their jurisdiction, which had been limited to members of that community, was now extended to all Jewish residents of Israel. Moreover, the Halakhah was established as the only law applying to marriage and divorce among Jews in Israel.[11] The Sabbath became the legal day of rest, with Friday an option for Moslems and Sunday for Christians. The state funded and supervised two school systems, one of secular and one of religious schools. A Ministry of Religious Affairs was set up to take care of religious needs. In fact, principles of the welfare state were applied to religious matters. The government subsidized religious services, building of synagogues, mosques, and churches. Salaries of religious functionaries were paid by the state or the municipalities. A vast body of vested interests developed within the religious establishment, dependent on the government apparatus and part of it.

Under these circumstances, it is no wonder that various religious groups—even those that had previously opposed Zionism and, in a sense, continued to consider the state religiously illegitimate—came to regard government as a constant source of fiscal benefits. Religious parties tended to become pressure groups for the interests of a variety of religious organizations and institutions.

The deeper problems following the transition from the voluntarily organized society of the mandatory period to statehood may be illustrated by two incidents which occurred in the early fifties. The first of these was the debate over the constitution. The first Knesseth (legislative body) was elected as a constituent assembly empowered to adopt a constitution. In accordance with European political tradition, most participants felt that the constitution ought, first of all, to be declaratory of the principles on which the state was to be conducted. The various parties strove to have their ideologies incorporated into the constitution. Only a handful of participants in these debates appreciated that the chief purpose of a constitution was to create the framework of a polity within which groups committed to clashing ideologies might be able to work together. All the religious parties opposed a constitution, some for opportunistic reasons—fear that it would severely restrict introducing halakhic principles into the law of the land—others on grounds of principle. The latter argued that the people of Israel already had a binding constitution, the Torah, and the adoption of any other constitution by the state of Israel would be an abrogation of the authentic constitution of Israel. These debates were replete with conceptual confusion. Many failed to appreciate the function of basic law in a pluralistic society. As Leibowitz held in other contexts, the community organized in the state of Israel ought to be the forum where basic issues of Jewish identity and of the norms of Jewish life would be fought out. It was not the function of the state to decide such matters.[12]

The other affair illustrative of the problems of statehood had to do with the education of children in the transition camps for new immigrants and later in their settlements. In the fifties massive immigration came to Israel from the Moslem countries. The vast majority of immigrant families were from a traditionally religious milieu. The parents were not yet used to their new surroundings. Without many qualms, the officials responsible for immigrant absorption set up secular schools in the transition camps and later in a good many of the villages in which these immigrants settled. At the time Leibowitz was a member of the executive committee of the Histadruth (General Federation of Jewish Workers), and he endeavored to convince his colleagues that this required rectification. He was dismayed by the utter disregard for the traditional religious background of the new immigrants. In his estimation, power considerations made it politically convenient to alienate them from their tradition. He was impressed by the etatism of David Ben Gurion, who would have the life of the nation center about the state and regarded religion, especially deep religious concern with the manner in which the state was conducted, as a nuisance.

The Kibiyeh incident of 1953 seems to have marked a turning point in Leibowitz's political thought.[13] It showed him that the state had become virtually an object of worship and, as a result, *raison d'état* would be a likely excuse for knavery of all kinds. In this situation, the task confronting religious Jewry was to constitute a bulwark against deification of the state and to conduct a struggle within the state over the religious national identity of the people of Israel. This did not imply that the demand for restatement of Halakhah so as to offer viable guidance to the conduct of the state was no longer valid, but its urgency was diminished by the need of the struggle over the substance of Jewish peoplehood. The battle was thwarted, however, by the status of the religious establishment as part of the machinery of the state, which prevented it from acting as a countervailing force within the community. Its efforts were spent in protecting narrow sectional interests. Problems of the Jewish people as the bearers of Judaism were beyond their concern. But precisely these problems were of the utmost importance. It was perhaps the supreme function of the state of Israel, as a Jewish state, to supply a framework in which the struggle over the identity of the Jewish people could be conducted. Integration of the religious establishment in the political structure tied its hands and limited its motivation. Concern with official status, fiscal benefits, and political influence made it vulnerable to corruption. In the interest of the integrity of Jewish religion, separation of religion and state now appeared to be a desideratum.

Zionism, the Arabs, and the Occupied Territories

The Arab-Jewish conflict, in Leibowitz's view, results from the clash of rival national aspirations. Both parties consider Palestine their homeland, each for good historic reasons. Neither is willing to live under the other's rule. One can hardly envisage a solution which would be entirely satisfactory to both sides. Thus Leibowitz is pessimistic about the prospects of resolving the conflict within the foreseeable future. Even if a settlement is reached, it is hardly likely to be a durable peace like that which obtains today between neighboring nations in Western Europe.

To construe the issue as one of conflicting *rights* is confusing and misleading. Talk of a right to a piece of property or a territory implies the existence of legal norms which confer the right, and of machinery for enforcing valid claims to such a right. Such rights pertain only to persons or to corporate bodies recognized as persons by law.[14] They do not apply to collectives as such. Zionism was never a violation of Arab "rights" to Palestine, though it came into conflict with the national aspirations of the Palestinians. Equally, the historic ties of the Jewish people to the land of Israel do not confer rights of sovereignty over the territory.

Partition appeared to be a feasible solution. As a matter of historic fact, the resolution of the United Nations was accepted by the Zionists but rejected by the Arabs, who attempted to thwart its realization by military action. Partition would not have satisfied the territorial aspirations of either Jews or Arabs, but it would have granted the Palestinians political independence just as it offered Jews the opportunity to establish the state of Israel. The current attempt to coerce the Arabs of the Gaza Strip and the West Bank into submission to Israeli rule can only lead to a permanent struggle for their independence. The adversaries, like all who undertook such struggles in the post-World War II era, will not be squeamish about the means employed. Another all-out war between Israel and the Arab states is likely. Hence repartitioning the land of Israel between Jews and Arabs is a *necessary* condition for peace, even though not a sufficient one.

In his assessment of the situation shortly after the war of 1967, Leibowitz exhibited remarkable foresight. He predicted that after a few years of occupation not a Jewish worker or a Jewish farmer would be left. The Arabs would be the working people and the Jews the administrators, inspectors, and officials. A state ruling a hostile population of a probable two million foreigners would necessarily become a police state with all this implies for education, free speech, and democratic institutions. The corruption characteristic of every colonial regime would also infect the state of Israel. The administration would have to suppress Arab insurgency on the one hand and acquire Arab Quislings on the other. Leibowitz found good reasons to fear that the Israel Defense Force, which had been a people's army, would degenerate as a result of being transformed into an army of occupation, and its commanders, who will have become military rulers, will resemble their colleagues in other nations. Twenty-one years later, in an overview of the state of the nation after forty years of political independence, Leibowitz could ruefully indicate that if his prognosis had not yet been confirmed in all its details by actual developments, its realization was close.

His gravest apprehensions concern the survival of Israel as a *Jewish* state. Unlike many other Zionists and especially religious Zionists, Leibowitz clearly discerns the implications of the modern state's territorial principle. A state can bear a national character by virtue of either of two factors. It may have a strong indigenous national culture to which newcomers tend to assimilate. This is obviously not the case in Israel, where the Arabs are not newcomers and have no wish to assimilate. Or the state may reflect the characteristics of the demographically predominant nationality. This indeed was the case in Israel before 1967. It would obviously no longer be so if Israel were to annex the occupied territories.

Even now, however, Israeli presence in Gaza and the West Bank undermines the capacity of Israel to fulfill the role of a Jewish state. In Leibowitz's view the Jewishness of the state could only consist in its concern with the problems of the Jewish people, both in the land of Israel and in the Diaspora. A state constantly engaged in suppressing potential or actual insurgency is focused on considerations of power which consume its material and organizational resources and distort its spiritual perspective. Most disturbing for Leibowitz himself is the debasement of religion by its use as a rationalization for vicious chauvinism and fetishistic irredentism.

Leibowitz is pessimistic about the prospects of genuine peace. Awaiting the agreement of the Palestinians to what the Israelis consider acceptable terms would result in its indefinite postponement. A continuing *status quo* will lead to progressive corruption of Israeli society, alienation of Jews in the Diaspora, and, in all likelihood, to out-and-out, possibly catastrophic warfare against a broad coalition of Arab countries. Meanwhile the military balance is shifting in favor of the Arabs, and continued occupation of the territories by Israel results in the constant deterioration of its standing in the international community.

This evaluation points to unilateral withdrawal of Israel from the occupied territories as the way to extricate Israel from the morass of occupation. As early as 1968, Leibowitz was arguing that the strategic benefits of occupying the territories have been exaggerated and that the occupation has, in fact, strategic disadvantages: the need to quell internal belligerence while facing the enemy across the borders. Only recently has his position come to be accepted by growing numbers of military experts.

Though many would agree with Leibowitz's diagnoses, few are ready to accept his proposal for a one-sided withdrawal. A common rejoinder is that withdrawal may be desirable, but is feasible only if certain safeguards are guaranteed. These require some kind of preliminary agreement between the adversaries. Certain questions, such as control of the water sources, which are not pressing at the moment, would constitute a *casus belli* if not settled prior to withdrawal. Furthermore, while such a withdrawal may have been possible in the early years of the occupation, today the vested material and ideological interests are so strong that it might be well-nigh impossible to implement such a policy even if the Knesseth and government were to adopt it. Leibowitz himself seems to feel that only strong external pressure of the powers, as in 1956 and again in 1973, could bring about some form of agreement.

Christianity

Leibowitz's view of Christianity as a form of paganism is not new. One can adduce good halakhic authority for such an evaluation, in particular that of Maimonides, just as it is possible to cite halakhic opinion to the contrary. However, his image of Christianity as the great historic adversary of Judaism, not merely its competitor, follows from his conception of the halakhic life as the essence of Judaism. If, as he believes, the founding documents of Christianity are the Pauline epistles rather than the Gospels, then Christianity originated with the abrogation of "the Law," in other words, with the negation of Judaism. He goes so far as to argue that in no true sense can Christianity be regarded as an offspring of Judaism. It originated in an entirely different spiritual milieu and the supposed ties with Judaism merely follow from the origin myth. But this myth had far-reaching effects. The caustic historic antagonism between Christianity and Judaism results from the claim of Christianity that it is the legitimate heir of Judaism. As Leibowitz puts it, the heir cannot admit that the testator is still alive. The very existence of Judaism is a scandal from this standpoint.

Leibowitz is not conducting a polemic against Christianity as a religion. Had the Marcionite heresy gained the upper hand and the Church repudiated the Hebrew Bible, coexistence of the two religions would not have involved the tremendous tension that has always characterized their relations. They would have been two separate and very different religions each going its own way. The stresses exist because Christianity claims to offer the true interpretation of the Hebrew Bible, and the Church contends it is the true Israel. Not only do Jews deny this claim, but the very survival of Judaism as practiced by Jews tends to refute it. It is a veritable stumbling-block. This *ressentiment* toward Judaism is deep enough to affect the thought even of the great Christian theologian Karl Barth, who certainly cannot be accused of anti-Semitism in the ordinary sense. A felt antipathy to Judaism is shared by many intellectuals, who can hardly be accounted Christian by faith but have absorbed the attitude from the Christian tradition.

The real butt of Leibowitz's polemic are what he calls Christianizing Jews, proponents of a liberal Judaism that would divorce their religion from the halakhic tradition. In his opinion, a Jew true to the spirit of Halakhah could have no interest in the Judeo-Christian dialogue which these representatives of liberal Judaism are keen on promoting. Such a dialogue is possible only between Jews who have become de-Judaized and Christians who have become de-Christianized. He is careful to note that his words apply to coexistence between Judaism and Christianity, not to coexistence and mutual communication between Jews and Christians outside the concerns of religion.

The discussion of "Hochhut's error" is an interesting projection of Leibowitz's tendency to carry an argument to its logical conclusions. This is certainly an *intellectual* virtue. But do people act under the guidance of such logic? As depicted in this discussion, the line of thought of Pius XII was as follows: Christian faith demands the annihilation of Judaism, not, of course, of Jews. But almost two thousand years of history indicate that, so long as Jews exist as a people, Judaism will not disappear. The Church would never initiate an extermination of Jews, but if another agent was doing this, the Church would not intervene to prevent an action which would bring about a result so desirable from its standpoint. *If* this was Pius's line of thought, it would explain his action, or rather inaction. But was this really his line of thought? And if it was, was it certain that he was prepared to carry it out?

The Leibowitzian Pathos

To the public, Leibowitz appears as the cold intellectual, oblivious of the deep emotional overtones of the issues he takes up, disregarding the nonrational elements of human situations. It is easy to see what promotes such an impression. Speaking from his extreme halakhic position, he dismisses the feeling-contents of the religious experience and the aspirations to salvation as peripheral, even misleading. He represents the ideal type of the Lithuanian *misnagued,* the opponent of the Hassidic "enthusiast," engrossed in the study of Torah and its application in life. His conception of halakhic religion as belonging to the "prose" of man's every day natural life and the disparagement of the religiosity of moments of uplift seem to confirm this picture. So do his affirmation of the life of halakhic praxis as itself the ultimate religious end and his denial of the religious value of the aspirations often associated with religion.

Most annoying to many is his capacity for thinking politically about politics: the ability to detach himself from the immediate emotional impact of the data, to take into consideration their practical implications for all affected, to assess policies from a long-range point of view. His readiness to attack "national policy" is taken to reflect lack of attachment to national values and goals. Objects of fetishistic worship such as the historic land of Israel are for him, when he is assessing them politically, elements in a rational calculation.

The assessment of coldness would be an extreme misrepresentation of the man. The most patent evidence against it is the vigorous nature of his polemic, which reflects the deep personal involvement in the issues he takes up. When he comments on instances of parasitism or corruption, one easily senses his indignation. The Lithuanian *misnagued* is no mere student. Much of what he studies has to be applied in life. His intellectual interest is never completely severed from real life. His conclusions drive him to action. No one has been more emphatic than Leibowitz in urging that a life of Torah is not just study of Torah but its practice. His theoretical conclusions are implemented on the practical level, in speech and writing, at every opportunity.

He has been accused of no longer being a Zionist by people for whom manipulation of meanings is part of their political arsenal. As Sir Isaiah Berlin so clearly perceived, his Zionism is deeply ingrained. On Leibowitz's own admission, the source for his conviction is emotional: as a Jew, he had enough of being ruled by *Goyim*. Zionism today calls for safeguarding the existence and welfare of the state of Israel. This requires careful analysis of the political situation, working out the consequences of alternative policies, and assessing the probable moves of the parties involved. The objective will not be attained by blind attachment to slogans or fixation on certain particulars, whatever the cost. Attachment to the state may be very deep even when its real interests are defined with critical deliberation.

On the purely religious level, Leibowitz himself points out the deep pathos animating the nonpathetic religiosity. There can be no deeper love of God than to forego human values in order to serve God. The rejection of hope for any radical transformation of the human condition, the readiness to conduct this service as part of man's humdrum existence, is a high peak of sacrificial religion. Whatever is attained is negligible in terms of ordinary human valuation. In the religious sense, it is the recognition of man by God and the sanctification of his drab natural life. Ironically, his discussion of the religiosity of the prose of life brings out a romantic streak in Leibowitz, incorporating Lessing's idea that the eternal search for the truth is preferable to the truth itself. To cap the irony, Leibowitz returns to the words of a Jewish mystic to say that the effort to attain the end is the only true end for man, since the end itself is God Himself.

PART I

FAITH

CHAPTER 1

Religious Praxis:
The Meaning of Halakhah
(1953)

M y approach to the subject of the Mitzvoth, and to Jewish religious praxis as a component of living religious reality, is not that of history or theology.[1] I will not elaborate a philosophic justification or rationale of the Mitzvoth, but intend rather to focus upon their meaning for Jewish religion as we live it and are capable of living it here and now. My theme is not historical; it is contemporary. To be sure, we are all influenced by the literary sources from which we learn what Judaism has been and what outstanding Jews have thought, but we shall not be bound by such sources. Citations and allusions to them will serve as illustrations, not as evidence. My contentions will be exemplified by selected citations, though I am fully aware that the sources include expressions of views and opinions which differ considerably from one another and are at times even opposed to those set forth here.

I will not talk about the substance of Halakhah, but rather about its religious meaning for the observant Jew. Nor will I expound specific laws, norms, reasons for various prescriptions and proscriptions, or the grounds for halakhic decisions. The Halakhah cannot be unambiguously defined in terms of its content. Although, as a system enduring over time, it is a totality, its details present considerable variation over the generations. Controversy and diversity of opinion abound within its framework, yet the opposed views are all regarded as "the words of the living God."[2] What characterizes Judaism as a religion of Mitzvoth is not the set of laws and commandments that was given out at the start, but rather the recognition of a system of precepts as binding, even if their specifics were often determined only with time. Moreover, this system of norms is constitutive of Judaism. The very being of Judaism consists in its imposing a distinctive regime on the everyday existence of the Jew, a way of life shaped by the Oral Law, which embodies human understanding, the understanding of men who aim at establishing the rule of Torah over their lives.[3] For this reason, the Halakhah is far from rigid. It is the intention of realizing the Torah in life that distinguishes the shaping of Halakhah by the preceptors of the Oral Law from its modification at the hands of the Reformers. In rendering their decisions, the former are guided by considerations which appear to them grounded either in the Halakhah itself or in the conditions necessary for halakhic observance. The latter act out of motives which reflect not a sincere attempt to understand the Halakhah itself but rather a desire to adapt the Halakhah to a variety of human needs, cultural, moral, social, and even political.

We characterize Judaism as an institutional religion, but not merely in the sense that it comprises institutions. That is characteristic of all religions. The description is intended to reflect the peculiarity of Judaism, for which the institutions of halakhic practice are constitutive. Apart from them Judaism does not exist.

Contrary to widespread and superficial belief, Halakhah does not exemplify religious fossilization. Credos and religious standards of value, as abstract principles, tend to petrify. The institutional religion whose principles and values are not confined to consciousness but are expressed in concrete manifestations in the lives of those who adhere to it is the truly living religion. The Halakhah represents Judaism in its full vitality.

Students of the history of religions and cultures differ as to the relation of myth and ritual in primitive religions. In the age of rationalism of the eighteenth and nineteenth centuries, it was axiomatic that primitive peoples fashioned rituals to express their world view and sense of life, which were embodied initially in their myths. Today many observers maintain the opposite view. Ritual is the primary phenomenon and myth is the attempt to interpret the ritual and attach meaning to it. In the case of Judaism, where religious belief and action are intertwined, is the religious praxis a superstructure erected on a foundation of religious values comprising both cognitive and emotional components, or is the spiritual and mental world of the Jewish religion a superstructure rising above a basis of religious practice? The answer to this question must be sought neither in dogmatic considerations nor in normative ones, but through empirical examination of historical facts. Within Judaism, the content of faith—the categories of religious cognition and sensibility—are interpretations of the system of Torah and its Mitzvoth. It cannot be emphasized too strongly that this approach does not detract from the primary element of faith inherent in the religious stance of the Jew. Whether one says, "I observe the Torah because I have had the privilege of recognizing the Giver of the Torah," or declares, "I have been privileged to recognize the Giver of the Torah as a result of having accepted the yoke of the Torah and its Mitzvoth"—in either case, one's point of departure is that of faith, which can only be grounded in the stance of Abraham: "and he had faith in God" (Gen. 15:6). The uniqueness of Judaism, the characteristic which distinguishes it from other faiths and religions, namely, its embodiment in the Torah and the Mitzvoth, cannot be understood at all if the Torah and its precepts are not construed as data preceding recognition of the Giver of the Torah "to whom there is no analogy whatsoever."[4] Judaism was embodied not in an abstract set of beliefs attained by many who had never heard of Abraham or of the Mosaic Torah, but in the Torah and the Mitzvoth.

Medieval Jewish philosophers, for whom rationalism was not a methodological postulate but a world view, defined the Jewish religious collectivity as one dominated by a common idea: *Qehal Hama'aminim* or *Qehal Hameyahadim*.[5] From a historic-empirical point of view this was completely erroneous. Articles of faith were the subject of violent dispute. The very idea of divine unity was interpreted in ways which were almost antithetic. Nevertheless, the unity of the community remained unimpaired. What Judaism created was a community that maintained the Torah and observed its Mitzvoth, a community that retained its identity despite extreme differences in theological opinion. Many great sages who succeeded Maimonides and are celebrated as saintly figures would have been regarded by him as idolaters, and he would, no doubt, have excommunicated them and regarded them as deserving extermination. Yet later generations through which Judaism was passed down considered the various opposed views to be words of the living God. It was thus not beliefs or opinions that determined the identity of Judaism. Its continuity was that of its religious praxis. This is why the Hassidic movement, which neither intended to create a new Halakhah nor did so in fact, remained an integrated and live member of the Jewish body, despite the psychic distance and abyss of enmity which separated Hassidim from their opponents, who went so far as to attempt to excommunicate them. Compare this with the fate of the Sabbatean movement, which, owing to its defection from observance of Mitzvoth, was ejected from the body of Jewry, its ideology remaining beyond the pale.

This empirically confirmed fact of Judaism as a distinct historical phenomenon, which preserved a constant identity, maintained its continuity over a period of three thousand years, and was embodied solely in the Mitzvoth systematically structured in the form of the Halakhah, will serve as a point of departure. Only by virtue of the Halakhah was Judaism delimited as a single independent and autonomous unit distinguishable from others. Within Judaism, faith is a superstructure rising above the Mitzvoth; the Mitzvoth do not subserve faith. Acceptance of the principles of Jewish theological beliefs by individuals or entire communities did not lead to their incorporation within Jewry. Such principles were discovered or conceived independently by individuals and groups who had no contact with Judaism. Furthermore, within Judaism precisely the articles of faith were subject to controversy. In any event, articles of faith were variously interpreted in different generations and even contemporaneously. The upshot was that Judaism as a historic entity was not constituted by its set of beliefs. It was not embodied in any specific political or social order. Contrary to the views of Samuel David Luzzatto, Ahad Ha'am, Hermann Cohen, and their followers, Judaism did not consist of a specific ethic.[6] Morality can be neither Jewish nor non-Jewish, neither religious nor irreligious. Morality is morality. The attempt to fuse morality and religion is not a happy one. Morality as guidance of man's will in accordance with his knowledge of nature and of himself (the Stoics; Spinoza), or in accordance with what the individual considers his duty toward man as an end-in-himself (Kant), differs radically from religious consciousness or religious feeling. From the standpoint of Judaism man as such has no intrinsic value. He is an "image of God," and only as such does he possess special significance. That is why Judaism did not produce an ethical theory of its own, was never embodied in a moral system, and made no pretenses of representing a specific moral point of view. The Bible does not recognize the good and the right as such, only "the good and the right in the eyes of God" (Deut. 12:28). The systematic ethical theories found in later Jewish sources (Maimonides; Bahya ibn Pakuda) were either adopted from non-Jewish sources or were guides to the systematic cultivation of the religious virtues, appeals to stricter adherence to the Torah and its commandments (Moshe Hayyim Luzzatto).[7] Judaism as a specifically defined entity existing continuously over a period of three thousand years was not realized in philosophy, literature, art, or anything other than halakhic living. Hence whoever is able to achieve religiosity only through the channels of Judaism, or whoever is interested in the Jewish manifestations of religiosity, must, willy-nilly, come to grips with the religious praxis of Judaism, with the world of Halakhah.

It may well be that a typological factor enters into the personal understanding of the relationship between the institutional aspects of religion (in the case of Judaism, the Halakhah), and the realm of values associated with faith and religious cognition. In other words, a good deal may depend upon the psychic propensities of each individual, and one cannot generalize and contend that in any given religion the institutional aspects or the abstract values have priority. Among the religious some believers may consider that faith precedes religion and others will say that religion antecedes faith. One person may proceed from a given realm of values—of principles of faith and abstract obligations—to participation in their realization in concrete manifestations. Another may reach the world of religious values as a result of taking up the yoke of Torah and Mitzvoth, the burden of institutional religion, the ideational content of which is formulated in terms of belief. However, one who is not naturally inclined toward religiosity will never attain religious faith and commitment to religious values except through the medium of institutional religion; if he is a Jew, through the religious praxis of the Halakhah.

A prevalent conception, which stems from a shallow rationalism, distinguishes kernel from husk in religion; the eternal ideational content of absolute value becomes incarnate in various external forms, which may, without loss, be exchanged for others and ought to be superseded from time to time to fit changing circumstances. This distinction is baseless. Substance is embodied in form. The essence of a given content is inseparable from the particular form which it takes on. Were it clothed differently, it could not be the identical content. An analogy with poetry is pertinent. Here, too, the distinction is sometimes made between substance and form. Shakespeare expressed his *eros* in the very specific form of his collection of sonnets—one of most moving masterpieces of world poetry. A naïve person may contend that it is possible to separate the essence of the Shakespearean eros from the artificial and intricate form in which he chose to express it. Such is not the case. Had Shakespeare chosen the form of the novel or the essay, the eros conveyed would not have been the same. His eros could be expressed authentically in no other medium than that of the marvelous form chosen by him. Similarly, the content of Jewish faith— the stance of man before God as Judaism conceived it—can be externalized in one form only, the halakhic system. The belief that the substance of Jewish faith can be retained when the Halakhah is adapted to human needs, whether these be material, spiritual, or mental, is mistaken. The essence of Jewish faith is consistent with no embodiment other than the system of halakhic praxis.

Apart from Halakhah, all flowering of creativity within Judaism was but episodic and fleeting. Consider one of the great religious manifestations in the history of Israel, the Kabbalah. A great inquirer into the history of Jewish faith, Gershon Scholem, revealed the significance and role of mysticism within Judaism. Thanks to his work we are aware, as never before, of the important role of this phenomenon. Scholem believed he had proved that Judaism had a fundamental aspect in addition to the halakhic one. It would appear, however, that he inadvertently proved the very opposite. The grand structure of the Kabbalah was created and developed after Judaism had already been delimited as a historic entity characterized by features which determined its continuous identity. Judaism existed long before the Kabbalah commenced and was not impaired after the wilting of the magnificent flowering of the Kabbalah and its almost total disappearance as a living pursuit. Moreover, even in its heyday, the Kabbalah was never identical with the whole of Judaism. Alongside it, and in opposition to it, grew various schools which rejected this mystic tradition. Thus the Kabbalah, probably the greatest extra-halakhic growth within the framework of Judaism, was only an episode and not a constitutive element in its identity. This identity and the persisting existence of Judaism were certainly never dependent upon some specific philosophy, ethic, world view, or theology. "Prophetic vision" and "messianic vocation" were never principal factors in Judaism or foci of its daily life. Even the medieval rationalists who tended to identify Israel as the Qehal Hameyahadim contributed nothing to an understanding of the phenomenon of Judaism.[8] Monotheistic beliefs were adopted by many outside the Jewish community independently of Jewish influence. For Judaism itself, the verse of Shema does not denote a proposition but serves as a slogan whose chief function is the rejection of idolatry in all its forms. As for the positive meaning of Shema, nothing was so hotly contested in the world of Jewish religious thought as the meaning of this verse ("Hear, O Israel, the Lord our God, the Lord is one"). Not only do the "One" of Maimonides and the "One" of Isaac Luria fail to coincide, they are incompatible.[9] How to understand that in the consciousness of religious Jewry both appear legitimate? The answer is that their differences did not affect the Halakhah. Recognition of the obligatory nature of the Torah and its *Mitzvoth* and of man's stance before God as determined by them was common to both interpretations. This framework, upon which both interpreters agreed, prevented a rupture. Hassidism did not become a schismatic sect either, despite the gulf separating it from the world of rabbinic learning. On the other hand, and precisely because it divorced itself from the halakhic praxis, Christianity tore away from Judaism and became a separate religion, in many respects alien and antagonistic to Judaism in spite of its recognition of the sanctity of the Hebrew Scriptures.

In yet another respect it is erroneous to describe the Jews as "the community of monotheists" (in the medieval style) and Judaism as a complex of "values," a formula favored by contemporary secular Jewish ideologies. Judaism is a collective reality. One cannot be a Jew *qua* isolated individual. A person is a Jew insofar as he belongs to the people of the Torah. But consciousness, sensibility, and valuation are radically private, not collective. "They shall be yours alone, and not shared by strangers."[10] In this domain there is no possibility of communication. A person's understanding and feeling derive from his own subjectivity, which differs from anyone else's. It is impossible for one person to communicate to another exactly what he feels: except for the formally defined terms of scientific discourse, the meanings of words and expressions of our common language vary from person to person in communication and in private thought. Hence there can be no collectivity of ideas or feelings. Collectivity is limited to the field of action—to cooperation in performance and achievement. Of course people will often jointly say or declare something. But it is only as acts that these declarations may be considered collectively performed. Hence if Judaism is a collective reality, not as the set of beliefs and the religious experience of individual Jews but as the religion of the Congregation of Israel, it can only consist in the common religious action—the halakhic praxis.

To base Jewish religiosity upon membership in the community of Israel and adherence to its institutional religion differs from the position of Maimonides yet does not contradict it. Maimonides maintained that religious perfection, which is man's ultimate perfection, consists of "cognitions," "neither in deeds nor in virtues." Cognitions are forms of personal awareness and are "his alone and not shared by strangers." All action and all the social aspects of human existence are reduced to the status of preparatory conditions which qualify man for the attainment of his true perfection.[11] Maimonidean anthropology, with its emphasis upon man's individuality, is at least partially a product of the historic situation of Jewry in exile, a community divested of independent social functions and deprived of civic roles and obligations. Vicious regimes in Spain and Morocco prevented Maimonides from engaging in any meaningful activity other than that of nurturing his inner quest for perfection and aiding other Jewish individuals in theirs. A gracious monarch in Egypt similarly liberated him and his fellow Jews from all concern with the political functions and from responsibility for the social needs. This enabled each one of them to concentrate on the attainment of personal perfection without fear of persecution. Had Maimonides, as the citizen of a free and independent Jewish society, been burdened with the tasks and obligations involved in the arrangement of political, economic, technical, and organizational public affairs—upon which rests the individual's ability to engage in personal matters—it is likely that his anthropology would have been less individualistic. Maimonides was torn between two conflicting tendencies. As against the personalistic and individualistic conceptions of religious perfection and of the meaning of religious observance, we also find in his writings a social interpretation of the significance of the Mitzvoth.[12] For our contemporary religious existence we can only accept his second interpretation.[13]

Today we are far more sensitive than was Maimonides to membership in the community as an essential aspect of a man's personality. Religious Jews must include the problems of state, society, and nation, of politics and history, within the sphere of religious concerns. I am a participant in the life of Torah and faith to the extent that I am a member of the community of Israel. As an individual I have neither the drive nor the capacity to create a religion and faith of my own. Since cognition and will are essentially personal, private, subjective, and individual, the religious community was not produced by beliefs or values. There are no communities of will, no general will, no collectivities of ideas. On the other hand, a common way of life is characteristic of most human groups. The endurance and continuity of the Jewish religious collectivity result from the objective factor of halakhic practice rather than from some form of subjective consciousness that is likely to change as its individual bearers succeed one another. Halakhah is founded on faith, yet at the same time constitutes this faith. In other words, Judaism as a living religion creates the faith upon which it is founded. This is a logical paradox but not a religious paradox. The Halakhah is not an external wrap clothing Jewish religion or faith. It is the sole form in which they can be embodied, the collective manifestation of Judaism.

Current attempts to identify Judaism with the Hebrew Bible, which is presented as proclaiming values, ideals, and a vision that "shine with their own light," are unrelated to the Halakhah and are independent of it. This kind of bibliolatry is Lutheran, not Jewish. Historically, Israel never lived or intended to live by Scripture, nor was it ever intended so to live religiously. Israel conducted its life in accordance with the Halakhah as propounded in the Oral Law. From the viewpoint of human values the above identification overrates the importance of the Bible. As instruments of moral education, Sophocles' Antigone or Kant's *Grundlegung* are possibly superior. As philosophy, the Bible's importance cannot compare to that of Plato or, again, Kant. Regarded as poetry, Sophocles or Shakespeare may surpass it. As history, Thucydides is certainly more interesting and profound. Only as the words of the living God is the Bible incommensurable with Sophocles and Shakespeare, Plato and Kant, Thucydides, or any other work of man. But what way have I of knowing that these twenty-four books are Holy Scripture other than through the Halakhah which canonized them? The decision about which books to accept as Scripture was not

made behind the veil of mythology or pre-history, but took place in
the full light of history and in the course of halakhic negotiation. We
are told that the Sages considered relegating certain books to the Apoc-
rypha. Only as a result of examination and discussion did they decide
to include them among the holy writings. The book of Ben Sira (Eccle-
siasticus), for example, at one time accepted as part of the canon, was
eventually rejected.[14] Were it not for the Halakhah as the authoritative
presentation of the religion of Israel, the individual could never know
what were the values and faith of this religion as found in Holy Scripture. The religion of Israel, the world of Halakhah and the Oral Law,
was not produced from Scripture. Scripture is one of the institutions
of the religion of Israel. Both religiously and from a logical and causal
standpoint the Oral Law, the Halakhah, is prior to the Written Teaching, which includes faith and values. In cybernetic terms one can define
the relation between the Bible and Halakhah as one of feedback: the
Halakhah of the Oral Teaching, which is a human product, derives its
authority from the words of the living God in Scripture; at the same
time it is the Halakhah which determines the content and meaning of
Scripture.

Thus far we have only discussed the historico-empirical role of the
Mitzvoth in Jewish history. What is the religious import of Judaism's
embodiment in Halakhah? How to understand the peculiar nature of
the religious faith for which Halakhah is the only adequate expression?
    The first mark of the religion of Halakhah is its realism. It perceives
man as he is in reality and confronts him with this reality—with the
actual conditions of his existence rather than the "vision" of another
existence. Religion is concerned with the status, the function, and the
duties of man, as constrained by these circumstances. It precludes the
possibility of man's shirking his duties by entertaining illusions of
attaining a higher level of being. The religion of Halakhah is concerned
with man and addresses him in his drab day-by-day existence. The
Mitzvoth are a norm for the prosaic life that constitutes the true and
enduring condition of man. Halakhic religion has no flair for the episodic excursions from the routine of everyday life, for evanescent
moments of solemnity. Halakhic praxis is oriented to the usual and
persisting, not to the exceptional, momentary, and fortuitous. The
Mitzvoth require observance out of a sense of duty and discipline, not
ecstatic enthusiasm or fervor, which may embellish one's life but do

not tell how to conduct it. Resting religion on Halakhah assigns it to the prosaic aspects of life, and therein lies its great strength. Only a religion addressed to life's prose, a religion of the dull routine of daily activity, is worthy of the name. This is not to demean the poetic moments, the rare occasions when a man breaks away from the routine, the experience of rising above the self spiritually and emotionally, the deeds performed fervently. It is quite possible that such moments mark the zenith of a human life. Nonetheless, the fundamental and enduring elements of human existence are in life's prose, not in its poetry. Molière's M. Jourdain discovered at the age of forty that he had unwittingly been speaking prose all his life. No one ever claimed to have been talking unwittingly in poetry. Only in full awareness and intention does one compose poetry, and such awareness and intention occur only at rare moments. A religion of values and concentrated intention is the religion of life's poetry, which can only adorn it. The religion of halakhic practice is the religion of life itself.

The Judaism of the Halakhah despises rhetoric, avoids pathos, abjures the visionary. Above all, it rejects the illusory. It does not permit a man to believe that the conditions of his existence are other than they really are. It prevents flight from one's functions and tasks in this inferior world to an imaginary world which is all good, beautiful, and sublime. Not by chance are so many of the Mitzvoth concerned with the body, procreation and birth, food and drink, sexual life, diseases, and the corpse. The largest section of the Mishnah, the first crystallized formulation of the Halakhah, is *Seder Taharoth,* which places man within the squalor of biological existence from which he can never extricate himself.

Most characteristic of the Halakhah is its lack of pathos. The Halakhah does not depend upon the incidence of religious experience and attaches little importance to the psychic urges to perform extraordinary deeds. It strives to base the religious act, even in its highest manifestations, on the permanent habit of performing one's duty. "Greater is he who performs because he has been commanded than one who performs without having been commanded."[15] Precisely this nonpathetic attitude hides a depth of intense pathos. How unfounded is the imaginary antithesis of the inner religious experience and the formalism of the halakhic praxis, an antithesis so popular amongst the opponents of the religion of Halakhah!

Two types of religiosity may be discerned: one founded in values and beliefs from which follow requirements of action, the other posited on imperatives of action, the observance of which entails values and intention. The religion of values and beliefs is an endowing religion—a means of satisfying man's spiritual needs and of assuaging his mental conflicts. Its end is man, and God offers his services to man. A person committed to such a religion is a redeemed man. A religion of Mitzvoth is a demanding religion. It imposes obligations and tasks and makes of man an instrument for the realization of an end which transcends man. The satisfactions it offers are those deriving from the performance of one's duty. The religious practitioner serves his God lishmah—because He is worthy of worship.[16] The two types of religiosity may be found within all religions, but religions differ from one another in the extent to which one type predominates. A religiosity of the first type is characteristic of Christianity. Its symbol, the cross, represents the sacrifice God brought about for the benefit of mankind. In contrast, the highest symbol of the Jewish faith is the stance of Abraham on Mount Moriah, where all human values were annulled and overridden by fear and love of God. The cross represents submission to human nature. The *Aqedah* (the near-sacrifice of Isaac) is man's absolute mastery over his own nature.[17] "Abraham rose early in the morning and saddled his ass . . . and set out" for the Aqedah. Don Isaac Abravanel, commenting upon Genesis 22:3, explains: "saddled his ass" means that he overcame his materiality, that is, his physical nature—a pun on the phonetically similar "hamor" (ass) and "homer" (matter).[18] This "matter" or nature includes all the benevolent sentiments as well as man's conscience; all the factors in man's makeup which an atheistic humanism regards as "good." In the morning benedictions, recited prior to reading the narrative of the Aqedah, we find the request: "Compel our *Yetzer* [inclination] to subject itself to you"—a request meant to apply to our benevolent as well as to our evil inclinations.[19] This would be a banal supplication were it concerned only with the evil inclinations. It was Abraham who first burst the bounds of the universal human bondage—the bondage of man to the forces of his own nature. Not everyone is Abraham, and not everyone is put to so terrible a test as that of the Aqedah. Nonetheless the daily performance of the Mitzvoth, which is not directed by man's natural inclinations or drives but by his intention of serving God, represents the motivation animating the *Aqedah*. From such a standpoint, the question "what does religion offer to me?"

must be completely dismissed. The only proper question is: "what am I obligated to offer for the sake of religion?"

In stark contrast to the Jewish religion, oriented as it is to the realities of human existence, stand religions which claim to offer the means of extricating man from the human condition and transporting him spiritually to a state governed by other categories of merit and obligation, of tasks and attainments. The Christian who believes in the event of the year 33 and has faith in it is redeemed; the very elements of his nature are altered. Among other things, he is liberated from the bondage of "the Law." Halakhic Judaism does not recognize such a redemption. The project it sets for man is permanent and endless. No religious attainment may be considered final; the project is never completed. Observance of the Torah in its entirety is merely the training of man for continuation of its observance. No religious achievement can change the human condition or the task.

A tremendous symbolic exemplification of this attitude appears at the close of Yom Kippur. At the end of the Day of Atonement, the culmination of a period of repentance when the people of Israel purify themselves before their father in heaven and are purified by him—at the close of the Ne'ilah service with the public utterance of the verse of Shema and the blowing of the Shofar—the first words of the weekday evening prayer are uttered: "And He is merciful and forgiving of sin."[20] Thus the basic situation of repentant man at the close of the Day of Atonement is exactly what it was the evening before. His sole achievement consists of the great religious effort invested in this day. Immediately after he must begin his preparations toward the next Yom Kippur. The cycle continues until the end of one's life. In like manner one's labor in study of the Torah is not a means for the attainment of any other goal. This very labor is itself the goal. "Until what period of life ought he to study Torah? Until the day of his death."[21]

Halakhah, as an expression of a religiosity which rejects all illusion, does not entertain man with the vision of some target at which he may aim and which, once attained, constitutes the fulfillment of his tasks. No human achievement affects the regime of religious praxis under which one lives from coming of age until death. Performance of the Mitzvoth is man's path to God, an infinite path, the end of which is never attained and is, in effect, unattainable. A man is bound to know that this path never terminates. One follows it without advancing beyond the point of departure. Recognition that the religious function imposed upon man is infinite and never ending is the faith which finds expression in the regularity, constancy, and perseverance in the performance of the Mitzvoth. The circle of religious praxis rotates constantly about its center. "Every day they will appear to you as new," for after each act the position of man remains as it was before. The aim of proximity to God is unattainable. It is infinitely distant, "for God is in heaven and you on the earth" (Eccles. 5:1). What then is the substance and import of the performance of the Mitzvoth? It is man's striving to attain the religious goal.

Halakhic observance as a way of life, a fixed and permanent form of human existence, precludes conversion of religion into a means to some ulterior end. Most of the Mitzvoth are meaningless except as expressions of worship. They have no utility in terms of satisfaction of human needs. No man would commit himself to such a way of life if he did not regard the service of God as an end in itself serving no extrinsic purpose. The Halakhah thus addresses a man's sense of duty rather than his emotions and inclinations. The Mitzvah of prayer—the obligatory routine prayer of institutional religion—can serve as proof. The concept of prayer has two different meanings: first, prayer in the sense of "a prayer of the afflicted when he is faint and pours out his complaint before God" (Ps. 102:1); second, prayer as defined in the prayerbook, which is more constitutive of Judaism than the Bible, since the latter was adopted by a large portion of humanity that did not embrace Judaism. The prayerbook, which determines the content of the Mitzvah of prayer, does not express the spontaneous outpouring of the soul. It contains a text of fixed prayer, imposed upon one as a duty and not conditioned by his spiritual or material needs or by his feeling. The same eighteen benedictions are recited by the bridegroom before his wedding ceremony, by the widower returning from the funeral of his wife, and the father who has just buried his only son. Recitation of the identical set of psalms is the daily duty of the person enjoying the beauties and bounty of this world and the one whose world has collapsed. The same order of supplications is prescribed for those who feel the need for them and those who do not.

The prayerbook is the outcome of a weighty religious decision. One of the Tanna'im (Sages of the Mishnaic period) demanded: "Do not make a routine of your prayer, but let it consist in supplication of mercy before God."[22] He opposed the fixed formulas of the prayer-book. But the halakhic decision was to regard prayer as the obligatory service of God, not as spontaneous expression. "Let him gird up strength like a lion to rise in the morning for the service of his Creator" (the first clause of the *Shulhan Arukh,* an authoritative code of Halakhah). Only as service can prayer be collective. "A prayer of the afflicted when he is faint" is individual and necessarily varies with the person and the changing contingent circumstances.

Proponents of an "authentic religiosity" maintain that the religious function of prayer can only be realized if the fixed formulas of prayer are abolished and each person prays only when he feels the need and desire to express his feelings and thoughts of the moment. The representative of institutional religion will reply that he has no religious interest in a prayer which is not the fulfillment of a religious obligation. Supplicatory outpouring of the soul is a psychological phenomenon, religiously irrelevant. That prayer is great which a person views as work and executes regardless of whether or not it suits his taste. Everyone is capable of reciting verses of praise when in good spirits. To utter many Hallelujahs when one finds no joy in nature or in his life is the act of the truly religious person, committed to prayer imprinted with the stamp of the Sages.[23]

The writings of Rabbi Kook assert the superiority of the Torah, that is, the Halakhah, to prophecy, the spirit of which he finds in Aggadah.[24] Prophecy occurs within the interior of a man's soul. Hence it may flow from the spirituality of man and be conveyed by man. The Torah, however, with its orientation to practice, must be given directly to God. This is one of the fundamental distinctions between Judaism and Christianity. The latter reversed the order of superiority and prefers the prophets to the Torah.

If the Mitzvoth are in the service of God, not of man, they may not be directed toward the satisfaction of human wants. Any attempt to ground them in human needs—cognitive, moral, social, and national—deprives them of their religious meaning. If the commandments were expressions of philosophic cognition, had a moral function, or were directed at the perfection of the social order or the conservation of the people of Israel, the observant Jew would be doing service to himself, to society, or to the nation. Instead of serving God he would be utilizing God's Torah for his own benefit as an instrument for satisfying his needs.

Consequently, the idea of "reasons for the Mitzvoth" is a theological concept, not a concept of religious faith. The rationale of a Mitzvah is service of God, not a utilitarian interest. Were the significance of the Sabbath social or national, it would be entirely superfluous. It was not to perform this function that the *Shekhinah* [the divine presence] descended on Mount Sinai; certainly not to replace politicians and intelligence officers in charge of national security. If its meaning is not holiness, the Sabbath has no significance whatsoever. But holiness is a category which is meaningless in a humanitarian or anthropocentric context.

The foregoing considerations apply equally to the ethical importance the secularists attribute to the Torah and its commandments. Ethics, when regarded as unconditionally asserting its own validity, is an atheistic category *par excellence*. A person who is ethical in this sense regards man as the supreme end and value, that is, deifies man. A person who perceives man as one among God's creatures and keeps in mind the verse, "I have set God always before me," cannot accept ethics as the overriding norm or criterion. Being moral, from the standpoint of a secular ethic, can have only either of two meanings; directing man's will in accordance with man's knowledge of reality—the ethics of Socrates, Plato, Aristotle, the Epicureans and especially the Stoics, and among the later philosophers Spinoza; or directing man's will in accordance with man's recognition of his duty—the ethics of Kant and the German idealists. Among the passages of the Shema we find the words: "that you seek not after your own hearts and your own eyes": "after your own hearts" is the negation of Kantian ethics; "after your own eyes" is the negation of Socrates'. The admonition: "I am the Lord your God" follows shortly thereafter. The Torah does not recognize moral imperatives stemming from knowledge of natural reality or from awareness of man's duty to his fellow man. All it recognizes are Mitzvoth, divine imperatives. The Torah and the prophets never appeal to the human conscience, which harbors idolatrous tendencies. No equivalent of the term "conscience" appears in Scripture. The counsel of conscience is not a religious concept. The "God in one's heart" which humanist moralists sometimes invoke is a "strange god."

Halakhah as a religious institution cannot admit the category of the ethical. Needless to say, it cannot admit the utilitarian justification, whether it be for the good of individuals, of society, or of the nation. "You shall love your neighbor as yourself" is the great rule in the Torah not because it is a precept transcending the formalism of law and above the Mitzvoth but precisely because it appears as one of the 613 Mitzvoth. As a guide rule, "You shall love your neighbor as yourself" is not specific to Judaism. Similar precepts were laid down in writing by thinkers who were not influences by Judaism and were not even acquainted with it, by the wise men of China, India, and Greece. Moreover, "You shall love your neighbor as yourself" does not, as such, occur in the Torah. The reading is: "You shall love your neighbor as yourself, I am God."

The duty of love toward one's neighbor is not a corollary of man's position as such but of his position before God. "You shall love your neighbor as yourself" without the continuation "I am God" is the great rule of the atheist Kant. The novelty and grandeur of this rule in the Torah consists in the framework within which the Torah places it. That context includes Mitzvoth as various as those occurring in the Ten Commandments, laws concerned with sacrificial rites, others regarding property rights or rights of a worker to prompt payment of his wages, prohibition of interbreeding species of animals and plants, and so on, all within the span of twenty verses (Lev. 15). "You shall love your neighbor as yourself" ceases thereby to be mere good counsel, a noble aspiration or sublime ideal. It becomes clothed in the reality of law, something one is compelled to take seriously as one must take police ordinances seriously. There is nothing deprecatory about this simile. None other than Rabbi Yohanan ben Zakai upon his deathbed blessed his disciples: "May your fear of Heaven be no less than your fear of human authority."[25] As misleading as the truncated quotation regarding love of neighbor is the distorted injunction, "And you shall do the good and right." The verse reads: "And you shall do the good and right in the eyes of God"! (Deut. 6:18).

What does the religious person achieve by observing the Mitzvoth? The last chapter of the prophetic books says: "Then you shall return and see the difference between him that serves God and him that does not serve him" (Mal. 3:18). Halakhic praxis is the active way in which man may serve God. It is the only way for man to acknowledge the

Kingdom of Heaven. So long as a person's religiosity expresses only his personal awareness, his conscience, his morality, or his values, the religious act is merely for himself and, as such, is an act of rebellion against the Kingdom of Heaven. Service of God through Torah and Mitzvoth and worship of "God in the heart" or the "conscience" of humanistic religion are in sheer opposition. The latter is worship of man, nothing other than the idolatry referred to by the verse "that you seek not after your own heart." Anything a man does to satisfy his own needs, whether material or spiritual, is self-service, not divine service. As such it is perfectly legitimate. But if a man attributes religious import to this act he is transforming God into a means and instrument for his own good. A man can worship God only by committing himself to observance of the Mitzvoth, which are the expression of the divine will and not means for the satisfaction of his needs, not even of his spiritual needs. A typical act of serving God would be the wearing of the phylacteries and, in doing so, observing all the detailed prescriptions pertaining to them such as the requirement that they be cubical, that the straps be black, and so on. For himself, a man has no motivation for performing this act and there could be no other motivation than compliance with the will of God, who commanded the wearing of phylacteries. The same is true of Sabbath observance, with all its strange precepts which serve no physiological, social, or psychological needs. The activities forbidden on the Sabbath are determined not by the energy expended or the effort required but by criteria internal to the Halakhah. The only significance of the Sabbath is one having to do with holiness—subordination of a seventh part of one's life to a special rule of living which has no roots in human nature, its inclinations, or its needs, but follows only from the decision to accept the "yoke of the Kingdom of Heaven."[26] This is not a way of life that is natural to man, and the precepts governing it emphasize and highlight this difference. Hence the Sabbath loses its religious significance if the precepts relating to it are adjusted to suit the inclinations or comfort of men. All these considerations apply as well to the laws governing the sexual life of man and wife and the restrictions forbidding certain foods. None have a physiological or psychological rationale. All constitute constraints upon human nature in the interest of the service of God.

It follows that the Halakhah cannot and ought not to be adapted to the interests and natural needs of man.

At this point the problem of Mitzvoth, which have no physiological, philosophical, or sociological basis and follow neither from man's intellect nor from his affections or volitions, comes to bear on the problem of man's freedom. What is the status of a man as an autonomous being if he is committed to the Torah and its Mitzvoth? The claim that a man who accepts the authority of the Halakhah is in bondage is only too familiar. But the concept of bondage no less than that of freedom demands semantic analysis. "The regularity of the world order is constant."[27] Events in the world and the order in which they occur are governed by law, and things are connected by fixed functional relations. Recognition of the world order within which man is ordained to live and act is a profound religious insight and a necessary condition for subjection to the rule of Halakhah—as against belief in repeated interventions from above. If the world possesses constant regularity, man is subordinate to the entire system of natural reality, which includes not only his body but his soul.[28] He is subject to it both physiologically and psychologically. Under these circumstances, what is man's freedom? Willing acceptance of a way of life which does not derive from human nature implies the emancipation of man from the bondage of raw nature. Among the many definitions of human freedom, Spinoza's was philosophically the most profound: freedom is activity arising from the necessity of one's own nature. But does man have a nature of his own? As a natural being he is part of nature as a whole. His own nature is only the last link in a causal chain of the forces of inorganic and organic nature which act upon him and within him. Where then is man's autonomy? Man activated by his "own" nature is, in effect, nothing but a robot activated by the forces of nature, just like the cattle grazing in the pasture, which are also "free from the Torah and the Mitzvoth"; that is, from any law externally imposed. The Amoraite Rava tells us: "All bodies are sheaths; happy is he who has won the privilege of being a sheath for the Torah."[29] No man is simply "himself." He is always a receptacle for something which is other than "himself." The individual who regards himself as free of any heteronomously dictated imperative and acts out of Spinozistic freedom is motivated by his nature, which is only one of the manifestations of nature in its totality. The psychological powers of man—his desires, inclinations, and volitions—are also part of his nature. From a religious point of view the triadic classification of being as nature, spirit, and God has no validity. There is only the dyad: nature, which includes the human spirit, and God. The only way man can break the bonds of nature is by cleaving to God; by acting in compliance with the divine will rather than in accordance with the human will. The latter is a natural factor. This disqualifies as idolatrous any religion oriented to values which reflect the aims and ideal vision of man. In contrast to its modern atheistic distortion, we must emphasize that the Hebrew Bible does not recognize the human spirit as the antithesis of the material. The well-known verse, which is nowadays usually quoted in a truncated form that perverts its meaning, does not confront matter with spirit but with the spirit of God: "not by might, nor by power, but by My spirit." The human spirit is part of the "might" and "power." The true meaning of the Tannaitic adage "None but he who busies himself with the Torah is free" is that he is free from the bondage of nature because he lives a life which is contrary to nature, both nature in general and human nature in particular. Hence there is neither a religious nor a philosophic need to assimilate halakhic practice to the concepts or interests of man. Their force lies precisely in their being alien to natural man. Rationalizations of the Mitzvoth and search for their origins are pointless. The only interest these researches serve is theological or psychological.

Emancipation from the bondage of nature can only be brought about by the religion of Mitzvoth. It cannot be accomplished by overcoming one's inclinations by rational or secular ethical considerations. True, the tendency to secularize all the traditional value-concepts has affected even the Aqedah. The term is prevalently used to designate heroic acts of self-sacrifice lacking any religious import, such as those of parents who sacrificed their children, or at least consented to their death, in the 1948 war of liberation. This is a misleading usage. The parents who overcame their pity and love suspended a human value out of deference to another human value which they themselves considered superior and justifying any sacrifice—the nation and the fatherland. This is entirely different from the Aqedah, in which all human values capable of being subsumed under the categories of human understanding and feeling were set aside before the "glory of the majesty" of God.

Many oppose halakhic Judaism for religious reasons, as a "commandment of men learned by rote." God desires the devotion of one's heart, and intention is more significant than anything else. Of what value is a religion which consists mainly in a way of life of exercise and training until it becomes second-nature? But bringing about second-nature is not a flaw in religion any more than it is in civic virtue. Only a small minority of men determine their way of life by conscious decision made in full awareness, and even they direct their actions by principles and conscious deliberation only on rare occasions—their moments of "poetry." The prosaic affairs of life are conducted as a matter of routine, in accordance with customary patterns to which one has become habituated and by which one is unconsciously directed. Let us not disparage this rule of habit, for it, and not the rare decision and intention which attain to full consciousness, is the chief barrier to barbarism and brutality. If certain human societies have attained a modicum of decency in interpersonal relations and civic order and have become communities of "law-abiding citizens," that is not due to their members' having suffered the perplexities and conducted the deliberations of Socrates in prison until they came to recognize that a person is obligated to abide by the laws of his state even when these are against his interests. It is the result of habituation to cultural practices. "That simply isn't done" is the classical expression of a norm learnt by habituation. Disparagement of "social superstitions," of "meaningless routines" or "empty conventions" has only loosened the reins and set free forces of darkness and agents of horror which had been restrained only by customary routine. Our generation especially has learned that men are incapable of living a life fit for men by their own decision and on their own responsibility. This is no less true of the religious life. Only the prophet Isaiah, whose eyes had seen the King, Lord of Hosts, could allow himself to despise "a commandment of men learned by rote." Most of us can only hope to put our lives in some relation to God through the traditionally communicated and habitually acquired formulas of halakhic practice. Once we are privileged to attain a religiosity of "commandment of men learned by rote" of "life in accordance with the *Shulhan Arukh*," so vigorously repudiated by the proponents of "authentic religion," we may continue to strive towards a religiosity of intention and consciousness. Contempt of religion which binds the religious experience with laws and regulations and pursuit of the free expression of this experience have led to the most abominable depravities. How great was the religious feeling and how deep was the religious experience of idolaters who sacrificed their sons to Moloch and abandoned their daughters to the whoredom of the worship of Ashtoreth? The Torah invalidates such free, spontaneous, and natural religiosity with its implications of idolatry, incest, and bloodshed.[30] It imprisons them within the confines of the Mitzvoth ("binds them with the straps of the phylacteries," in the words of Saul Tchernikhowsky) and has no qualms about the danger of becoming an artificial system accepted as "a commandment of men learned by rote."

Life molded on the halakhic model demarcates a domain of things and deeds that pertain to holiness. Holiness, in the religious sense of this word as against its figurative secular meanings, is nothing but halakhic observance; the specific intentional acts dedicated to the service of God. Any other deed—whether regarded as good or bad, whether material or spiritual—that a man may perform in his own interest or for the satisfaction of a human need is profane. Sacred and profane are fundamental religious categories. Within institutional religion, the religion of Halakhah, the distinction between them is an essential aspect of religious perception. Conversely, the idea of holiness as an immanent property of certain things—persons, locations, institutions, objects, or events—is a magical-mystical concept which smacks of idolatry. There is no holiness outside the sphere of divinity, which is the sphere shaped by the divine imperative, not by human values; a sphere in which human action is dedicated to service of God. "God has nothing in his world beyond the four ells of Halakhah"—the sphere of actions directed by His commands. Nothing is holy in itself. There is only that which is "holy to God"; that which is sanctified by the distinct purpose of serving God. Only this meaning of "holiness" can be accommodated by halakhic Judaism. "You shall be holy" is demanded at the beginning of a portion of the Torah concerned mainly with Mitzvoth. "For you are a holy people" occurs in a context devoted in its entirety to halakhic practices.

One of the most cunning wiles of anthropocentric secularism, which hides behind the mask of "authentic religiosity," is to obliterate this distinction and to extend the rubric of the holy to cover natural functions and human values. If holiness is incarnate in aspects of natural reality itself, or if forces and drives within man are holy, there is no room for "the holy God" who transcends natural reality, since then reality itself is divine and man himself is God. Abrogation of the distinctive religious category of holiness and imputation of sanctity to human functions and drives is one of the most vicious phenomena of our times, socially, educationally, and morally. This generation has been witness, as none other before it, to the evil which may be perpetrated in the name of fatherland, nation, honor, liberty, equality, and any other human value to which holiness is attributed when men lose sight of the great truth that holiness is resident in a realm which transcends human values. Hence the tremendous educational significance of the Mitzvoth, which demarcate the realm of the sacred in human life and are a constant reminder that anything outside that realm lacks sanctity and is unworthy of religious adoration. Our generation must keep nothing more constantly in mind than this.

Although it is only halakhic praxis which creates a sphere of the sacred within human life, outside this domain flourish many good deeds and events of grandeur and sublimity. They are good, great, and sublime, but cannot be sacred. They are always subject to evaluation and criticism from a religious standpoint, for only a religious requirement sanctioned by Halakhah is sacred. Fatherland, security, nation, liberty, honor, loyalty, beauty, conjugal love, parental love—if not defined and imposed by religious precept—may not be sanctified or represented as absolute values in the name of which anything may be permitted and for the sake of which everything must be done. By distinguishing the sacred from the profane the Halakhah functions as a bulwark against idolatry in all its manifestations and a defense against the corruption associated with it. For idolatry is simply the representation of things profane as sacred, as possessing supreme and absolute worth. Consider the nature of the "sanctity" of national security or the "sanctity" of military loyalty and discipline, in the wake of which we have Kafr Kassem.[31] The tendency to sanctify elements of the profane, such as natural states or events, psychological drives, certain natural relations between man and man or man and society, is identical with the evil inclination of idolatry, of rebellion against the Kingdom of Heaven, of the deification of the world, of nature, and of man himself.

From a religious, theocentric life perception and world view, it follows that all that derives from man—his volitions, needs, and drives, whether material or spiritual—is profane and may not be sanctified. This is the meaning of "You shall not take the name of the Lord your God in vain" when its full implications are understood. This understanding requires the Halakhah to determine what is holy, from which we may infer what is not holy.

Sanctification of natural reality expresses a world perception which is antireligious, atheistic or pantheistic. Thales of Miletus, the materialistic polytheist who declared that all things are full of gods was the spiritual father of the idea that "There is no place at all empty of Him."[32] The echoes of this type of perception in Jewish mysticism are incompatible with halakhic Judaism. If holiness inheres in natural reality, there is no room for the introduction of sanctity from a source transcending nature, and none for the service of God by observance of the Mitzvoth.

From a didactic point of view, it is probable that a religion oriented to halakhic practice is capable of exerting a greater educative force than a religion consisting solely of beliefs and values. No doubt a religion of values, an "endowing religion" such as Christianity and forms of Judaism which resemble Christianity, is capable of gratifying certain psychic needs. Today, "seekers of religion" or "seekers of God" in order "to fill a vacuum in the soul" are legion. Such a religion is likely therefore to attain some popularity. It will never become an educative force. Men like comforting religions which require no effort, but they do not revere them or take them seriously. It is a basic psychological fact that men respect and adore only that which is demanding, which requires sacrifices and imposes duties. Comforting and congenial teaching is not likely to have a penetrating impact. Why do most people revere the fatherland? Not because of the benefits it confers, but because it requires its citizens to be ready to die in its defense. In like manner, the effectiveness of the "demanding" religion as an educative force is greater than that of the "endowing" ones. The great weakness of religious Jewry in the last generation is a result of having forgotten this truth in its education and propaganda. Instead, they tried to make Judaism acceptable to the public, and especially to the young people, by persuading them of the great benefit and utility the individual and the Jewish community at large may derive from observance of the Torah.

We do not claim that education through halakhic practice guarantees the success of religious education. There is no recipe for attaining a desirable result through education analogous to getting a definite outcome from a chemical reaction. But there are factors which open up certain educational possibilities and others that block them. Jewish religious education is possible only if centered on the Mitzvoth, not otherwise.

Living in accordance with the Halakhah, demarcating a sphere of the sacred through halakhic practice—is this the ultimate end of the religious life? The answer is both yes and no. On the one hand, there can be no doubt that the end and perfection of religiosity, which the prophet calls "knowledge of God" and the psalmist "nearness of God," are not a matter of conduct: "to this ultimate perfection there do not belong either actions or moral qualities . . . it consists only of opinions to which speculation has led and that investigation has rendered compulsory" (Maimonides).[33] The quest pertains to consciousness and inward intentionality. Accordingly, Maimonides identifies the Mitzvoth of the Torah, as it would seem, not with the "ultimate perfection" but with the preparatory perfections. In this sense, halakhic praxis is not the end of religion but only a means and method. But with a penetrating dialectic Maimonides converts the instrumental status of the Mitzvoth into the end of religion: "Know that all the practices of worship, such as reading the Torah, prayer and the performance of the other commandments, have only the end of training you to occupy yourself with His commandments, may He be exalted, rather than with matters pertaining to this world; as if you were occupied with Him, may He be exalted, and not with that which is other than He."[34] After nine chapters (chaps. 26–34 of *Guide* III) discussing the "intention of the Torah," which is to say the purpose of the Mitzvoth, and after fifteen chapters (35–49) devoted to clarifying the rationale of the particular precepts in terms of their utility for perfecting the condition of individuals and of society, Maimonides reveals the secret: the purpose of the Mitzvoth is to educate man to recognize that knowing God and cleaving to him consist in the practice of these very precepts, and this constitutes the worship of God! This is also the meaning of the sentence in his commentary to the tenth chapter of the mishnaic Tractate *Sanhedrin*, "There is no other end to the (acquisition of) Truth than to know that it is true, and the Torah is true, and the purpose of knowing it is to observe it."

At the same time, the "ultimate perfection" of religion can never be realized. It always remains an eternal signpost indicating the right direction on an infinitely extended road. Man cannot observe the Torah in its entirety because it is divine, not human. Even the perfect man is unable to cleave to God, since he will never be able to remove the last barrier separating him from God, "his being an intellect existing in matter." Hence what is meant by "observance of the Torah" can only be the perpetual effort to observe it. In this respect the religious life resembles the work of the housewife; her job is endless, because whatever she does today she will have to do once more tomorrow. The eternal striving toward the religious goal, which is never attained, is embodied in the halakhic practice, which never ends. After all the effort invested in it, the scope of the remaining task is never diminished and the goal is never nearer no matter what distance one has covered in one's attempt to advance toward it. Every morning one must rise anew to the service of the Creator—the self-same service that one performed yesterday, and at the end of every Yom Kippur—after the great realization of repentance and atonement—the annual cycle of weekday Mitzvoth toward the next Yom Kippur begins anew. Thus halakhic observance, in itself a means to religious perfection is, in respect of man, the ultimate religious perfection of which he is capable.

One of the finest European writers and thinkers, Gotthold Ephraim Lessing (1729–1789), said that if God gave him the choice between the truth and the eternal search for the truth, he would choose the latter, "for the genuine truth is known to God alone." Similarly, a great Jewish leader of the socialist movement said in regard to socialism: "The movement itself is everything, the goal nothing at all." In like manner, one representing the "religion of Mitzvoth" would say to the proponents of "authentic religiosity": the eternal pursuit of the religious goal by persevering in religious praxis is the be-all and the end-all of religion for man. "The end of the matter, when all is said and done: fear God and keep his Mitzvoth for that is the whole [attainment] of man" (Eccles. 12:13). The end itself is hidden by God. Rabbi

Kook put it this way: "If man is always likely to stumble . . . that does not detract from his perfection, since the essence of his perfection is the aspiration and the constant desire to attain perfection."[35] His disciple, Rabbi Jacob Moshe Harlap, elaborates on this statement almost in the same words as Lessing's, whose works he had never read: "the desire is more of an end than is the achievement, especially according to Maimonides, who explains that there is no end other than He, may his Name be exalted. It follows that, essentially, the end is the aspiration to attainment of the goal . . . and we must prefer the search for wisdom to its attainment."[36] "Precisely the mediacy is the goal . . . to know how to appreciate the effort more than the attainment of the imaginary end; for, truth to say, there is no end and mediacy is the chief desideratum and the truest end."[37]

CHAPTER 2

Of Prayer

(1960)

"A prayer of the afflicted when he is overwhelmed and pours out his complaint before God" (Ps. 102:1) is diametrically opposed to "Let him gird up strength like a lion to rise in the morning for the service of his Creator"; the first is the heading of one of the psalms and the second, the very beginning of the *Shulhan Arukh,* which serves as an introduction to the laws of prayer.[1] These two symbolize and highlight two critically different meanings of prayer.

The first is a human-psychological phenomenon, the expression of an impulse from within, an action which springs from man himself, from an experience he has undergone, or from the circumstances in which he finds himself. It is an action performed for a man's own need, whether material, intellectual, or emotional. This is prayer for one's own benefit, a service to oneself. There is nothing worshipful about it. It does not represent acceptance of "the yoke of Heaven." In other words, it is not essentially a religious act although, like many other psychologically determined events, it may occur in a religious context as a natural outcome of human manipulation of religious categories.

Prayer, as shaped in the prayerbook, is an entirely different matter. It is obligatory and fixed. Consider what these two properties imply. As obligatory, it is not what a person desires but what is demanded of him; not prayer initiated by him, but one imposed upon him. As fixed, it does not vary with the changing circumstances or states, objective or subjective, in which the praying individual finds himself. Hence it does not reflect the state of mind or situation of the praying person. Such a prayer is not intended to satisfy a need. No two people have identical emotional needs or perceive their position before God in the same way. Their needs and perceptions could not be expressed in the same words at the same moment. Moreover, in the life of a single person no two moments are identical in respect of what he feels or needs. Yet the prayerbook does not take these differences between individuals or between the varying circumstances of the same person into account. The same morning, afternoon, and evening prayers are imposed upon the Jew every day of his life, the only variation being the additional prayers of Sabbath and holidays and the Ne'ilah service of Yom Kippur. The Jewish prayer—inasmuch as it is a distinctive religious institution, determined by religious considerations and a constitutive element of halakhic Judaism—is not intended to serve as an outlet for the feelings and thoughts of man. It is not the spontaneous outpouring of one's soul which necessarily varies with individuals, their moods and states of mind. It is more than an expression of a psychological need which has been granted due place in the religious life. The radical difference between these two kinds of prayer is well brought out in the words of a Tannaite, who apparently was dissatisfied with the kind of prayer embodied in the prayerbook: "Do not make a routine of your prayer, but let it consist in supplication of mercy before God." But the opposite opinion eventually prevailed and was prescribed by the Halakhah.

The sole meaning of prayer as a religious institution is the service of God by the man who accepts the yoke of the Kingdom of Heaven. His acceptance becomes real through his assumption of the burden of Torah and Mitzvoth. Only the prayer which one prays as the observance of a Mitzvah is religiously significant. The spontaneous prayer ("when he is overwhelmed and pours out his complaint before God") a man prays of his own accord is, of course, halakhically permissible, but, like the performance of any act which has not been prescribed, its religious value is limited. As a religious act it is even faulty, since he who prays to satisfy his needs sets himself up as an end, as though God were a means for promotion of his welfare. As in the case of any Mitzvah, prayer—especially prayer—is religiously significant only if it is performed because it is a Mitzvah. Its religious value is minimal when it is performed out of free inclination.

The grandeur and power of prayer, prayer that is mandatory and fixed by Halakhah, lie precisely in setting aside all of man's interests and motives out of awareness of man's position before God, a position

which is always the same regardless of any personal circumstances. Man
relinquishes his own will in the recognition of the duty of worship.
The same set of eighteen benedictions is required of the bridegroom
as of the widower returning from his wife's funeral.[2] The same series
of psalms is recited by one enjoying the world and one whose world
has collapsed. The identical supplications are required of those who
feel the need for them and those who do not.

This characterization of halakhic prayer is not contradicted by its
formulations of praise of God and request for the fulfillment of needs.
The wording is the ritualistic form prescribed for man's worshipful
stance. It is not necessary to request satisfaction of one's needs or to
praise God. But because there is a deep religious reason for praying at
fixed intervals using unchanging formulas, the carrying out of this prescription has been given the form of praise and supplication. This can
be understood by way of analogy with Maimonides' discussion of the
sacrifices, which the fixed prayer has come to supplant. There is no
reason for sacrificing exactly two sheep or thirteen oxen on a given day.
But because there were significant religious grounds for instituting the
sacrifices, one form had to be chosen from among the many which, in
themselves, were of equal value (or of no value). Moreover, prayer
cannot be comprehended otherwise than as having a ritualistically
determined content and form. Whoever worships the Creator who has
no body and cannot be corporeally conceived cannot imagine that he
can truly praise God or that he need inform Him of his needs. He will
certainly not seek to influence God, an idea which comes short of being
blasphemous only because of its naïveté.

The great religious duty of "intentional prayer" is meaningless unless
construed in terms of the general intention to worship God in praying
and in employing the fixed formulas of the prayerbook.[3] It is impossible to demand of every man, in each specific life situation, to recite
the prescribed words with wholehearted intention when in many of
these situations the prescribed praise or the requests are entirely inappropriate. Conversely, to pray because one is obligated to do so, and
not because one is prompted by personal feelings and needs, is an
entirely fitting expression of one's assumption of the yoke of the Kingdom of Heaven and the Mitzvoth. The discussions and controversies
in both halakhic and aggadic sources concerning "intention" and *Iyyun
Tefilah* while praying are highly ambiguous.[4] Is Iyyun Tefilah praise-

worthy or to be avoided? From a thicket of what seem to be contradictions and confusion, one may glean two meanings of "intention"
and two of lyyun Tefilah. The great principle governing intention in
prayer is: "He who prays must direct his heart to Heaven." The
required intention is to serve God by observing the Mitzvah of prayer,
not attention to the supplications or praises recited.[5]

Several of the greatest Amoraites testify that they were at times
unable to concentrate on the content of their prayer. They regarded
themselves as properly praying by virtue of their intention to observe
the Mitzvah of prayer. The Tossafists make a careful distinction: "There
are two kinds of lyyun Tefilah—awaiting that one's request be granted
[which is discreditable] and directing one's heart to Heaven [which is
praiseworthy]." As summed up by Rabbi Solomon ben Adreth: "Not
all intentions are identical."[6]

A controversy reported in the Midrash brings into clear focus the
great difference between these two distinct conceptions of prayer.
"Our rabbis declared: it is forbidden to pray more than the three
prayers instituted by the patriarchs [or instituted in lieu of the daily
sacrifices] . . . One may not pray more than three time daily." By way
of contrast, R. Yohanan said: "Would that one might spend the entire
day in prayer."[7] The first view is illustrated by a conversation reported
between Rabbi Judah the Prince and the Emperor Antoninus, in which
Rabbi Judah explains that "One is forbidden to pray at any time [he
may be so inclined] . . . so as not to assume a disrespectful attitude to
the Almighty . . . that one may not disturb Him whenever he may
wish."

For these reasons there is no point to demand that liturgical formulas be modified to fit the needs of men or the mental climate of the
times. Prayer cut to fit the needs and current attitudes of men loses its
religious importance and becomes one of the activities men carry on at
their pleasure to satisfy their spiritual needs, much like poetry, music,
or the art of cinema. We, of course, recognize that the formulation of
our prayers did not descend from heaven and has no special sanctity in
itself. It was phrased, arranged, and redacted by men like ourselves in
accordance with what appeared to them the most appropriate way of
observing the Mitzvah of prayer. Only by virtue of this halakhic decision did the set forms and locutions of prayer acquire their sanctity. In
this respect, prayer does not differ from any other religious institution

or practice determined by halakhic deliberation within the framework of the Oral Teaching and by virtue of its authority. No doubt, by virtue of this same authority, the formulary of the prayer may be modified, if this appears necessary to the community of those who maintain the Torah and observe its Mitzvoth and who, like the Sages who maintained and shaped the Oral Teaching throughout the ages, sincerely believe that their innovation is called for by the Torah itself. The legitimation of the Oral Teaching depends upon this belief, which is also the condition that permits human decisions on Halakhah to be regarded as the words of the Living God. It is quite different to modify the prayerbook so as to make prayer more palatable to those who participate in it, to adapt it to the spirit of the times or to the prevalent moral and aesthetic values. Such a revision does not perfect the act of prayer; it negates its religious substance. The demand for such reform is not expressive of a religious impulse but of the desire to free oneself from the yoke of the Kingdom of Heaven.

The various "occasional prayers" composed to lend a religious halo to personal or collective interests—"prayer for the welfare of the state," "a prayer for the parachutists," "a prayer for submarine crews"—are ludicrous and insipid. All these are either national-religious play-acting or expression of fears which have nothing to do with religious consciousness. By the nature of things as implanted in them by their Creator, if the girls assigned to folding the parachutes perform their work conscientiously and the parachutist follows his instructions carefully and skillfully, he will land safely. If not, the special prayer will be of no avail. "The foolishness of a man perverts his way, and his heart frets against God" (Prov. 19:3). To pray as one who has faith in God, not as one who worships an idol, one must recognize that "the regularity [implanted by God] of the world-order is constant," and that prayer is not the silly and impudent demand that God change the world's regularity for the benefit of the person praying, but is rather a token of man's cleaving to God by serving Him, no matter what occurs in his natural environment. In the words of the Psalmist, "I am continually with you, you hold my right hand . . . Whom have I in heaven but you and there is none that I desire on earth besides you . . . My flesh and my heart fail, but God is the strength of my heart, and my portion for ever" (Ps. 73).

By understanding prayer as a worshipful stance and not as an attempt to bring about God's intervention in His natural order, we are able to solve a problem which arises in religious education regarding prayer: why does not prayer—at times, even the prayer of the saintly and just—evoke a response? The answer is, simply: no prayer is without response! Since true prayer is the expression of one's intention to serve God, in praying one carries out this very intention. In other words, "prayer which evokes a response" is a tautology and "prayer without response" an absurdity. This is true whenever one prays with proper intention, the intention of worship. "God is near to all those who call upon him, to all who call upon him in truth" (Ps. 145:18). He who prays without proper intention, with the intention of deriving some ulterior benefit from his prayer, is likely to be disappointed: "they shall fret themselves and curse their king and God" (Isa. 8:21).

The great contrast between prayer expressing consciousness of man's position before God and prayer as request of man's wants is highlighted in the prayers of the Days of Awe.[8] The mandatory portion voices man's apprehension of the glory of God's majesty, which leads to longing and hope that his great Name shall be magnified and sanctified in the world; all this without reference to a man's own concerns and troubles (see the prayers beginning "Now, therefore, impose Your awe," "Reign over all the universe in Your glory," and especially "It is incumbent upon us to praise," which is the praise of thanks for Israel's privilege of worshiping God). The essence of the Yom Kippur experience is the consciousness of becoming purified before God and the awareness of the uniqueness of man's position before Him, even though man in himself is as nought. However, popular religiosity was unable to bear this sublimity of faith, and embellished this essential liturgy with prayers expressing man's anxiety about his fate, the fate of the people of Israel, and his relation to God, conceived as master over this fate. Most popular of all is the prayer U'netaneh Tokef.[9] The concern with "who shall live and who shall die," "who will be impoverished and who enriched," and so on, is a general human concern that has no religious bearing. In this respect the man of faith does not differ from the infidel. Nevertheless, this prayer has been accepted as legitimate.

A striking statement of this distinction was made by one of the great latter-day rabbis:

> On Rosh Hashanah all men of Israel pray that the Kingdom of Heaven may return to Jerusalem and that God may reign over the entire world. However, in thus praying, not all intend the same thing. One person loves God with all his heart and prays for the enhancement of his glory. Another has in mind the return of Israel to its land . . . Yet another is insensitive to the troubles of the Exile and prays for his own welfare, which prayer is but a "commandment of men learned by rote." With reference to this the divinely inspired poet proclaimed (Ps. 102:18) "He heeds the prayer of the destitute"—that is to say, of him who, from the depth of his soul, desires to awaken the divine mercy for the sake of the glory of Heaven, and yet "does not despise their prayer," namely the prayer of the many who pray only for their own benefit or merely out of habit.[10]

The Reading of Shema

(1981)

I know of no ways to faith other than faith itself. The formulation "ways to faith" could be interpreted as implying that faith is a *conclusion* a person may come to after pondering certain facts about the world—facts about history, nature, or consciousness. If that were the case, one could lead a person to this conclusion by presenting these facts to him and pointing out their implications. I, however, do not regard religious faith as a conclusion. It is rather an *evaluative decision* that one makes, and, like all evaluations, it does not result from any information one has acquired, but is *a commitment to which one binds himself.* In other words, faith is not a form of cognition; it is a conative element of consciousness. Faith, therefore, cannot be taught. One can only present it in all its might and power.

I shall discuss faith, not ways to faith. There are no ways to faith, since faith is the supreme, if not the only, manifestation of man's free choice. Man can assume the yoke of the Kingdom of Heaven, the yoke of Torah and Mitzvoth and he can repudiate it. No method can guide him in this. Nothing he could experience would lead him to faith if faith did not spring from his own decision and resolve. Signs and wonders, "the mighty hand and the stretched-out arm," God's deliverance and even the revelation of the Shekhinah—none of these sufficed to inculcate faith in the generation that witnessed them. The prophets who appeared among the people of Israel subsequently, men of God through whose mouths the Shekhinah spoke, failed to reform even one soul. Conversely, long after them, scores of generations that saw no miracles and never in their lives beheld any testimony of divine gov-

ernance, who witnessed neither reward of virtue nor punishment of sin
and had not experienced deliverance, nevertheless conducted their lives
in the fullness of faith. It is not nature or history that give origin to
religious faith. In that case, faith could have no meaningful value. It
would impose itself on man even as the findings of science impose
themselves on any mind that understands them, leaving no room for
choice, deliberation, and decision.

In taking up the subject of faith, I am struck by the emphatic claim
that "faith and religion are not identical concepts." I assume that the
authors of this statement wish to distinguish a specific psychological-
conceptual content of the religious consciousness from its concrete
institutionalized embodiment. I disagree with this intention, and my
main purpose in what follows is to contest it. I contend that, for Judaism, faith is nothing but its system of Mitzvoth, which was the embodiment of Judaism. In other words, the assumption of the yoke of the
Kingdom of Heaven is nothing other than the assumption of the yoke
of Torah and Mitzvoth. Faith, in Judaism, is the religion of Mitzvoth,
and apart from this religion Jewish faith does not exist.

In thus depicting Jewish faith, I appeal to the primary document of
faith for Israel, the Shema. Nothing is clearer, more unequivocal, and
more familiar to us than the reading of Shema. Not only is it the primary document of Jewish faith, it is also the subject of the first halakhic
discussion in the Torah of Israel, the Oral Torah, which opens with the
question: "From what time may one recite Shema?"[1] Moreover, the
reading of Shema is the first commandment a Jew must perform when
he reaches the age of thirteen. The first Mitzvah that he is bound to
perform on the eve of the last day of his thirteenth year is the reading
of Shema.

It would seem that nothing new could be said here about the reading
of Shema. During some hundred generations, all that could be said has
been said. Nevertheless it is worth repeating these things, following
the example of Moshe Hayyim Luzzatto, who, in the opening of his
The Path of the Upright, informs us that he has come not to innovate,
but to remind people of what they already know.[2]

The reading of all three parts of the Shema poses difficult questions.
Because reading Shema has become a matter of habit for those who
practice religion and must read it twice daily, these questions tend to
be overlooked although they had already been pointed out by the great

Jewish thinkers. In the ensuing pages I shall be guided by the greatest
of Jewish believers since the biblical age, Maimonides.

The initial question pertains to the first two portions, which are also
included in the *Mezuzah*.[3] In the Pentateuch they are not far apart, and
in the prescribed recitation of Shema they are read consecutively. This
is very perplexing. Ostensibly, one cannot imagine a sharper contrast
in quality of faith than that between the first and second portion of the
Shema. The types of faith they represent seem to be worlds apart. Yet,
in Deuteronomy they are close to each other, and even the unbelieving
critics of Pentateuchal sources do not deny that both parts derive from
the same source. In the halakhically prescribed recital they are read
contiguously as constituting a single unit.

The contrast between them is profound, one might say abysmal. My
comments on the first part do not refer to the opening verse (Hear O
Israel, the Lord our God, the Lord is One), which is a slogan of faith
rather than its content. The content of the first part is in the second
among its six verses: "And you shall love the Lord your God with all
your heart, and with all your soul, and with all your might." Here, love
is faith.

The commandment to love God is presented here as an absolute
demand, a categorical imperative. No justification of the imperative is
offered and no claim is made that is necessitated by any facts. It is not
bolstered by sanctions. There is no hint of benefits to be incurred by
fulfilling this commandment nor is there any threat of punishment that
would follow its violation. The imperative is presented as self-validat-
ing. It represents what the post-biblical tradition calls *lishmah*—the service of God for His own sake. This tremendous verse of the written
Torah received its authentic elucidation by the greatest figure of the
world of the oral Torah, Rabbi Akiba, who said "'with all your heart,
and with all your soul, and with all your might'—even if He take way
your soul."[4]

The second portion, beginning with the words "And it shall come
to pass, if you will hearken diligently," stands starkly opposed to all
that is implied by the first. The observance of the commandment to
love God and to serve him now seems to require bolstering by sanctions. The word "if" at the beginning and the word "lest" in its sequel
suggest the alternative, that of violating the Mitzvah. The imperative
thus ceases to be categorical and becomes hypothetical. The first por-

tion, in which the imperative is presented as categorical, makes no mention of the possibility of its violation. The second part offers a utilitarian motivation for the assumption of the yoke of Heaven and of the Torah and Mitzvoth: "If you will hearken diligently . . . then will I send the rain for your land in its due season"; and "Take heed to yourselves lest your heart be deceived . . . For then God's wrath will be kindled against you and he will shut up the heavens," and so on. This is diametrically opposed to the first part, as construed by Rabbi Akiba. One might say that "If you hearken" represents the religiosity of Elisha ben Abuyah, who was also one of the great Torah sages, Akiba's colleague and Meir's mentor. He became *Aher* or "alienated" after he saw how a Mitzvah which was supposed to confer longevity on one who observed it might in fact be the cause of his death.[5]

How could both "Hear O Israel . . ." and "if you hearken" be included in the Mitzvah of reading Shema? Answers to this question were proffered by many, but *the* answer was given by Maimonides. It is an answer which penetrates to the very depths of religious faith. The great issue epitomized in the confrontation of the two constituent portions of the reading of Shema is pivotal for Maimonides' conception of faith. He discusses it repeatedly—sometimes referring explicitly to one or both of these portions and sometimes only by implication.[6]

Central to this discussion is the sharp distinction between lishmah and not lishmah. Without this distinction the world of Jewish faith constituted by the Torah and Mitzvoth cannot be fully comprehended. God may be worshiped at two levels, representing two different types of motivation. In the terminology of ethical theory, one might say that faith and Torah may be conceived deontically, and also along consequentialist lines. The Torah admits both levels. The first part of the reading of Shema is the expression of faith for its own sake, which is called "love." This faith has no instrumental function and no ulterior purpose. It cannot be rationally explained. If it were capable of being justified for ulterior reasons, it would lose its character as a categorical imperative. What a person does for a specific reason is not, in itself, the direct outcome of his decision.

The explanation of the nature of the faith, which is identical with love, is repeated by Maimonides wherever he takes up the subject: "human perfection—*that they should fear God* (the fear of His grandeur) *and should know who is with them*"; "that the purpose of all the Mitzvoth is the attainment of this passion, namely, fear of Him, may He be exalted"; "that the purpose of the Torah in its entirety is the single end of leading to fear of the Exalted and Awesome One"; "and what the Exalted One demands of us is that we adopt this as our end: 'and you shall love the Lord your God.'"[7] This love was the virtue of Abraham, and because of this it was said of him, "and he believed in God." It is what he proved in the Aqedah by accepting the yoke of the service of God, even though no "advantage," in the sense of the satisfaction of a need, or any imaginable reward could accrue from it. Any punishment for disobedience would be insignificant compared to the sacrifice demanded of him. The duties of faith take precedence over all human needs, interests, and values, even those of the divine promises embodied in visions of the future (the abrogation of the Covenant of the Pieces! [Gen. 15]). Abraham "believed in truth," and it was not a "truth" that is used as a tool or an instrument or means for the satisfaction of a need. "Towards the attainment of this way [of serving God] one must aspire," and the first portion of the reading of Shema is conducive to arousing such aspiration.[8]

We must pay strict attention to the wording: Maimonides does not say that a person ought *to conduct himself* in this manner, but rather that he should *aspire* to this way of conducting himself. He distinguishes between the end itself and the striving toward it. Maimonides is aware that the goal indicated in the first portion of the reading of Shema is "an exceedingly high and difficult achievement which only the very few attain after highly elaborate preparation"; "that not all persons apprehend the truth as did Abraham, and therefore the masses have been *permitted*—in order to confirm them in their faith—to perform the Mitzvoth out of hope for reward and to refrain from transgression for fear of the punishment . . . until one may apprehend and know the truth and the perfect way."[9] "Permitted" is the key word to understanding "If you will hearken." "What the Exalted One *demands* of us" is set forth in the first portion of Shema.

The distinction between the two levels at which faith may be conceived removes the *prima facie* internal contradiction that some find in the doctrine of Maimonides concerning the purpose of the Mitzvoth. Some twenty chapters of the *Guide* appear to be concerned with rationalization of the Mitzvoth, each of which is interpreted as possessing utility for the individual or society or as an efficient educational instru-

ment. But after all this Maimonides comes out with his stupendous
statement: "Know that all the practices of the worship, such as the
reading of Torah, prayer and the performance of the other commandments, have only the end of training you to occupy yourself with His
commandments, may He be exalted, rather than with things pertaining
to this world; you should act as if you were occupied with Him, may
He be exalted, and not with that which is other than He."[10] Thus,
contrary to Maimonides' previous discussion, the purpose of the service of God is now seen to be not the improvement of the world and
human life; the service itself is the very purpose! But, in point of fact,
there is no contradiction here but rather a clear distinction between the
two concepts of faith: as an end-in-itself and as instrument; a distinction corresponding to that between lishmah and not lishmah; between
"Hear O Israel" and "If you will hearken."

From Maimonides we turn back to our very first source, to Genesis,
where we shall already find the two senses of "the fear of God," both
in the same portion of the Torah. In his confrontation with Avimelekh
the king of Gerar, Abraham talks in terms the ruler would understand:
"Because I thought surely *the fear of God* is not in this place; and they
will slay me." Yet approximately sixty verses later, when Abraham
stands before God after the awesome experience of the Aqedah, he is
told: "for now I know that you fear God." There is no need for many
words to explain the difference between these two "fears." The former
is the fear of the supreme chief of police, the latter is the fear of God,
and that, according to Maimonides, "is the intention of the Torah and
the fundamental intent of our sages." In His graciousness toward His
creatures, the Giver of the Torah does not reject a person who abides
by the Torah even if he has not attained understanding of its "intention." The joining of the two portions of the Pentateuch into a single
unit, the Shema, so as to express both the faith of him who serves God
in acknowledgment of His divinity and the faith of him who serves
God because he attributes to Him the governance of human life, was
an act of profound significance. That the intention of the Torah is the
service of God lishmah ("out of love") was never in dispute among the
rabbinic Sages. The subject of their disagreement was the evaluation
of the service of God "not for its own sake" ("out of fear"). Some
approve of it and even recommend it as a way of serving God suitable

to a person who has not attained perfection of faith. Maimonides himself, the greatest believer among the Jews since the patriarchs and the
prophets, lends his authority to this view. "A man should always
occupy himself with Torah and Mitzvoth though it is not for their own
sake, for in consequence of doing so out of an ulterior motive one
comes to perform them lishmah."[11] Moreover, we even find a statement of our sages to the effect that "If a man declares 'this *sela* [a coin
of the talmudic period] be for charity in order that my son may live,'
he is completely righteous."[12] Perhaps this saying is to be construed as
sarcastic in intent but, even if we understand it as a straightforward
utterance, it can hardly be taken as consonant with the true intent of
the Mitzvah of charity. As against such remarks, which condone the
service of God for ulterior reasons, we find vehement denunciations of
such worship. Thus it is contended that only Torah lishmah is a life
potion to man, while "he who occupies himself with Torah not for its
own sake—it becomes poison to him."[13] Whoever regards the service
of God as a means for fulfilling his wishes—be they "life, children, or
nutrition" or the satisfaction of an emotional need ("a prayer of the
afflicted when he is overwhelmed and pours out his complaint before
the God")—is seeking his own advantage and not applying himself to
the service of God. Even observance of the Torah for the purpose of
expediting redemption falls under the category of Torah that is not
lishmah. Perhaps this was already the meaning of the harsh words ending the prophecies of Hosea: "for the ways of the Lord are right, and
the just shall walk in them: but the transgressors shall stumble therein."
"Therein"—in the ways of God! Care must be taken in how one follows the ways of God.

Two thousand years, and perhaps more, after the prophet uttered
these words, we find in the confession of transgressions listed in the
Sephardic prayer book for the Days of Awe: "We performed Mitzvoth
not for the sake of Heaven." The performance of Mitzvoth (!) not for
the sake of heaven is perceived as a transgression in need of atonement.

Now that we have tried to understand the difference between the first
part of Shema and the part of "If you will hearken," let us revert to
Shema as a whole and attempt to plumb the depth of its meaning.
There is no doubt but that it centers on the great injunction "and you
shall love." But what is the meaning of the "love of God" when it is

demanded of human consciousness? "Love" is a constituent of consciousness and one of the natural tendencies of man. It is as many-faceted as are its variegated objects, all of which are presented to him in sensation, conception, or imagination. A man may love himself, a woman, wealth, or honor. He loves his country and may love cake topped with whipped cream: anything he senses, conceives, or imagines. Is it appropriate to apply the human category of "love" to man's relation to that which is not given in sensation, conception, or imagination? Seeing it as a human phenomenon, we are capable of understanding a pagan's love for his idols, which he can envisage with his senses. We can also understand the love of a Christian for his lord, who is a human figure. But how can one love God who is not conceivable in terms of any attributes and is analogous to nothing whatsoever? What is the meaning of the austere demand presented in Shema to the believing Jew? Does it have any meaning in terms of human categories?

The Torah spoke in language spoken by men.[14] In this tongue it conveys notions whose meaning cannot truly be rendered in such a manner. The unintelligible verse "and you shall love the Lord your God" is elucidated through its sequel: "And these words which I command you this day should be in your heart." The acceptance of the yoke of Torah and Mitzvoth is the love of God, and it is this that constitutes faith in God. Man's faith in a God who eludes all predication of attributes and the love he bears for a God who cannot be imagined can only mean the readiness of man to serve God by observing his Torah and its precepts. This must be explicitly stated in order to remove the error afflicting the naïve (or those who feign naïveté), who contend that one can separate faith from religion; that faith is one thing, and religion, in the sense of the institutional system of Torah and Mitzvoth, another; that, when faith and religion appear together, adherence to Torah and Mitzvoth is a kind of superstructure built upon faith; and that there could be a belief in God unaccompanied by the observance of the commandments. To them one may retort: who is the God you "believe in"? If it is not a pagan idol or the Christian deity, but rather "the Lord He is the God" (as in the profession of faith elicited by the prophet Elijah and repeated yearly at the end of the Day of Atonement), without shape or figure—then there is no other content to the faith in God and the love of God than the assumption of the yoke of the Kingdom of Heaven, which is the yoke of Torah and

Mitzvoth. The Lord is giver of the Torah, and the belief in him is man's acknowledgment of the obligation to abide by the Torah. Since the Mitzvoth have no utilitarian significance and are not intended to satisfy human needs, their observance by man is an act of sheer love. Take away the obligation to perform the commandments from the faith in the God of Judaism and it turns into a belief in the Platonic demiurge or in a supervisor of world affairs who, from his seat in heaven, pulls strings on earth. Such a conception might be of cosmological interest, but it is devoid of religious content. Hegel, whose position between atheism and Christianity is difficult to determine, said, "If there is no world, God is no God." But in our prayerbook we find "Lord of the universe, who reigned before anything was created," and also "You were before the world was created and are since its creation." The world and all it contains are insignificant before God.

The meaning of the relation between "and you shall love" and "these words which I command you" in the first paragraph, and of the relation between this portion and the one beginning "if you will hearken," are illuminated by the addition of the third portion, the one about *Tsitsith,* to these two paragraphs. This portion is concerned with remembering and doing. It explicitly directs attention not to the subject of God and man, but to the issue of Mitzvoth and man ("and remember all the commandments of the Lord and fulfill them"; "To the end that you may bear in mind and perform all my commandments"). Remembrance is a matter of the heart, and one might suppose that it could be conjoined with "faith" and "love" in the abstract sense of these terms; but Scripture makes clear that remembrances means nothing other than the performance of the Mitzvoth. The remembrance of God exists in the consciousness of the believer on one of two planes: that of Shema (faith lishmah), and that of "If you will hearken" (faith not-lishmah but in God as the supreme minister of finance, health, and security). However, the man who remembers God on the level of Shema and the one who remembers Him in the sense of "If you will hearken" are both obligated to perform the Mitzvoth.

The end of the portion relating to Tsitsith, with which the reading of Shema ends, brings forth a notion which is specifically religious: the notion of holiness, "and be holy." This notion has no meaning outside the domain of religious faith. Although it has penetrated into everyday secular usage, as in the sentence: "the memory of my late mother is sacred to me," in such contexts the expression is merely an emotionally charged figure of speech. Originally, and in its authentic sense, "holy" refers to God. Hence it is not amenable to explication in terms derived from ordinary discourse, and it cannot be applied to anything that exists as part of the world. In human reality the category of holiness cannot be applied except as indicating an activity which is directed toward "the Holy" and connoting the service of God, the performance of the Mitzvoth. It signifies both the goal toward which we must strive, and the striving itself. But it does not denote any existing entity. Within the confines of human reality there is only functional holiness. Essential holiness pertains to God alone. Whoever applies the notion of holiness to a natural or artificial being—to man, land, an institution, a building, or an object—is engaging in idolatry. He thereby exalts that object or fact to the rank of divinity. This is the great significance of the demand set forth in the Tsitsith: "To the end that you may bear in mind and perform all my commandments and be holy." Man is not intrinsically holy; his holiness is not already existing and realized in him. It is rather incumbent upon him to achieve it. But the task is eternal. It can never be fulfilled except through a never-ending effort.

At this point it is appropriate to quote one of the greatest Torah scholars of recent generations, a man of true piety who devoted profound thought to the subject of faith, Rabbi Meir Simhah Cohen of Dwinsk, the author of *Meshekh Hokhmah*.[15] The contention that "there is nothing holy in the world . . . Only God, exalted be His name, is holy, and He alone is worthy of glory and worship" is repeated frequently and with great emphasis in his book: for example, "There is no holiness in any creature; only in the Creator, blessed be He"; "All holy things—the land of Israel, Jerusalem, the Temple Mount, the Temple, the Tablets, are not intrinsically holy, and they are not sanctified except by the performance of the Mitzvoth." Consequently, when Jews repudiate the Torah and violate the Mitzvoth, they are all deprived of holiness and become profane. He makes this point insistently: "Do not imagine that the mountain is a holy thing"; "That they should not suppose that there is a sanctity inhering in the building itself"; "and do not imagine that the Tabernacle and the Temple are things holy unto themselves." Other passages in the same vein may be found in the work. It is as though he foresaw that "religious" Jews, fifty years after his death, would degrade and violate the notion of "holiness" by taking advantage of it as camouflage for the satisfaction of human needs and interests, whether private or collective.

It would seem that the Torah wanted to illustrate the profound significance of "holiness" for faith in placing the story of Qorah immediately after the portion of Tsitsith. Only three verses separate the great programmatic affirmation of faith by Moses ("and you will be holy") from the programmatic statement of faith by Qorah: "all the congregation are holy"—holiness being regarded by him not as an end whose achievement is demanded, but as already given, established, and residing in the people as they are. The great notion of holiness is thus desecrated and given a pagan connotation.

CHAPTER 4

Fear of God in the Book of Job

(1974)

I t is a mark of the universal significance of the Book of Job that neither the book nor its author can be traced to a definite place or time or to a specific historic-cultural milieu. This characteristic of the powerful work precludes not only identification of its author, but even a learned guess as to where and when he wrote. The author's words seem appropriate to all times and all places, to the human condition in any society and culture. Although the protagonists in the Book of Job have names suggestive of specific places and particular families, they remain unidentified. It would seem that the anonymous author intended to blur or efface all trace of incidental facts, and to build his narrative upon that which is beyond time and place: a man— not necessarily Jewish—aware of standing before God, in the sense of the great closing statement of the Yom Kippur Ne'ilah prayer, "You have distinguished man of yore . . . and recognized him so he may stand before you."

Some of the rabbis, according to a midrashic-aggadic source, were so bold as to attribute the Book of Job to Moses. Others, including recent scholars, have ascribed to Job (actually, to the Book of Job) dates ranging from the time of the patriarchs to that of the Persian rule in Judea—in other words, dates ranging over the entire biblical era. Ultimately we have to agree that Job never existed in fact but was merely a parable.[1]

The author offers us clear hints as to the meaning and intention of this parable. From them we can infer that he *was not Moses*. The Pentateuch was clearly before his eyes, Genesis in particular. Moreover, his entire narrative fastens on the Aqedah, the story of the attempted sacrifice of Isaac, with which he tries to draw an analogy. The trial of Job is a duplicate of the trial of Abraham; both stories seek to teach the meaning of fear of God, which is attributed to Abraham after the Aqedah and is announced in the very first verse of the Book of Job. As the Sages themselves remarked, "That which Abraham said is what Job said."[2] They further stated that "it is said of Job 'one that feared God,' and it is declared to Abraham 'thou fearest God;' just as 'fear of God' with Abraham indicates love, so 'fear of God' with Job indicates love."[3] The first conspicuous clue to this correspondence is found in the opening verse of Job, namely, "There was a man in the land of Uz." Now why Uz of all places, a land mentioned in the Bible only in passing, one whose imprint on the biblical world is nil?

It appears that the author placed Job in "the land of Uz" as an allusion to the Uz whose name appears in the Book of Genesis in the verse immediately following the Aqedah episode: "And it came to pass after these things, that it was told Abraham, saying, Behold, Milkah, she also has born children to your brother Nahor: *Uz* his firstborn" (Gen. 22:20–21). This serves to apprise us that Job's trial is the continuation of the trial of Abraham.

At a later stage in the narrative the author of the Book of Job introduced an additional figure into the debate between Job and his friends, naming him "Habuzi" ("Elihu the son of Barakh'el the Buzite"). Surely he meant to follow up on the verse succeeding the Aqedah: "Uz his firstborn and Buz his brother." It is inconceivable that such parallels are accidental. They reflect a definite intention.

What is the common element in the trials of Abraham and Job, of whose fear of Heaven there could have been no doubt even *prior to their trials*? They are both tested as to the nature of this fear. Do they fear God because they are enjoined to fear and worship Him under all conditions and circumstances, or is their fear the result of the attributes and functions ascribed to Him as the monitor of man's actions and provider of his needs?

Abraham is put to the test when fulfillment of the divine demand requires that he renounce all human values; not merely personal values such as those involved in the relationship of a father to his only son, but also promises bearing on his seed for all generations to come. He is expected to forgo the Covenant of the Pieces.

Job is put to the test when God appears to him not as the guardian of his fate who metes out reward and punishment, but *in His sheer divinity;* Job experiences God directly and hears the words the author quotes as God's own at the end of the book. Abraham and Job are tested to determine whether their faith is faith for its own sake, manifested in the worship of God for His sake, and unlike the religious faith of the mass of believers who conceive God as acting for their sake. Both Job and Abraham pass this test of true fear born of true love. Scripture testifies that Abraham "believed in God" and that he "feared God," and the prophet Isaiah calls him "lover of God." Job attains the same level after God's revelation to him, and God testified that he spoke "the thing that is right."

Chapter 28 is perhaps the climax of the Book of Job from the human point of view, which is the perspective from the beginning until that point (in contrast to the divine aspect presented in the book's final chapters). It constitutes Job's main argument. The argument rises to a level which becomes both loftier and more profound during the course of the three rounds of Job's debate with his friends. It begins with Job's cry of protest against the iniquity in the governance of the world by its Creator, and his urgent demand for justice. Gradually, a new note is insinuated, which becomes more and more explicit as the argument proceeds. Job's suffering is no longer the focus of his protest; rather, it is his inability to comprehend the meaning of his suffering, which is but one detail within an incomprehensible world.

Without quite resigning himself to the way the world is conducted, Job is now inclined to accept it with its inherent iniquity as being part of God's world. But he is ready to accept it only if he may gain an insight into the meaning of this awesome world of God. Job is convinced that a profound wisdom—the wisdom of the Creator in whom he believes with every fibre of his being—underlies the horror inherent in the world's course and in the fate of its creatures. But this wisdom is concealed from mankind. The plea he addresses to God thus shifts from justice to illumination. Job demands that God reveal to him why the world is as it is. The inscrutability of the creation, and of human fate in general and Job's in particular, has become a source of anguish deeper than the torment of the sense of iniquity. Hints of this modification in Job's attitude occur already in chapters 13, 19, and 23 ("and understand what he would say unto me"), but in chapter 28 his remonstrance to God bursts into the open, and is presented with incomparable force.

Job describes the wisdom of man as displayed in mankind's great achievements. Man's power and his art, stemming from his wisdom, are manifest in technology: control over nature, the extraction of metals from their ores, the diversion of the course of rivers, the bringing under cultivation of wasteland. The power to control nature, however, does not endow man with the knowledge and understanding of nature or of the purpose of creation, of which he has become the master. This lack of knowledge oppresses and troubles him. But for this suffering there is no remedy. The Creator of the world concealed from man its meaning, knowledge of which is the true "wisdom." This is the great accusation that Job levels at the Creator: He treats His world like a despotic ruler who exacts from his slaves blind obedience to his decrees. True enough, the decrees have a profound significance. Job never doubts this (see 28:23: "God understands the way thereof, and He knows the place thereof"). But the Ruler does not heed man's distress and does not reveal the true meaning to him. It is this accusation that is ultimately answered by God, an answer that satisfies Job and makes him revoke his accusation.

In the last chapter Job passes the test to which he was put in the initial chapters. He commits himself to faith in God and dedication to His service purely in respect of His divinity, much like the stance of Abraham at the Aqedah. Job began by crying out against the iniquity found in creation, and addressed his protest to God and man. Gradually he came to understand that the cause of his suffering was not so much his afflictions as his inability to comprehend their meaning. Henceforth he addressed his argument to God alone, of whom he demanded an explanation of the horror caused by the seeming pointlessness and injustice of the world. In chapter 28 he accused God of concealing true wisdom from man, and so doing a great injustice to His creatures. Job constantly repeats his demand that God reply to his questions and reveal to him the wisdom underlying the course of the world, the sense and meaning of His Providence which is incorporated in it.

Job's request and pleas evoke a response: God appears to him and answers him out of the whirlwind. His request was therefore granted, at least partially. Was it fulfilled completely? According to Job himself—his few words in the last chapter—God's response satisfied him and answered his charges. But how should we construe the satisfaction that Job derives from such a response? Our understanding of the test to which Job was put and of how he proved himself, indeed, the significance of the entire book, hinges upon this point.

The response ascribed to God by the author of the Book of Job in the last three chapters is, at first sight, irrelevant. It does not answer the question "whence shall wisdom be found." It does not discuss man and his fate. It does not refer to the problem of justice and equity, of strictness and leniency, reward and punishment. It leaves physical reality unaccounted for. It describes being as it is without judging it. It presents the cosmic and terrestrial world, from the inanimate to the living, from the splendid and wondrous to the awful and monstrous—especially the monstrous phenomena—without hinting at any purpose in this amazing creation, or any secret intention underlying the monstrosity. Such is the Creator's Providence, and this is what satisfies Job. The following are the words of Maimonides whose explication of the meaning of the book of Job is the most profound: "In the prophetic revelation that came to Job and through which his error in everything that he imagined became clear to him, there is no going beyond the description of natural matters—namely, description of the elements or description of the meteorological phenomena or description of the nature of the various species of animals, but of nothing else."[4]

It is precisely for this reason that Job is able to grasp what God demands from him and the import of the trial through which he was put: "I have heard of you by the hearing of the ear, but now my eye sees you" (42:5). All his life Job believed in God in the way prevalent among the masses, who believe in God and undertake to serve Him because He—in their conception—acts for their benefit, a deity whose essence is the fulfillment of the functions of supervisor of their affairs. That is the faith "by the hearing of the ear." But now Job's eye "saw" a deity whose divinity is his very essence, and whose world, precisely as it is, is His Providence. This providence manifests itself in natural reality itself; It is not intended or directed toward any specific purpose or goal, not even toward the needs and wishes of Job. Having thus "seen" God with his "eye," Job understands that he must decide whether to commit himself to faith in God and to His service in the world as it is, to believe in Him and to serve Him not for his (Job's) benefit, but because of His divinity. Thus Job's trial proves to be identical with that of Abraham, of whom, already prior to the Covenant of the Pieces, it was said that he "believed in God."

Once again we shall cite the words of the great believer Maimonides summarizing the meaning of the Book of Job:

> The latter [Job] said all that he did say only so long as he had no true knowledge and knew the deity only because of his acceptance of authority, just as the multitude adhering to the Law know it. But when he knew God with a certain knowledge, he admitted that true happiness, which is the knowledge of the deity, is guaranteed to all who know Him and that human beings cannot be troubled in it by any of all the misfortunes in question. While he had known God only through the traditional stories and not by way of speculation, Job had imagined that the things thought to be happiness, such as health, wealth, and children are the ultimate goal. For this reason he fell into such perplexity and said the things he did. This is the meaning of his dictum: "I had heard of you by the hearing of the ear; but now my eye sees you; wherefore I abhor myself and repent of dust and ashes." It is because of this final discourse indicative of correct apprehension that it is said of him after this: "For ye have not spoken of Me the thing that is right, as my servant Job has."[5]
>
> The notion of His providence is not the same as the notion of our providence; nor is the notion of His governance of the things created by Him the same as the notion of our governance of that which we govern. The two notions are not comprised in one definition . . . and there is nothing in common between the two except the name alone . . . you should not fall into error and seek to affirm in your imagination that His knowledge is like our knowledge or His purpose and His providence and His governance are like our purpose and our providence and our governance. If a man knows this, every misfortune will be born lightly by him. And misfortune will not add to his doubts regarding the deity and whether He does or does not know or whether He exercises providence or manifests neglect, but will, on the contrary add to his love, as is said in conclusion of the prophetic revelation in question: "Wherefore I abhor myself, and repent of dust and ashes." As [the sages] may their memory be blessed have said: "Those who do out of love and are joyful in suffering."[6]

The love of God is the key word. The author of Job alluded to the closeness of Job to Abraham by putting as last words in Job's mouth: "[I] repent in dust and ashes." "Dust and ashes" were the words used by Abraham in his argument with God: "Behold now I have taken upon me to speak to God, who am but dust and ashes" (Gen. 18:27).

CHAPTER 5

Divine Governance:
A Maimonidean View

(1972)

This chapter is a meditation on the following texts:

"At four seasons judgment is passed on the world . . . On *Rosh Hasha-nah* all creatures pass before Him one by one" (Mishnah Rosh Hasha-nah).

"This means that a balance is drawn up for human beings, and they are sentenced to health and disease, to death and life and to the alternative states pertaining to the various circumstances of human life. The literal meaning of this is clear as you may see, *but its secret and true meaning is indeed very difficult*" (Maimonides' Commentary on the Mishnah).

"The meaning of *knowledge of the Name* is apprehending Him" (Maimonides, *Guide of the Perplexed*).

"So that man has no preeminence above a beast: for all is vanity. [Yet] You have distinguished man of yore and recognized him so he may stand before you" (The Ne'ilah prayer).

Those who perceive themselves as "standing before God," in the sense of the prayer that concludes the Day of Atonement, interpret the meaning of this "standing" in different ways. Some see it as a gift. Others regard it as a demand.

Some people perceive their "standing" as "receiving," whether in the sense of something given, or in the sense of expecting, wishing, intending, or making an effort to be given something. In any case, this person's standing before God is *for his own good*. It does not matter whether he envision this "good" as a material benefit for the individual or for the community ("life, children, nutriment," or the redemption of Israel) or as a spiritual good (perfection, or elevation of a person or of humanity). In either case he intends nothing other than the satisfaction of human needs. Such a belief in God is seen to be a means to an end, the good of oneself (or his community).

Others, however, may regard themselves as being called upon to "give," because the "standing" is itself the end, the service of God for the sake of which all man's resources, material and spiritual, are but means.

According to the first approach, the crucial aspect in "man's standing before God" consists in what descends from above—providence, as this is understood in common usage. The crucial aspect of the second approach is what ascends from below, which is love.

The traditional formulation of the contrast between these two conceptions is the distinction between lishmah and not lishmah, or, in a sharp midrashic phrasing, between "the wicked who subsist on their God" and "the just on whom God subsists." After the patriarchs and prophets, and Rabbi Akiba's exposition of the Mitzvah to love God with all one's soul, the idea of faith lishmah, for the sake of God, was given its most eloquent expression, its most profound and sublime formulation, in the doctrine of Maimonides, especially in his conception of Providence.

Maimonides foreshadows his critique of the accepted notion of providence in his remark in the commentary on the same Mishnah in which Rosh Hashanah (the scriptural "day of blowing the horn") is presented as the day of judgment. It is implied more clearly in his lengthy introduction to the tenth chapter of Tractate *Sanhedrin*. It is stated concisely in an extremely concentrated fashion in his responsum to Rabbi Obadiah the Proselyte in connection with the talmudic adage "All is in the hands of Heaven, save the fear of Heaven."[1] In the *Guide of the Perplexed* Maimonides develops his doctrine of providence systematically in the chapters that are explicitly devoted to this topic and to the discussion of the book of Job.[2] However, in these chapters—in accordance with the method described in the "Instruction with respect to this Treatise" and the "Introduction"—he typically reveals one truth to those capable of understanding, while he conceals others. The last four chapters of the *Guide,* which are illuminated by the sublime last chapter of the *Book of Science,* epitomize the Maimonidean faith in providence in all its power.[3]

Two terms that occur frequently in traditional discourse are presumed to express religious notions: "general providence" and "individual providence." What do they mean? Since each person is merely a particular item within an encompassing genus or whole (that is, humankind or even the entire world)—do not these two concepts, if taken literally, contradict one another? Can one reconcile the concept of providence (in both its modes) with another notion also current in the same religious tradition, (free) "choice"? Is it possible to reconcile the belief in providence with objective reality—with the regularity of nature, with the course of history, with the fate of the community and the individual?

These problems have notoriously preoccupied and tormented religious thinkers, from the patriarchs and the prophets to the contemporary men of faith. The conceptual wealth of Judaism and the boundless breadth of its spiritual world are reflected in the plurality of opinions and views, the diversity of conceptions, and the often conflicting doctrines on these matters. Nonetheless, all of them have become entrenched and have acquired legitimacy within the domain of faith that is founded on the acceptance of the yoke of Torah and Mitzvoth. However, in respect of the power of faith, none of these doctrines measures up to that of Maimonides.

More than any other religious thinker and believer Maimonides was compelled to struggle with two grave difficulties related to the notion of providence, difficulties that arose in consequence of his own anthropological views juxtaposed with his theological doctrine.

By nature the individual human being participates fully in all the life processes, from nutrition and sensation to desire, imagination, and thought. This contradicts the popular theory, which splits up the personality by according freedom of choice to man in the domain of faith and morality, while imposing the decree of providence on his remaining activities ("all is in the hands of Heaven save the fear of Heaven").[4]

The theological problem arises from true faith's credo that "He alone is true being," and "the truth of His being" is not contingent upon any other existing entities, among which "there is no true being like His other than He."[5] The prevalent idea of providence, however, implies faith in a deity that performs certain functions in the world: a God *for* the world (or for man). It is precisely in response to these difficulties that Maimonides set forth the great answer of faith.

General providence is, in effect, "The course of the world." Whatever exists in reality, or is necessitated by the causal structure inherent in nature, falls under providence. In this respect, the fate of humankind—as one type of natural beings—is no different from that of any other species, whose existence is secured by the general scheme of causality (final cause!). The individual too, of course, is subject *by nature* to this reality. "The contrary of this is impossible." The consequences of all human deeds are necessitated by the nature of men's actions, the regulation of which is the manifestation of providence. Man's fate and the events which befall him that are not the fruits of his actions are incidents that are also necessitated by the nature of the reality to which he belongs and within which he exists. Man cannot demand something that is self-contradictory: to be part of natural reality and at the same time transcend its laws and processes. God's general Providence in the world is *Hessed, Mishpat,* and *Tsedaqah* ("loving kindness", "judgment" and "righteousness"). But when these are attributed to God they do not designate a disposition (as they do when used to qualify human behavior). They rather denote the manifestation of providence in the nature of reality. Thus the very existence of the world is God's loving kindness. The existence of living things possessing powers implanted in them is righteousness. "Judgment" refers to the sequence of events succeeding one another by the necessity inherent in the relations between them.[6] Insofar as man's natural existence is concerned, he is as subject to general providence as an animal ("so that man has no preeminence over the beast").[7]

Nevertheless, man has been chosen, because of a "power" (capacity) given him, which is what distinguishes him from the animal: the ability "to use his mental powers [all natural] for one purpose" which is *knowledge of God* ("to stand before you"). The actualization of this potentiality is up to each individual and depends upon his concentration of will and effort toward this goal. He who knows God cleaves to him with a strength which is proportionate to the extent of his knowledge ("according to the knowledge shall be the love"), *and it is this knowledge and this cleaving to God that constitute "individual providence."* In the relation between man and his maker individual providence is

not a datum of human nature. It is not bestowed upon man from above
in virtue of his humanity. Rather, each individual must achieve it by
his own endeavor, that is, through the perfection of his rational power
and of all the "powers of the soul" related to it (since "the soul of man
is one"!) and through a supreme effort in exercising his capacities for
this purpose. The notion of "individual providence" has no meaning
except in reference to the truly wise person, who is also the veritably
righteous man—he who makes the supreme effort and is always in the
"proximity of God"; "he is with God and God is with him." He who
is not close to God is beyond the scope of individual providence, and
is subject only to general providence—"is like the beasts who perish"
(Ps. 49:21). God knows man only insofar as man knows Him, "for
God knows the ways of the righteous" (Ps. 1:6).

The full religious depth of this conception can be comprehended
only if one discerns that individual providence is not a result of the
adherence to God or a reward for cleaving to Him. Individual providence is *identical* with this adherence. The sublime summary of Maimonides' various discussions of providence, both by way of allusion
and explicitly, is to be found in *Guide* III 52.

> Man does not sit, move, and occupy himself when he is alone in his house
> as he sits, moves, and occupies himself when he is in the presence of a
> great king; nor does he speak and rejoice while he is with his family and
> relatives, as he speaks in the king's council. Therefore he who chooses to
> achieve human perfection and to be in true reality *a man of God* must give
> heed and know that the great king who always accompanies him and
> cleaves to him is greater than any human individual, even if the latter be
> *David* and *Solomon*. This king who cleaves to him and accompanies him
> is the intellect that overflows towards us and is the bond between us and
> Him, may He be exalted. Just as we apprehend Him by means of that
> light which He caused to overflow towards us—as it says, "In thy light
> do we see light" (Ps. 36:10)—so does He *by means of this selfsame light*
> examine us; and because of it, He, may He be exalted, is constantly with
> us, examining from on high: *Can any hide himself in secret places that I
> shall not see him?* (Jer. 23:24). *Understand this well!*[8]

The "light" wherein man apprehends God is the very light by which
God examines him and sees him. It is in this sense that man is under
the guidance of providence—"his God is within him," and "he whose
God is within him will not be touched by evil at all." Many have failed

to see the point of these statements of Maimonides, including some of
his important interpreters, who took it for granted that he is referring
here to concrete events in a person's life. Thus they were perplexed as
to how these views of Maimonides can be reconciled with what is common knowledge regarding human fate and the nature of things, and
with the cries of protest by the pure and the holy in face of "a righteous
man who suffers." But Maimonides did not wish to contend that the
person who achieves personal providence, that is, the person who
knows God and cleaves to Him, is protected from the sway of the
forces that represent general providence. Natural things do happen,
and at times cause harm. The apprehension of God and the adherence
to Him are not means toward the attainment of a "good"; rather, they
are "good" itself, compared to which all the necessary evil encountered
in experience is as nought, as though it did not exist. Providence, as
far as man is concerned, is essential rather than functional.[9] The presentation of the good not as a reward for man's righteousness but as
identical with his righteousness is also the gist of Maimonides' clarification of Job's predicament.[10]

Maimonides' faith in providence is the faith of the first believer, who
"believed in God" and went with his son to the Aqedah. It is the faith
of the divine poet Assaf, "And I am continually with you" (Ps. 73) (*not*
"you are continually with me"!), and this trust is "holding me by my
right hand." Assaf does not demand or expect that because of his cleaving unto God he will benefit in any concrete fashion. On the contrary,
he knows that perhaps "his flesh and his heart fail" from grief and
suffering, "but God is the strength of my heart and my portion for
ever." "But it is good for me to draw near to God." The Psalmist does
not say that "because I draw near to God I benefit." The proximity of
God itself is the good.

Hence the lesson for the approaching Day of Judgment. Man passes
sentence on himself with respect to closeness to God or remoteness
from Him. That is the "secret" Maimonides alludes to in his commentary on the Mishnah of the Day of Judgment (see above).[11] The genuine aspiration to be "under the governance of providence" is to be
found in the prayers for awakening man's awe in the presence of God,
in those which express a worshipful attitude and recognition of God's
majesty. It is not expressed in man's concern for his welfare which is
found in the U'Netaneh Toqef prayer and in "and on Rosh Hashanah

will be inscribed . . . who shall live and who shall die . . . who will be tranquil and who will be tormented."

It should also be noted that the emphatic imperative "understand this well" occurs *verbatim* also in the chapters on prophecy in the *Guide,* which present prophecy not as a miraculous invasion from the higher world into the lower (as in R. Judah Halevi's doctrine of prophecy), but rather as an ascent of man from the lower to the upper world of the knowledge of God through the effective use of man's natural faculties. In the doctrine of Maimonides, the apprehension of God, the love of God, prophecy, and providence are one and the same.

CHAPTER 6

Lishmah and Not-*Lishmah*

(1977)

This chapter is the author's abridged rejoinder to the lengthy criticism by M. S. of his book *Judaism, the Jewish People, the State of Israel*. It was published in several installments in the literary section of *Ha'aretz* and highlights some of the views against which he directs his most acrimonious polemics.

Whoever occupies himself with the Torah for its own sake, his learning becomes an elixir of life to him . . . But whoever occupies himself with the Torah not for its own sake, it becomes to him a deadly poison.

B.T. Ta'anith 7a

Whoever dismisses these propositions that we have elucidated, which are founded upon the most basic of principles, and searches among the Aggadoth or the Midrashim or in the remarks of one of the Geonim of blessed memory in order to seek out an isolated phrase with which to rebut our rational and well-grounded assertions is committing (spiritual) suicide.

Maimonides' Responsa

This is the truth which all who choose to admit the truth will believe, for the several statements will testify to one another and are instructive, one with respect to the other.

Maimonides: Guide of the Perplexed

It is not proper method to set aside a ruling applied in practice and search out rebutting considerations and rejoinders. Likewise, one ought not dismiss plausible opinions which have already been confirmed by evidence and appeal to some statement of a single savant, who may have been mistaken, or whose words were not intended to be taken literally, or were pronounced as applying to a given context and its specific conditions.

Maimonides' Epistles

Theoreticians are prone to succumb to the error of disregarding the obvious.
                                    Eugene P. Wigner

E xamination of the components of a system one by one cannot reveal the nature of the system in its totality. A component of a whole takes on a different meaning when it is seen by itself. A system can never be properly understood unless it is first perceived in its totality. Only then can one proceed to determine the place or functional contribution of each component. A system is a totality which is both logically and causally prior to its parts. Thus a biological organism is prior to its organs not only logically and causally, but even chronologically. This is the meaning of the second, third and fourth citations from Maimonides at the head of this chapter. Maimonides was referring to "Judaism" and its embodiments in detailed thoughts and deeds in all the domains of human life.

The concept of the whole and the parts applies to use of sources. I never base my views on isolated citations. By so proceeding, one could find grounds for *any* opinion and *any* view. My citations and references do not serve as evidence but solely as illustrations. I regard it as legitimate to illustrate what I have to say by suitable statements occurring in the sources, in full awareness of the possibility of extracting from these very sources formulations of other opinions, even contradictory ones. In so doing, I follow Maimonides' instructions to construe particular assertions in terms of their meaning within the system in its totality.

My argument is directed against people like M.S., whose perception is shaped by the wish that Judaism provide for their own psychic needs: the need for gratification conceived in terms of the categories of humanistic atheism, and furthering the interest of the people of Israel, as seen from the standpoint of a secular nationalism. M.S. discusses religion (the religion of Israel) and religious faith not as oriented to the service of God—which is an endeavor to break through the bounds of a meaningless natural existence to that which transcends it—but as meant to gratify the cravings of the natural creature, "man," and to serve the interests of a construct of human consciousness, "the nation." He *wishes* to regard Judaism as an instrument for satisfying these desires and interests. To this end he selects from the huge complex of ideational and practical elements of historical Judaism just those elements from which one might construct a secular-nationalist theology of the kind he desires.

His expectations of religion are that it satisfy the spiritual needs of man: his "happiness," "perfection," "morality." As a person whose spiritual world lies beyond the orbit of religion, M.S. fails to appreciate that the clash between the outlook of religious faith and that of atheistic humanism is necessarily reflected in differences over the construal of these concepts. He is unable to grasp either the idea, basic to Jewish religiosity, that perfection consists in the very effort to serve God by observance of the Torah and its Mitzvoth, or the contention of the greatest of ethical theorists (Kant) that a "morality" based on religious faith is no morality at all. As an observer of religion from the outside, M.S. can perceive only "what religion offers man." Utilitarianism has become his religion. Similarly, he is incapable of acknowledging the phenomenon of religious faith as anything other than "man's need of religion." He is unable to understand religion on its own terms but only in terms of what he takes to be the psychology of the believer. He fails to distinguish between needs and values and does not realize that the satisfaction of a need may be of no value and that a utilitarian conception of religion depletes religion of all *religious* import and makes it otiose from a humanistic-ethical standpoint.

At this point let me emphatically repeat Wigner's warning against overlooking the obvious in the effort to seek out the hidden aspects of one's subject. The efforts of religious (or pseudo-religious) anthropologists, sociologists, psychologists, humanists, and proponents of "liberal" religion to extract from religion some contribution to human welfare are likely to veil the obvious fact that the substance of the Torah of Israel is a demand made of man and an obligation imposed upon him; the essential content of Jewish faith is the recognition of this demand and the acceptance of this obligation (acceptance of the yoke of Heaven and the yoke of Torah and Mitzvoth). All the rest is supplementary, problematic, or subject to controversy.

Not only does a Judaism of personal eudaemonism masquerading as religiosity render religion superfluous, but it becomes deleterious and vicious because of its fusion with a collectivist eudaemonism and utilitarianism—Judaism as the ancilla of Jewish nationalism. The two principles of this sort of Judaism are to provide gratification for the Jewish individual, and to accommodate the national interests of the people of Israel.

The central aspect of "Judaism," as the empirical datum existing *in actu* in the life of the Jewish people and in its history, has been the struggle over the Torah and its Mitzvoth conducted both internally and between Israel and the other peoples, a struggle which shaped the image and fate of Israel. Precisely this is what M.S. would like to discard. He *wishes* that for the religious person "the motivation of . . . religious life or . . . religious life itself" were "the satisfaction of a profound psychic need . . . to be happier, more perfect or moral." But these "values" are not unfamiliar to the pagan or the atheist—why, then the attachment to Judaism? Are not the votaries of Baal, Astarte, the Moloch, Zeus and Apollo, or Jesus, "religious"? Religious fervor was not lacking among those who conducted human sacrifices or among the Crusaders and the inquisitors! If M.S. evinces a greater interest in Judaism than in Canaanite or Olympic paganism or in Christianity, this is not because of any specific content of Judaism but because it is the national form of "religiosity" of the Jewish people, whose interests are the really important matter (in the spirit of the silly adage of Ahad Ha'am, "the Sabbath preserved Israel far more than Israel observed the Sabbath").

In contrast to this attitude is the daily stand of the religious Jew. Throughout his life, he rises early every morning *to observe the Mitzvah of prayer with the congregation* even when he feels no need to "pour out his complaint before God," and perhaps has never felt the need in his life. He may do so even though he knows that there is no need to inform the Omniscient of his needs and despite his understanding that as a frail human he cannot effectively praise and glorify the Almighty; he prays, it may be, contrary to his perception that there is no relation between his prayer and the events which befall him or occur in the history of Israel. If one day he or one of his children falls ill, he consults the physician and resorts to the science of medicine as would any atheist, without diminishing the sincerity with which he recites the benediction "who cures the sick of his People of Israel." To provide for his livelihood he makes use of all the means employed to this end by the atheist, even though in the morning he recites in perfect faith the verse,

"You open your hand and satisfy the desire of every living being." If he is deeply concerned about the welfare and security of the state of Israel, it never enters his mind that if the chief-of-staff were to put on his phylacteries daily or never in his life, it would in any way affect his plans of operation. The Jew who regularly prays his daily prayer does so in recognition of the obligation to pray, as an aspect of his obligation to serve God. M.S., in his contempt for Torah and Mitzvoth, has the audacity to call this Jew "a man who is religious without believing in God."[1] He himself defines the "belief in God," upon which he would found his Judaism, "as what religion grants man." This indeed was the faith of those who worshipped the golden calf: "These are your gods o Israel." The calf need not necessarily be of gold; it can equally be embodied in a nation or a land. It is the "religiosity" of Gush Emunim, the religion of chauvinistic patriotism—but with a difference. The Gush appeal to religious motives and anoint their trinity of land-nation-state with a coating of religious terminology; for M.S. land, nation, and state suffice for the constitution of "Judaism."[2]

Consequently, M.S. ignores the obvious when he comes to interpret the rejection of Christianity by Judaism. In the spirit of a secular historiosophy he attributes this repudiation to political motives: "Christianity attempted to discard the *national underpinning* of Judaism and detach it from its *earthly roots*" (my emphases), and the Jews repudiated the attempt. But the earliest authentic Christian documents, the Epistles of Paul (which anteceded the Gospels by thirty to fifty years) clearly and unambiguously present a strategy of removing the barrier between Israel and the Gentiles by abrogating the Mitzvoth (the "Law"), a strategy similar to that of Antiochus Epiphanes two hundred years earlier. Christianity originated in opposition to the principles of Judaism. Detachment from Judaism marked its very beginning.

The first document in which the faith of Judaism was formulated is the "reading of Shema," with its three parts extracted from the Torah. The Mishnah, the crystallization of the oral Torah, the empirical manifestation of Judaism—as distinct from the various ideologies about Judaism—also opens with the precept of reading Shema. The first two parts of the Shema belong to two levels of faith. The existence of these two levels and the contrast between them is among the most profound aspects of faith, and this difference is entrenched in the religious tradition of all ages and in the spiritual life of all the eminent religious men of thought in Judaism. It is the contrast between service of God lishmah, for its own sake, and not for its own sake, a contrast which, up to a point, overlaps that between "love" and "fear." The first part, in its six verses, presents the demand of absolute, unconditional faith: "And you shall love ... with all your heart." This is a categorical imperative that is not grounded in any presumptions, and is unaccompanied by any promise or threat. The second part suggests persuasive utilitarian reasons for serving God ("I will grant the rain in your land in due season") as well as threats in the event of transgression. How could these two adjacent portions of the Torah be reconciled? They are, indeed, incompatible and there is no sense in trying to harmonize them. Both were given us and joined together for reasons of religious opportunism (a term used here without any negative connotations) as pointing to the two levels of faith that exist in the mental and spiritual life of believing Jews. The first is the *demanding* faith. Acceptance of this demand, and it alone, is the religious perfection of man. The second one is the mode of belief that is permitted to those who are incapable of attaining the first level. The Torah proposes it to him as a psychological-didactic aid on the arduous road toward religious perfection. The Torah and the tradition resign themselves to the second way, perhaps as a transitional phase in the believing man's religious education. Thus we have the oft-quoted saying of the Talmudic Sages "that in consequence of performing them not-lishmah one comes to perform them lishmah."[3] But in the spiritual world of the Sages there is also an emphatic negative valuation of this religiosity represented by another dictum that is seldom quoted: "for him who preoccupies himself with Torah for its own sake it becomes a life potion; if not for its own sake, it becomes poison to him."[4]

The third part of the reading of Shema refers to the Mitzvoth, which are a common denominator for the one who attains perfection and the one who falls short of it. The Torah thereby enjoins every Jew, both the believer lishmah and the believer not-lishmah," to "remember all the commandments of God and fulfil them." He who fulfils them, whatever the level of his faith, is regarded as having assumed the yoke of the Kingdom of Heaven, for he has undertaken the yoke of Torah and *Mitzvoth*.

The space will not suffice to indicate the profusion of sources, from among the earlier and later authorities, which express the basic idea of faith lishmah. Out of this abundance I shall gather odd items for purposes of illustration, and I shall begin with the greatest of Jewish believers.

The end of the truth is nothing but to *know it to be the truth.*[5]

And the Torah is true, and *the purpose of knowing it is to observe it . . . so that one should truly believe truth itself,* and that is what is called to serve out of love . . . this is a very difficult matter, and not every person can grasp it . . . they therefore *permitted* the masses, in order to foster their faith, to observe the Mitzvoth in the hope of reward and to refrain from transgressing for fear of punishment.[6]

Know that all practices of the worship such as reading the Torah, prayer and the performance of the other *Mitzvoth, have only one end of training you to occupy yourself with His commandments, may He be exalted,* rather than with matter pertaining to this world; you should act *as if you were occupied with Him,* may He be exalted, and not with that which is other than He.[7]

Some six hundred years later, in the world of the Lithuanian Yeshivoth founded by the disciples of Rabbi Eliyahu of Vilna, we come across the following statement: "For the reward of the Mitzvah is the Mitzvah itself given to one as a reward, and that is the light enveloping him, and he truly sits in Paradise . . . for he is *now in the world to come as he performs the Mitzvah,* and this is achieved by man himself, *for the Mitzvah is the very reward,* and the light is Paradise in the lifetime of man, and that is his reward—and understand!"[8]

This is the "idea of Judaism" in its original sense, the spirit animating the world of Halakhah. Conversely, in a theology of "not-lishmah," the deity is the caretaker of the world, of man, and of the Jews. The Jewish religion thereby becomes a pursuit of interest—the satisfaction of human needs and the fulfillment of man's aspirations.

Nevertheless, I do not feel free to ignore M.S.'s construal of Maimonides completely. His interpretation reveals both ignorance and misunderstanding, and a malicious intent to present the foremost figure in Jewish thought as a propagandist for the state of Israel. The above quotations should suffice, as exceedingly concise statements illustrative of the conception of faith informing the *totality* of Maimonides' work, to indicate how in Maimonides' thought faith and Halakhah coalesce. As Rabbi Meir Simhah Cohen puts it, contrary to the opinions of Shlomoh Pines and Leo Strauss, "the statements of our teacher Maimonides in all his books, the *Mishneh Torah,* the *Guide,* and the *Commentary on the Mishnah,* are imbued with one spirit."

Maimonides provides detailed methodological instructions for interpreting his treatise (the "Introduction" at the opening of the *Guide* and the warning appended to it). Very clearly he apprises us of the *two planes* on which he conducts his discourse. On the heuristic-didactic level, things may have to be said "using many means that occur to him [the teacher] or gross speculation . . . He will not undertake to state the matter *as it truly is* in exact terms, but rather will leave it *in accord with the listener's imagination* that the latter will understand only what he now wants him to understand." But on the second plane, "the obscure matter is stated in exact terms and explained as it truly is." "In speaking about very obscure matter it is necessary to conceal some parts and to discuss others . . . the author accordingly uses some device to conceal [the contradiction] by all means."[9] And the final warning is: "Know this, grasp its meaning and remember it very well so as not to become perplexed by some of its chapters."[10] M.S. did not heed this warning. As a result, Maimonides' apprehensions came true in his case. Similarly, M.S. ignores Maimonides' explicit accounts of the two planes of the service of God and observance of the Mitzvoth, namely, the "welfare of the body" (ethics and politics!), which is only of functional and instrumental importance, and the "welfare of the mind" (the recognition of the truth for its own sake!) which is the essence of the Torah and the goal of man. Maimonides used a felicitous phrase in speaking of "the truth that will be believed by whoever chooses to admit the truth."

"He who chooses to admit the truth" can discern when Maimonides discourses on the plane of faith which is not-lishmah, a faith Maimonides concedes and even recommends for reasons of *religious opportunism,* and those in which he is referring to faith lishmah—the *true end of religion.* M.S., however, for reasons of *pseudo-humanistic national opportunism,* desires precisely the faith which is not-lishmah. The discerning reader will understand why Maimonides on some occasions discusses the Mitzvoth in their functional significance as educational and instrumental in promoting the welfare of society (the *Guide* III, chaps. 29–49), and at other times, in quite a different vein, presents them as the end itself ("Laws of Repentance," chap. 10). He who comprehends this will know why Maimonides did not include the "vision of messianic redemption" among the "Laws Concerning the Basic Principles of the Torah" and why, in the discussion of the good that is in store for the servants of God ("Laws of Repentance," chap. 9), that vision is not mentioned except in connection with the reason why "all Israelites, their prophets and sages, longed for the advent of messianic times." Such a reader will also understand the implications of the last chapters of the "Laws Concerning Kings and Wars" and of the dictum about "the legend themes . . . and the midrashic statements bearing on this and the like subjects." It will likewise be clear to him why the discourse on redemption, which concludes the vast enterprise of the Code of Maimonides, should end with the verse from Isaiah (11:9), "for the earth shall be full of the knowledge of God as the waters cover the sea."

The perfect expression of M.S.'s scheme to reduce Judaism to a mere adjunct of Jewish nationalism and Israeli patriotism is this shattering phrase: "If there is no Messiah there is no Torah!" There is no hint in his words that by messianic redemption he intends what Maimonides described in the words of Isaiah. On the contrary, it is clear from what he says that the "Messiah," to M.S., is the unpartitioned land of Israel.

The fatuous impudence (or the impudent fatuity) of such a declaration notwithstanding, it must be dealt with in the context of the messianic idea as an empirical datum throughout the history of Judaism. Following Wigner's dictum, we must avoid disregarding the obvious: the content of Judaism in theory and practice has been the struggle of Jews to live a life of Torah and Mitzvoth, in which the "nearness of God" is attained *in the world as it is,* that is to say, in man's natural mode of existence in the world and in history. "The world as it is," including human nature and history, is intrinsically indifferent. Though this world follows its natural course, it is the framework within which the Jews as a nation and as individuals are enjoined to serve God. In this arena the nation and its individuals have to struggle unceasingly to maintain their way of life. This is the deep meaning of the eternity of the Torah. The entire Halakhah refers to nothing but the duties of man in the world as it is. It is this that distinguishes Judaism from Christianity, the literal meaning of which is "Messianism." Christianity loathed this constant struggle, and sought to liberate the believers from its toils through the redeeming action of its Messiah. Judaism does not permit man to free himself from the effort to serve God through the burden of "the Law." From its point of view man does not stand in need of "redemption." By the very effort he makes to serve, he stands before God, and standing before God in this way constitutes his religious perfection, or "redemption." But Jews struggled thus to serve God under historical circumstances and conditions that were far from being redeemed in any possible construction of the word, a world that refused and still refuses to acknowledge God and His Torah. On the level of natural human reality, Jews suffered failures because of their human frailty, and because of the suffering and misery inflicted on them. The bondage and exile of the Jewish people were also interpreted as humiliation of the Torah of God which is addressed to them. The continuing allegiance of the Jews to the life of Torah was attended by expectation of victory "in the end of the days"—to be brought about by the will and power of the Lord of history who gave this Torah to His people. This victory was conceived in a variety of images: as mundane and as spiritual, as a cosmic event, in terms pertaining to humanity as a whole or specifically to Israel, as a transition from the course of the world with its natural blemishes to a better world, or from human nature as we know it, with its tainted inclinations, to a perfected humanity. All this was envisioned as being accompanied by restoration of the Torah and the people of the Torah to their former glory. Included in such visions were the elevation of the world in the kingdom of God, the victory of Judaism, the manifestation of the truth of the Torah of Israel, the delivery of the people of Israel from bondage and its return to its land, the full observance of the Torah among all the Jews (or by the entire world), the glory and splendor of the redeemed people.

In this complex of hopes, expectations, and visions of "messianic redemption," the line of demarcation between religious faith aimed at the service of God and psychological yearnings for the satisfaction of human aspirations was constantly blurred. Judaism hardly benefited from the vision of redemption. "The messianic vision" tended to undermine the motivation to serve God in the world as it is. But so long as it was unmistakably projected upon "the end of days" (*the end of history*), recognition of the obligation to serve God in ongoing history was not affected. On the contrary, such a vision lent courage to many who, without it, would have despaired. There were periods of Jewish history when the study of Torah and personal religiosity were intense, and yet these times were marked by almost complete neglect of the vision of messianic redemption, even though it always remained an article of faith. From time to time, however, the historic situation made it so difficult to persist in the halakhic service of God that the religious consciousness and sensibility turned to the vision of redemption as though it were the core of the faith. This was a form of escape from the strict religious demand of the Halakhah to visions which satisfied a psychological need of the believer. In other words, it was a transition from faith lishmah to faith for the sake of human hopes or national aspirations. Whenever the vision of redemption became pivotal to the religious consciousness, a severe crisis set in. The believers' hearts were completely set upon the vision of glory and grandeur of the Jewish people and of the victory of the Torah; they were no longer capable of living the cheerless day-to-day practice of Torah and Mitzvoth. Ultimately they severed themselves from Judaism. From such *sincere* religious ardor for personal salvation sprang Christianity and split away from Judaism. From the *sincere* religious ardor for immediate national redemption emerged Sabbateanism, which led its adherents to apostasy. Converting the service of God lishmah into the service of God for the sake of the redemption of Israel and its land is bringing forth Gush Emunim. Who can foresee where they will end up once they recover from the messianic intoxication?

Although M.S. points to "their standing with both feet on the ground of the service of God through Torah and *Mitzvoth*," it is not for *this* reason that he identifies with the Gush Emunim, but because of the nationalism and patriotism he shares with them. I am not at all relieved by their religious fervor, for the precedents are frightening. The faith of Gush Emunim is not-lishmah but is fueled by national ambitions. For the incipient Sabbatean movement (prior to conversion), redemption had become the core of the faith, and the People of the Torah the People of Redemption. This paved the way to apostasy. For Gush Emunim, the land and its conquest are becoming the core of the faith, and the people of God are for them the people of the divine land. As for their ardor in the observance of the Mitzvoth—does not M.S. know how great a religious revival the early Sabbatean movement effected among the Jews? Is he not aware of the "great repentance," which involved regret for past transgressions and a renewed commitment to strict observance the Mitzvoth by multitudes anticipating immediate redemption; all this only a few months before the catastrophe?

It is a mistake to point to Rabbi Aqiba in connection with the messianic awakening. The place of the greatest of the Sages is established by his work in the domain of the oral Torah, by his decisive influence on the shaping of the Halakhah. But M.S. and his colleagues admire Rabbi Aqiba for his support of a revolt which he conceived in terms of messianic redemption and which brought disaster upon the Jews.[11] Don Isaac Abravanel, whose zeal for the vision of messianic redemption in *time to come*—as opposed to the false Messianism of Christianity—was unequalled, has this to say about Rabbi Aqiba's being seized with enthusiasm for redemption in his own time: "What happened to him is what often happens to the wise—that he will believe that for which his soul longs and yearns."

The profound religious meaning of the messianic idea consists in presenting a goal and a purpose towards which one must strive eternally. The Messiah is essentially he who always *will come,* he is the eternal future. The Messiah who comes, the Messiah of the present, is invariably the false Messiah.

M.S. does not want Judaism as the service of God, but Judaism as a service to human individuals and collectives. But the significant content of Jewish history for several thousand of years has been precisely the relation of the people to Torah and Mitzvoth as the sole manifestation of the service of God, and the struggle within the people of Israel over its observance. From the standpoint of national interests, often a crypto-fascist standpoint, Judaism has been a disturbing and divisive factor, which constantly undermined the unity and strength of the nation. Such was the case during the first and second commonwealths, in the Diaspora, and today in Israel, where a Jew who observes Mitzvoth and a Jew who has thrown off this burden cannot eat together at the same table, cannot marry (because of the precepts regulating the "purity of the family"), and where a Sabbath observer has difficulty working jointly with a person who desecrates the Sabbath. Had M.S. been faithful to himself, he should have rejected Judaism in its totality and spurned the main part of Jewish history, much as did the overt "Canaanites," or like the covert "Canaanite," Ben Gurion, who clearly voiced his aversion to Judaism and the historical Jewish people and instead adhered to the "Bible," a Bible that he fabricated for himself, with a tinge of Karaism [the doctrine of a sect that rejects the Oral Teaching], a tinge of Christianity, and a tinge of atheism; a Bible without a Torah, in which even the prophets are not exponents of the demand to serve God, but are champions of the "messianic vision."

But M.S. is not candid. He will not renounce "Judaism" as a cover for the nakedness of nationalism. He needs Judaism to endow nationalism with the aura of sanctity attributed to the service of God. He therefore makes desperate efforts to ignore the obvious about Judaism, that it is actually a system of halakhic praxis, a program fixing detailed arrangements of the everyday, and that the effort to carry out of this program is what constitutes its "faith." The content and meaning of the great verse of the Shema "and you shall love," are revealed only in the succeeding verse: "And *these words which I command* you this day, shall be in your heart." Were it not for the second verse, the first would merely be a vacuous phrase. Love of God is but the observance of the Mitzvoth. Their justification is *not* "national" and *not* "moral" and *not* social. Their sole point is the service of God (see the quotations from Maimonides which head this chapter). Had the rationale of the Mitzvoth been national welfare, fulfilling them would express love of Israel. Had it been moral, their observance would indicate the love of mankind. Had it been social, observing them would serve important human needs. But M.S., who desires to present nationalism and perhaps also "morality" as supreme values, is compelled to empty Judaism of its content as manifested in the Halakhah. Since "nothing is shown a person in his dreams save what his heart desires," M.S. apparently succeeded in deceiving himself. There is no other way of understanding his quoting my words: "Judaism does not exist except insofar as it imposes on man a specific everyday regime and lifestyle," and following up with the rhetorical question whether there is anything here "that distinguish Judaism from vegetarianism. Vegetarianism also dictates to its believers an everyday regime and life-style." For I have

repeatedly contended that a life governed by the Mitzvoth is not comparable to any life-style motivated by human inclinations and urges. It
is the assumption of the yoke of the Kingdom of Heaven, not the yoke
of human nature. Therefore, by observing the Mitzvoth, one in a sense
subdues nature and frees himself from subjection to it. "No one is free
except he who occupies himself with Torah." I can only presume that
the anthropocentrism or, more precisely, the ethnocentrism of M.S.'s
way of thinking compels him to regard *any* way of life of a person or
group as an expression of the inclinations of that person or that group;
this is how he regards the undertaking of the way of life prescribed to
the individual Jew and to the Jewish people by the Torah. In other
words, M.S. is utterly incapable of grasping the religious meaning of
the halakhic life.

I cannot understand what kind of faith it is that M.S. talks about at
such length and which, according to him, I lack. It would seem that
belief in God in his sheer divinity, is totally foreign to him, and that he
therefore is quite incapable of apprehending the existence of faith lishmah, which is not dependent on the world and on God's relation to it.
M.S. wishes to locate the Judaic faith in God's unity and uniqueness
along a set of coordinates equally applicable to atheistic, pantheistic,
pagan, or Christian faiths that have in common the conception that
the world (nature) is primary, and the deity is an agency that brings it
into existence or helps human consciousness to understand the world
and the processes of nature. Thus the deity is regarded as the world
itself, or as the demiurge who set it up, or as the formal or teleological
cause of the world, or as a functionary who pulls the strings of nature
or of history, or as a deity who penetrated natural reality by incarnating
itself in man. These are all variant forms of faith which is not-lishmah.
They are not faith in God, but faith in the representations of attributes
or divine functions *in which man is interested.*

In contrast to Hegel's "Without a world God is no God," the morning benediction of the prayerbook (to which M.S. wishes to appeal for
support) states: "You were ere yet the world was created, and are the
same since its creation." God's divinity is entirely intrinsic to Him and
does not consist in his relation to the world, whose contingent existence adds nothing to God's divinity. And similarly, it says, "Lord of
the universe, Who reigned before ought was created." What did He
reign over? Clearly, his kingship is essential to Him. God is a king even
in the absence of a world in which He reigns.

The belief in the existence of God and in His kingship as independent of the world may lead man to recognize his duty to serve God *unconditionally,* and such a decision might withstand all the trials to which man may be put by the nature of things. A recognition of God which is dependent on what man conceives as His manifestation in nature or in history is egocentric and bound to collapse. Moreover, belief in God conceived in terms of His "involvement in the world" is inadequate as a basis for the decision to serve Him. Even if one could be absolutely certain that the world was created by the will of God, and that He liberated our forefathers from Egypt, and that He revealed Himself to them on Mount Sinai, and that the Torah was given from Heaven, one may still refuse to serve God. As against the theories of atheistic students of religion who locate the source of faith in God (or gods) in the specious explanations man gave to natural phenomena inexplicable to him, or to amazing historical events, our Sages knew the great psychological truth than man may believe in God as revealed in His actions, and nevertheless refuse to worship Him. Scriptural historiography teaches us that events in which "the finger of God" is incontestably manifest do not inevitably lead to faith and service of God. The generation that witnessed wonders and miracles in Egypt and by the Red Sea and to whom the Shekhinah was revealed did not believe. Forty days after the revelation at Sinai they made the golden calf. The prophets who rose in Israel and delivered the word of God did not succeed in influencing even one person to repent. On the other hand, during many periods in Jewish history multitudes of men and women adhered to God and to His Torah, and sacrificed their lives for them even though the Shekhinah never revealed itself, no prophets rose among them, and miracles were never performed for them. They experienced no deliverance; still they believed. There is no correlation between what occurs in nature or in history, even if it is recognized as the finger of God, and man's faith in God and his willingness to serve Him. Faith and worship are born of the resolve and decision of man to serve God, which is the whole of Judaism.

M.S. talks a good deal about God and about the attributes and functions that the religious person ascribes to God, and in particular about "God's will." His loose use of theological terms and concepts is appalling. Religious faith can be pure and profound without the believer engaging in theological reasoning. Such reasoning is almost absent in the Bible. If, however, a religious person's thought turns to theological

reflection, he is not at liberty to forego analysis and criticism of theological terms and concepts and must master their meanings which are
necessarily different from their meanings when they are used in dis-
coursing of nature and man.

M.S. writes as if Jewish theology had not devoted its efforts for
hundreds of years to the purification of these concepts and terms from
the popular theology that clung to them. Is he really unfamiliar with
the problematic of "will" when applied to God? As a category applicable to man, willing does not refer to what already exists, but is rather
an aspiration, an inclination, an intention towards something that
should or ought to be. Conversely, "He has done whatsoever he has
pleased"; we are in no position to distinguish His will from given reality. It thus follows that in its profound sense, the expression "to do
God's will" asserts nothing about God, but is rather an expression of
the believer's recognition of his duty to serve God.

In reflecting and speaking about man's standing before God, the
believer (the man of faith lishmah) tries to refer minimally to God,
who has no image at all, and makes an effort to direct his religious
consciousness to himself as recognizing his duty to his God. That is
the practice of the men of Halakhah. The pagan, however, and he who
serves God not-lishmah, direct their attention to an imaginary notion
of their god and to the understanding of his attributes and actions.
This is the mystical approach which is represented in Judaism by the
Kabbalah.

How are Judaism (the Torah) and the Jewish people related?

M.S.'s theologico-political doctrine devaluates Judaism by secular-
izing it—by shifting its center of gravity from adherence to God and
His service to loyalty to the nation, in order to further its political
interests. He identifies Judaism with Jewish nationalism. In other
words he reduces Judaism to Zionism, but still wishes to take advantage of the repository of spiritual and mental powers inherent in Judaism as a religion of the service of God. To that end, he balances the
devaluation of Judaism through secularization by inflating the value of
Zionism through its sanctification. He presents us with Zionism gar-
nished with religious embellishments (to which he himself assigns no
importance), and rejects my prosaic definition of Zionism as the totality of the aspirations and actions that were directed toward the attain-

ment of Jewish political and national independence and now serve to preserve it. The flaw M.S. finds in this definition is the absence of any religious pathos. It should be noted, however, that my definition amounts to a tautology, because only these general aspirations and actions are common to all Zionists. Values, on the other hand, whether general human values or specifically Jewish values for which, supposedly, the political sovereignty is a framework, excite controversy and profound disagreement among Zionists. Consequently, none of them may alone claim the title of "Zionism." They represent, in effect, the different and opposing tendencies and orientations which characterize the attitudes of contemporary Jews toward *Judaism*.

Through the establishment of the state and its continued existence, the Jewish people are freed from subjection to the rule of others, even if not all Jews choose to live in Israel. However, the state alone cannot determine the quality and nature of the political entity. The national character of the people in its state, its social structure, its way of life, and its human and Jewish consciousness are determined by the individuals constituting the politically organized community, not by the governmental apparatus. The problems of *Judaism* lie outside the orbit of state action or political decision. With this in mind I have denied that the state has any religious significance, and contended that it is rather the fulfillment of our human aspiration to national independence. This aspiration, common to many observant and non-observant Jews, is a legitimate aspiration in every respect, but it is not a function of religious belief, and its actualization does not constitute a religious act. *No act has any religious significance unless it is done for the sake of Heaven*. This too is a tautology.

The two great value systems of humanity, which oppose each other in almost every way, are united in their assessment of the institution called "the state." The religious value system requires that the problems of man and society and the efforts to solve them be approached with a view to man's consciousness of standing before God. The humanist-atheistic value system seeks to approach these problems and their solutions from an exclusively human perspective. From the standpoint of both these value systems, the government apparatus, that is, the "state," has no intrinsic worth. Its value is purely functional and instrumental. It is an instrument for the satisfaction of certain conditions (not all!) for the existence and welfare of the individual and of society.

Matters of intrinsic value are excluded from the jurisdiction of this apparatus.

In addition to these there is also a fascist value system, according to which man's relation to the governmental apparatus—to his state—provides the definition of his problems and shapes their solution. This value system identifies Judaism as a function of the Jewish people organized in its state. To this identification M.S. assigns religious significance, and thereby alters the historical character of the nation as this was embodied in Judaism. No longer is it a people whose sanctified national uniqueness consists in the task it is obliged to fulfill—the service of God—but a people that is holy in itself; nationality as a faith and a religion.

The original author of this notion of the "holiness of Israel" was Qorah the son of Izhar, who declared: "all the congregation are holy, everyone of them (Num. 16:3). Throughout Jewish history runs a line of thought that endows this people with "holiness" as an objective attribute. It has been represented by such outstanding figures as Judah Halevi, Maharal, and Rabbi Kook. In the thought of their epigones, religious faith and national arrogance are fused, at times even with racist ingredients.

However, as against the verse expressing Qorah's religiosity and his sense of holiness, we have, four verses from it, a statement that articulates the religion and concept of holiness taught by Moses: "and do all my commandments, and be holy unto your God" (Num. 15:40). You yourselves are not holy, but the task eternally to strive toward holiness is laid upon you. The task is the Torah, which is eternal, for its realization is never completely attained. This is the holiness of Israel, as it is represented in the reading of Shema by Maimonides, and by the implications of Halakhah as a structuring of Jewish life. This task is binding upon us in the present, and in every forseeable future, no less than it was in the past. It is binding on Jews in exile and in Israel, under imposed subjection to the rule of others, and in the condition of national independence.

In the contemporary situation, the choice between a conception of Israel reflecting Qorah's idea of the sacred community and that taught by Moses is of the greatest consequence.

CHAPTER 7

The Uniqueness of the Jewish People
(1975)

> And what one nation in the earth is like your people, like Israel.
> (2 Sam. 7:23)

> There is a certain people.
> (Esther 3:8)

King David and Haman son of Hammedatha emphasized the "uniqueness" of the Jewish people, and their words found their way into the daily prayer of supplication, the Tahnun, and into the Sabbath Minhah (afternoon prayer). The expressions "one nation" and "one people," implying uniqueness, have become catchwords of traditional religious parlance. In literary sources of Jewish thought and in various pronouncements of Jewish thinkers to this day, these expressions have come to represent basic tenets of faith. "Uniqueness" is interwoven with other concepts such as "election," "being cherished," and even with "holiness" in usages made obscure by the ambiguity of these expressions. Adherence to this idea of uniqueness may lead to great religious exaltation. But its indefiniteness invites perversion, distortion, and eventual corruption. Today, this is an imminent danger. We must therefore examine carefully the meaning of the entire edifice of spiritual and emotional associations that has arisen around this vague idea.

The very formula "the uniqueness of the people of Israel" requires elucidation. Is the people of Israel mentioned here an ideal concept, or

are we concerned with the *phenomenal* Jewish people? Are we dealing with the people of Israel as an *a priori idea,* or with the Jewish
people as a historical *entity*? Is the people of Israel a nation whose
uniqueness is a goal to be achieved, or an entity whose uniqueness
is an empirical datum? If the subject is the historical people of Israel,
are we concerned with the continuum of its history, or with the
present generation, whose problems do not necessarily coincide
with those of preceding ones? In other words, is the "uniqueness
of the people of Israel" conceived as initially determined or as
a contingent factuality? Is it an entelechy predetermining Israel's
vocation or a product of its history? What came first, the uniqueness that produced a people or a people that shaped its own uniqueness?

The term "uniqueness" itself is most perplexing. Only one uniqueness is absolute, and it is mentioned in the first verse of Shema. Within
human reality there is no absolute uniqueness. Jews are human beings
like all the rest, and they cannot be peculiar by nature, since by nature
we are all—Jews as well as Gentiles—children of Noah. Jews could not
possibly possess aptitudes that are not inherent in man *qua* man. The
notion that Jewish man is endowed with characteristics that non-Jews
lack (the prophetic faculty described by Judah Halevi, the "soul of the
nation" proposed by Rabbi Kook, and the like) derogates the significance of Judaism.[1] If by nature there is something special about a Jew
that distinguishes him from the non-Jew, then Judaism is not a *task
and a vocation* but a *factual datum.* Given facts, as such, are devoid of
value; they are axiologically neutral. Values are not rooted in reality;
they are objects of aspiration beyond reality toward which one must
strive from within reality. It follows that to claim inherent uniqueness
for the people of Israel is to deprive this uniqueness of all significance.

Some people argue that the Jewish people is empirically unique,
since the Jewish fate is singular and has no counterpart among the
other nations. In other words, the uniqueness of the people of Israel
does not consist in a Jewish essence, but rather in the history of the
Jewish people, which is an oddity in the context of general human
history. If so, one should explore the sources of this uniqueness and
not evade the empirical inquiry by invoking a special calling and arguing circularly that the Jewish people was destined for a special fate,
therefore its fate is peculiar.

The belief that the history of the Jewish people differs from that of all other people hinges on the use of the term "people." The existence of different people is a fact we take for granted without giving it much thought. Only rarely does it occur to us to ask ourselves what indeed is "a people." Why does a conglomeration of human beings, each of whom differs from the others, constitute a particular nation, while others, who do not differ from these individuals more than they differ from one another, do not belong to this people? A "people" is not a *natural* entity. It is a *being of the mind*. A nation exists insofar as there is a consciousness of its existence—the awareness of particular human beings that their communal existence has a framework which is "the nation," *their* nation. It is characteristic of such a framework that it does not exist *ad hoc*, for a limited period and a specific purpose. It rather persists and endures continuously over generations, throughout changes in conditions and circumstances.

The consciousness of national life is related to history. But what is the source of this shared self-consciousness? Why do the numbers of a particular human group consider themselves (and are usually considered by others) a "nation"? It seems to me that no objective answer to this question applies validly to all human groups that consider themselves "peoples" (and are so regarded by others). It also seems to me that no historian or sociologist has succeeded in proposing a criterion that would determine whether a certain human group was or was not a nation. Several defining characteristics have, indeed, been listed: racial origin, language, territory, state, and so forth. But many and diverse groups are considered "nations" and, although they lack one or even several of these characteristics, no one doubts their status as "nations." It is instructive to compare the Swedish people and the German people (the Austrians? the Swiss?), the Indian people (who lack a "national language"), the Arab people, the Palestinian people, and so on. Can an objective account be given of the peoplehood of all of these national groups?

Where does the Jewish people stand in view of these considerations? Its existence has been an empirical fact for the last 3,000 years. Despite variations, changes, and structural metamorphoses, it has preserved its self-identity and continuity for approximately a hundred generations. It retained them not only in the self-consciousness of the Jews but also in the consciousness of non-Jews. Up to the end of the eighteenth century it occurred to no one to raise the question whether a Jewish nationality existed. The fact of its existence was taken for granted. What were the defining characteristics of the historical Jewish people during these hundred generations?

The biological criterion does not apply. The Jewish people is a multiracial melange. Today we can clearly discern typical facial features of all races among people who are Jews in every sense of the word "Jew." Even from the standpoint of the traditional perception, the sons of Abraham, Isaac, and Jacob have no racial or even familial peculiarity which would distinguish them from the Ishmaelites, the Edomites, the Arameans, and the Moabites. As for language, the significance of Hebrew for the Jewish people is unlike the significance of the national tongue for other peoples. During most of their history the Jews did not speak Hebrew. Even their monumental collective national literary composition, the talmudic literature, is written mostly in Aramaic. In the contemporary world, the greater part of the 13–14 million people who are considered Jews, both by themselves and by others, do not know or speak Hebrew. Yet Hebrew undoubtedly was, and is even today, the national language of the entire Jewish people, because every Jew knows that the Torah was given in Hebrew, even if he reads it in translation, and that the Shema and the daily prayer are in Hebrew.

The historic Jewish nation is not defined by territory either. Most of its history is not specifically related to the land of Israel, and today, too, most Jews have no actual tie to the land of Israel. Moreover, the heroic period of the Jewish people is precisely the period of exile. Needless to say, the historical Jewish people is not definable in terms of statehood. During the greater part of its history it had no state of its own. Even today only a minority of Jews are citizens of the Jewish state.

The Jewish people, as it existed in history, is definable only by reference to its Judaism—a Judaism that was not a mere idea in the mind but the realization of a program of living set forth in the Torah and delineated by its Mitzvoth. This way of life constituted the specific national content of Jewishness or, in other words, the *uniqueness* of the Jewish people. The Jew practiced a way of living that was exclusively his. His style of eating was not that of the Gentile—the Jewish kitchen differed from that of all other people. The sexual practices of Jews were peculiar to them since they were governed by the laws and rituals pertaining to the menstrual cycle and the "purity of the family."[2] In the practical domain of work and industry, the observance of the Sabbath set them apart. Unlike the identities of the peoples that are characterized by race, language, territory, or state, the national identity of the historic Jewish people is *Judaism,* the actuality of which is life according to the Torah. It is not surprising that a people distinguished by a criterion absent from the defining characteristics of all other peoples should also have a history which was different from that of other nations.

The distinctiveness of the Jewish people as a historic national entity began to be blurred some two hundred years ago. Until then a Jew who cast off the yoke of Torah and Mitzvoth usually recognized that he thereby loosened his ties with the Jewish people.[3] The innovation of recent generations is the phenomenon of Jews—a great number of them, and today the vast majority of those considered Jews—who have abandoned the Jewish way of life without severing themselves from their people. There is no authentic "Jewish" content to their lives that might distinguish them from that of Gentiles. Nevertheless, they continue to regard themselves as Jews, to present themselves as Jews and to be regarded as such by the others. Consequently a question that was hitherto meaningless arises: who is a Jew? Who and what is the "Jewish people" with which they are affiliated? Not only is there today no Jewish national identity that actually distinguishes a Jew from a Gentile, but even among those held to be Jews, the common constitutive element that would render them *one* people is lacking. Jews who abide by Torah and Mitzvoth and Jews who have cast off their yoke cannot dine at the same table, have difficulty working together (Sabbath), and even marriage between them is problematic when both parties do not agree to observance of the laws relating to "purity of the family." Thus the appeal to national solidarity of all Jews is nowadays merely verbal and declaratory. It reflects no living reality. Even the legal halakhic criterion for inclusion in the Jewish people is inadequate at present, since only a minority among those who consider themselves Jews regard the Halakhah as binding.

In our times we lack an objective criterion, independent of the subjective beliefs, views, and opinions of those who apply it, to determine whether someone is a Jew. In other words, we have no mark by which to define Jewish identity today. Consequently even the continued existence of the historical Jewish people is not guaranteed. The problem of the uniqueness of this people vanishes. There is a strong tendency in the religious camp to ignore this harsh reality by hiding it behind a screen of national-religious and pseudo-mystical ideology expressed in misleading phraseology. This ideology does not address itself to the real Jewish people but to a semi-mythological entity, "the nation," whose eternity is guaranteed in abstraction from the persons composing it.[4] The perverse use of traditional terminology in these circles reaches its peak in application of the phrase "the eternity of Israel" to the alleged perpetual existence of Israel. When the prophet Samuel used this phrase (1 Sam. 15:29), he was not referring to an attribute of Israel, but to the God of Israel who transcends all categories of human existence.[5]

The doctrine of Rabbi Kook identifying "the soul of the nation" with *Knesseth Israel* (the community of Israel), which in kabbalistic context is the Shekhinah (the divine presence), or *Malkhuth* (kingdom), the tenth *Sefirah* (emanation) has been a calamitous stumbling block. In Rabbi Kook's kabbalistic conception, the Jewish People is no longer an empirical-historical datum. From a factual reality it has been converted into a symbol of a completely different order of reality. The (intended or inadvertent) confusion of mystical and real categories is the great flaw in Rabbi Kook's doctrine that misled his disciples and continues to mislead theirs. It is imperative that we overcome this tendency to shroud reality with high-flown phraseology. There is no "soul of the nation." There are Jews who are living human beings. And the great crisis of the nation, "The hurt of my people" (Jer. 8:21), is that today we cannot tell *what* it is that makes them Jews.

The uniqueness of the empirical people of Israel is that their laws (the laws of the "King of kings of kings") are different from all peoples, whose laws are "the king's laws" (Esther 3:8). The problematic connection between the uniqueness of the actual life led by the people, and the uniqueness which the people is *intended* to achieve, can be highlighted by contrasting two adjacent verses:

> You have avouched the Lord this day to be your God and to walk in His ways and to keep His statutes and His commandments and His laws and to hearken unto His voice.

And God has avouched you this day to be His peculiar people as He has promised you, and that you should keep all His commandments.

(Deut. 26:17–18).

Is there an implied cause and effect relation between these two verses? Which would be the cause and which the effect? I have no communication with what occurs behind the curtain which conceals the divine intentions, and have no opinion on the precise meaning of "God has avouched you." I am familiar, however, with the fact that "You have avouched the Lord" was the commitment of many Jewish generations. In the opinion of the greatest man of faith after the patriarchs and the prophets, these two verses should not be regarded as two distinct propositions but rather as two formulations of one proposition. In his doctrine of providence, Maimonides conceives of God's providential relation to man as identical with the state of man when he is aware of God. It is *identical* with it and not just a consequence. Similarly, one might say that the election of the people of Israel ("And God has avouched you") is identical with the assumption of the yoke of the Kingdom of Heaven by the people of Israel ("You have avouched").

Accordingly, the uniqueness of the Jewish people—also called the "holiness" of Israel—is not something that was given to the people as an abiding and an enduring possession, but is rather a demand, an assignment and a task with which they are charged—a goal toward which they are to strive eternally, without any guarantee of ever attaining it. The question is not "Did God bestow holiness upon the Jewish people"? but rather, "Is the Jewish people striving toward holiness by assuming the yoke of Torah and Mitzvoth?"

This view has been strongly opposed by many who were incapable of such lofty faith. The first to object to it was Qorah, who declared that "All the congregation are holy" (Num. 16:3), implying that the uniqueness of the people of Israel is a given fact: Israel is essentially a holy nation. The holiness of the Jewish People is not, however, a reality, but rather an end or goal which transcends reality. In reality itself there is only eternal striving towards this goal. Holiness is dependent on the doing of "all my commandments"—a condition that clashes with human nature. The author of the *Shulhan Arukh* advisedly opens his work with the words: "Let one gird up strength to rise in the morning to the service of his Creator." One cannot say simply, "man should rise in the morning to the service of his Creator," for it may well be that man is incapable of attaining the goal of serving God, but man can be charged with the trying and the effort to achieve it.

The Judaism of Moses is arduous. It means knowing that we are *not* a holy people. The Judaism of Qorah is very comforting. It allows every Jew to be proud and boast that he is a member of the holy people, which is holy by its very nature. This obligates him to nothing. There is no greater opposition than that between the conception of *Am Segulah* (a chosen people) as implying subjection to an obligation and Am Segulah as purely a privilege. He who empties the concept of the Jewish people of its religious content (like David Ben Gurion) and still describes it as Am Segulah turns this concept into an expression of racist chauvinism.

As thus understood, the concept of the uniqueness of the Jewish people requires us to choose between two traditions of interpretation. One is represented by Judah Halevi (as the author of the *Kuzari*, not as the divine poet of the *Selihoth* and the *Yotzeroth*), some centuries later by Maharal, and, in our times, by Rabbi Kook and Ben-Gurion. The other tradition has descended from Moses, via Maimonides, to the *Shulhan Arukh*.[6]

The uniqueness of the Jewish people is not a *fact;* it is an endeavor. The holiness of Israel is not a reality but a task. "Holy" is an attribute that applies exclusively to God. It is therefore inapplicable to anything in the natural or historical domain. He who does so apply it is guilty of idolatry. He exalts something natural or human to the level of the divine.

The uniqueness of the Jewish people is a direction and a target. Were it a reality, it would have no value. The people of Israel were not the chosen people but were *commanded* to be the chosen people. In what does its being chosen consist? This is made perfectly clear in the wording of the benediction "who has chosen us from among all peoples and has given us His Torah."[7] The Jewish people has no intrinsic uniqueness. Its uniqueness rather consists in the demand laid on it. The people may or may not heed this demand. Therefore its fate is not guaranteed.

What has been said about the holiness of the people is also valid with regard to the holiness of the land. Exalting the land itself to the rank of holiness is idolatry *par excellence*. For a full understanding of the meaning of "holiness of the land," "the holiness of Jerusalem," and so on, one must refer to the Mishnah: "There are ten degrees of sanctity: the Land of Israel is more sanctified than all other Lands." We are not told that the land is holy but that it is sanctified. The crucial point is what its holiness consists of: from it are brought the *Omer* and the first fruits and the two loaves of bread.[8] These things are brought from the land of Israel not because it is a holy land. The land is sanctified by the act of fulfilling the commandment to bring the offering of the Omer and the first fruits and the two loaves of bread. Similarly, the Mishnah tells us that "the area within the walls (of Jerusalem) is more sanctified than the rest of the country, since minor sacrifices and the second tithe are eaten there," and so on. The holiness of Jerusalem thus consists, among other and similar things, in the commandment enjoining the pilgrimage to Jerusalem. The Mishnah proceeds through ten stages up to the Holy of Holies, whose holiness lies in the prohibition of anyone's entering it except the High Priest on the Day of Atonement. It is only in this sense that we find holiness in the world (in nature, in sites, buildings, objects, and persons). By contrast with the intrinsic Holiness of God, there is no holiness in the world except sanctification through Mitzvoth ("who has sanctified us with his commandments"). "The Torah and faith are the very principles of the Jewish nation, and all the sanctities—the Land of Israel, Jerusalem etc.—derived from the Torah, and are sanctified by the holiness of the *Torah*. Therefore, there is no distinction of time and place relevant to any matter of *Torah*. Thus it is the same in the Land of Israel and abroad . . . *Ultimately: nothing is holy in the world* . . . only the name of God is holy . . . and every sanctity stems from a commandment of the Creator."[9]

This is what distinguishes pagan religiosity from true religiosity. For pagan religiosity the land itself may be holy. I am aware that this paganism is spreading like wildfire today, affecting even many who, subjectively, are believing Jews. But a genuine religiosity recognizes that, in regard to the land, we are bound by certain obligations. Only the One is holy who is thrice declared holy in the Qedushah [a prayer centering on Isaiah 6:3]. Nothing other than He is holy, neither in history, nature, or man, though by virtue of their role in the service of God they may be sanctified.

CHAPTER 8

The Individual and Society in Judaism

(1967)

I t is doubtful whether any one of the many views from Jewish
literary sources concerning the individual and society represents
the definitive outlook of Judaism. Each is the perception of certain Jews. Each is held in common by Jews and non-Jews and was not
necessarily derived from the authoritative Jewish sources. The problems of values and morality as such are not uniquely Jewish.

There is no specifically Jewish morality, no specifically Jewish politics, no specifically Jewish conception of society. Jews and Gentiles
have been equally divided on all these matters, and the dividing line
does not separate Jews from Gentiles, but individuals from one
another. Controversy between Jews and Gentiles as such had to do
only with the issue of serving God through the observance of Torah
and Mitzvoth. Moreover, it is not even possible to classify the thinkers
whose ideas appear in the Jewish sources on the basis of their stand on
the question of the individual and society. A thinker associated with a
certain approach or conception, or who is thought to represent a distinct trend in Judaism, is likely to change his position for pragmatic
and heuristic reasons. He is likely to say something today and the
opposite tomorrow with reference to any political, social, or moral
problem—each statement appropriate for the needs of the time, the
place, and the misguided views of his interlocutors. The one invariant
motive governing such shifts in position is the demand to serve God
by performance of the Mitzvoth.

Consider, for example, the prattle about the prophetic conception
of the people of Israel and the national-political aspects of its life. In

truth, prophecy is not at all concerned with these questions. If it were, it would not be sacred but secular. Prophets did, of course, take a stand on these questions because they addressed men who were deeply steeped in the life of nation, state, and politics. But this is not what interested the prophets.

Neither Isaiah nor Jeremiah had a specific political-historical ideology with regard to the Jewish nation and its fate, only the principle to heed the word of God. When conditions and circumstances changed, heeding the word of God demanded different responses to problems of the nation, land, and state. In his historical context Isaiah proposed resistance to a foreign invader, and Jeremiah, in his, proposed that an invader be propitiated. What is true of "the prophets of truth and justice" is also true of all the thinkers in later Judaism, insofar as they represented the thing that constituted the identity of Judaism and enabled it to persist throughout the historical and cultural changes of 3,000 years.

In like manner we may understand the seemingly contradictory attitudes toward the institution of kingship. The contradictions are resolved only if we realize that, for the Torah and prophets, kingship *per se* is irrelevant. Such an institution exists, and under certain conditions may even be required. If it is required and exists, there are Mitzvoth which pertain to it. Is this institution mandatory from a religious standpoint? The dispute among the talmudic Sages over this question devolves upon the interpretation of the verse: "You shall appoint over you a King" (Deut. 17:15). Is this a prescription or a permission? The fact that later halakhic authorities, following Maimonides, decided that it is a prescription is not the final word, because many outstanding scholars and thinkers who were familiar with all the talmudic sources rejected this view. Most radical in his rejection of monarchy was Abravanel.[1] One of the later rabbinic commentators, Hanatzir, states in his commentary on the aforementioned verse that the Torah and prophets appear to indicate that monarchy is not in accord with the spirit and intention of the Torah. However, in certain circumstances it may be required for reasons of national welfare and even the nation's very existence. In such circumstances, establishment of a monarchy becomes a Mitzvah.[2] The negative attitude toward monarchy must give way to the exigencies of national survival, very much as proscription of work on the Sabbath is overridden by the imperative of saving a human life.

The Halakhah does not, therefore, give an unequivocal answer to the question of the desirable form of rule.

Some would begin the discussion of the problem of the individual and society in Judaism with the story of the creation of man in the image of God. The significance of that creation can be interpreted in very different ways. It can be given a collectivist interpretation, that all of mankind is like one person. It can, of course, be given an individualist interpretation. Moreover, it is not even possible to say that having been created in the image indicates something about the value of man. Man is only the image of God, without intrinsic essence, much as the picture hanging on the wall is only a surface treated with paint and meaningful only as representing something else. If what that picture represents is something I don't recognize, or that, in my opinion, doesn't exist or has no value for me—then the painted surface has no value. In other words, the very fact that man is created in the image of God deprives man of intrinsic value. Man is not divine, but only an image of God. He is not valued as an end-in-himself, and his significance consists only in his position before God. This is in extreme contrast to the view of Kant, for whom man replaces God, and the human individual becomes the highest value.

Those who insist on discovering the authoritative view of Judaism on the problem of the individual and society frequently turn from the Bible and the Halakhah to aggadic Midrashim and sayings of the talmudic Sages. They often cite the words used by the courts in admonishing witnesses, to the effect that, in the beginning, only one individual man was created to indicate that one life (according to one textual reading), or one Jewish life (according to another version) is equivalent to that of a whole world.[3] However, citation of isolated statements as authoritative is inadmissible, even if they are very penetrating and expressed with great pathos. We should never forget Maimonides' advice (in a letter to Obadiah the proselyte), that whoever seeks support for a certain view in a single verse among the many in the Bible or in one Aggadah or Midrash or a saying of one of the Sages, "only commits intellectual suicide." Principles and opinions on fundamental matters can be determined only by examination of the total material, and this totality, in Judaism, is represented only by the Halakhah. As for the Halakhah, it is impossible to determine definitively whether it centers on the individual Jew or on the Jewish community which observes it. The significance of the Halakhah is neither anthropological nor sociological but religious. It is concerned with man as he stands before God, not with man by himself nor with human society. Both are regarded as natural data, not as values.

In the Judaism of Torah and Mitzvoth, one aspect seems to be unambiguously collectivist: the institutionalized worship of God in sacrifice and prayer. The divine worship of Yom Kippur as prescribed in Leviticus, chapter 16, has meaning only as the service of the community and as atonement for the Congregation of Israel, in which every Israelite is included as a member: "and there shall be no man in the Tent of Meeting" except for the High Priest, who, on that occasion, represents and symbolizes the Congregation of Israel. These remarks apply not only to the service on Yom Kippur, but also to the daily sacrifices and the additional sacrifices of the Sabbath and holidays, which were communal and were never contributed by individuals. Similarly, the obligatory prayer instituted to replace the communal sacrifices is communal. Its occasions, forms, and content are prescribed for every individual as part of the praying community. There is no place for the expression of personal feelings and needs arising from the situation and condition of each individual. All this seems to express an extremely collectivist religiosity.

However, in our discussion of Yom Kippur, we are not concerned with archeology but rather with living Judaism. The Day of Atonement—over the past two thousand years a definitive expression of Jewish religiosity, the legitimacy of which has never been questioned—has the Ne'ilah prayer as its climax. The sacrificial service is recalled only as a historic memory in the Mussaf prayer. The essential concern of Ne'ilah, its unique content, is the sin and repentance of each individual. The community is mentioned only in the opening and concluding benedictions, which are the same for all prayers of Yom Kippur. Ne'ilah is the expression *par excellence* of individualistic religiosity, and, in this respect, the contrast between it and the Mussaf prayer of Yom Kippur is most interesting. However, it is meaningless to ask which of these two aspects of Yom Kippur is more acceptable, legitimate, or authentic. There is only one Yom Kippur in Judaism in all the transformations of its history, and nothing severs the Yom Kippur of "there shall be no man in the Tent of Meeting" from the Ne'ilah prayer of each individual

Jew of our present Yom Kippur. The continuity of Judaism and its identity were neither diminished nor undermined when this Yom Kippur was substituted for that. Here, too, we cannot draw any conclusion about individualism or collectivism in Judaism.

An analysis of the prayers of the Days of Awe reveals the same truth. The obligatory prayer of Rosh Hashanah reiterates the motif "We must praise . . . therefore we will hope . . . to see speedily the glory of Your might," and so on.[4] This prayer does not single out the individual or even the Jewish community. Its content and meaning are universal, almost cosmic; its theme is the Kingdom of God in the world. The individual and his unique personality do not appear in it at all. However, good and worthy Jews who did not have the ability to serve God solely from the aspiration "to see quickly the glory of Your might" composed the prayer U'netaneh Tokef, which expresses anxiety concerning "who will live and who will die," and so on. From a formal standpoint the two prayers must be evaluated quite differently. Only the former is halakhically obligatory, whereas the latter is optional, included by custom in the service of some Jewish communities and omitted in that of others. However, as constituents of living, empirical Jewish religiosity, both are legitimate, and the Jew need not choose one and reject the other. He can say both prayers with intentional devotion (*Kavanah*) despite the contrast between the types of religiosity they represent.[5]

What is true of Halakhah is equally true of every other field which has become an inseparable part of Judaism. We have, on the one hand, the great Mussar literature (devotional morality), ranging from *The Duties of the Heart* of nine hundred years ago to *The Path of the Upright* of two hundred years ago.[6] These books were greatly popularized by the Mussar movement of recent generations. They are documents of extremely individualistic religiosity. Society, and even the community of the Jewish people, plays no role in this religious life. Moreover, for the author of *The Duties of the Heart,* social reality, with its obligations, tasks, and problems, is a disturbing factor. All these distract a person from "his duty in his world," and he who cares for his soul will avoid them. On the other side is Maimonides, whose work is axial for all attempts to systematize Jewish religious thought. Maimonides, as is his wont, conducts his discussion on two levels. Failure to distinguish them is the source of many misconstructions of Maimonides' philosophy. One level has to do with needs, the other with values. As in every other area, here, too, needs and values are practically antagonistic concepts. Maimonides deals with Judaism from both standpoints, and he does not explicitly distinguish between the two approaches. He confuses them intentionally and shifts from one level to the other without indicating this explicitly, to obscure matters for the reader who is not capable of understanding his teaching. This teaching is intended for the reader whose understanding is sufficiently penetrating to distinguish the two levels.

Maimonides' discussion has a utilitarian and a mystical dimension. On the utilitarian level Maimonides is an extreme collectivist: "It will not be possible that the laws be dependent on changes in the circumstances of the individuals and of the times . . . On the contrary, governance of the Law ought to be absolute and universal, including everyone, even if it is suitable only to certain individuals and not suitable for others, for if it were made to fit individuals, the whole would be corrupted."[7] In other words, the proper agent of religious behavior is not the individual but the community. Similarly, Maimonides emphasizes the importance of social improvement as a condition for the very possibility of attaining the religious *telos:* "For man cannot know the truth nor perform the Mitzvoth when he is sick or hungry or fleeing his enemies"—and, after all, penury and fear, and to a large extent also sickness, are only functions of social conditions. However, on the level of the Torah as that which alone is intrinsically valuable, he describes true human perfection as something which is "yours alone and no strangers' with you" (Prov. 5:17). The individual who has attained perfection wishes to be alone with God and "will regard all people according to their various states with respect to which they are undoubtedly either like domestic beasts or like beasts of prey. If the perfect man who lives in solitude thinks of them at all, he does so only with a view to saving himself from harm . . . or to obtaining an advantage that may be obtained from them."[8] The purpose of the Torah is not social improvement, and the ultimate ground for the Mitzvoth is not concern for man's needs in his social existence; it is for the individual (every individual) to attain perfection by rising above everything that is not an inherent part of this perfection: "Know that all the practices of the worship, such as reading the Torah, prayer and the performance of the other Mitzvoth, have only the end of training you to occupy yourself with His commandments, may He be exalted, rather than with matters pertaining to this world; you should act as if you were occupied with Him, may He be exalted, and not with that which is other than He."[9] The contradiction between these two approaches of Maimonides is only a seeming one: social organization is indeed necessary, and the Torah regulates it, but social regulation is not a value. It may be compared to health. Digestion and excretion are vital needs, and woe to the man whose digestion or excretion are not functioning properly. Nevertheless, they are not values.

Our subject has a practical aspect relating to the place of the Jewish religion in the state of Israel or—reversing the perspective—the place of the state in the religious life. We must distinguish between the historical exilic existence of the Jewish people and its present existence as possessing political autonomy. Previously, the individual conscious of his Jewish identity could not live his life as a Jew except through complete immersion in the Jewish collective—the religious community. Outside this community there were no institutions for the realization of the Jewish identity. Jewish life was expressed concretely in the synagogue and the cemetery, the *Mikveh* (ritual bath) and the slaughter house, through study of the Torah and the Yeshivah—and above all—in observance of the Sabbath. Our generation has created a framework for Jewish existence which is not religious, which is not conducted by religious institutions, is not committed to religious values, and has no religious meaning. We must examine afresh the significance of religion for a Jewish person and for the Jewish people and its state.

One contemporary approach, widespread is to regard the Jewish religion as a factor in the survival and welfare of the Jewish people, and to evaluate it from the standpoint of its contribution to satisfying the needs and forwarding the interests of the nation and the state. This attitude was shared by the agnostic David Ben-Gurion and the official religious leadership alike. In truth, this approach renders the Jewish religion otiose and even exhibits it as harmful. The state of Israel and the unity of the nation within it are based on nonreligious foundations: the identity card and passport, the service of our children in the IDF (Israel Defense Force), the secular civil and criminal law, which are accepted by the religious community in Israel. The Torah and *Mitzvoth*—the Jewish religion—divides us. This is the great crisis of the Jewish people in its state and the great obstacle to national unity and political consolidation. Therefore only he who does not regard religion as a collective national-political manifestation, but views it as setting personal goals and values, is capable of surmounting the crisis. He will not voice the false claim that "it is good for Jews" to be religious, but will rather urge the claim of the first paragraph of the *Shulhan Arukh* that to be religious is the obligation of a Jewish person in his world, whether it is useful or not to the national, political, or economic interests of the state of Israel and the Jewish people. No nation and no community, no state, not even the Jewish nation and its state are supreme values. All are fictions or human constructs which satisfy man's objective or spiritual needs. But even spiritual needs and human values such as homeland or liberty are only human and of no religious significance. Therefore, if in the exilic history of the Jewish people the collective aspect of the Jewish religion was emphasized, it is our obligation today to emphasize its personal aspect. Religious education and the struggle for dissemination of Jewish religion should concentrate on the personal element.

CHAPTER 9

Ahistorical Thinkers in Judaism
(1980)

A lecture delivered at the Annual Conference on Jewish Thought, Jerusalem, 1980.

The expressions "Jewish thought" and "the biblical point of view" are used repeatedly as if they pertained to a coherent system of ideas. Conversely, some thinkers deny the existence of any single system of ideas that deserves the name "Judaism." This is correct. Nevertheless, Judaism is a well defined entity whose continuous existence for several thousands of years is a fact.

If we are to talk meaningfully about Judaism, we must attend to its actual manifestations rather than to its various interpretations. We must ask: what was Judaism in fact? What would a visitor from Venus or Mars perceive as the continuous and abiding nature of this entity? I submit that such an uncommitted observer, free of evaluations, beliefs, and opinions, will be struck by the fact that Judaism manifested itself in a *particular way of serving God, and not in any particular conception of man, of the world, or of history.* Not only did the conceptions change and replace one another throughout the ages, but divergent and contradictory conceptions existed side by side. Moreover, we regard them all as legitimate, yet none as binding. Judaism, *in actu,* is the service of God in a particular way, to wit, through the Mitzvoth. Only that can be called simply "Judaism." Historically, various viewpoints, opinions, and values were entertained by the Jews against the background of the practice of Mitzvoth. Every such system of ideas, however, was a fleeting episode in Jewish history and, what is crucial, was not considered authoritative. It is only from this perspective that I can address the issue of historic or ahistoric conceptions in Judaism. The formulation "ahistorical thinkers in Judaism" is to be taken in a loose sense. I shall not discuss particular thinkers but will examine various conceptions, some of which were formulated by identifiable persons, and others that were held collectively.

The abiding and constant element in Jewish history, the Halakhah, is essentially ahistoric. It does not reflect a vision of historical reality, and the changes and modifications it underwent throughout the ages do not necessarily reflect changes in the historical situation. The foundations of the Halakhah are themselves of halakhic nature, and its transformations throughout the ages reflect factors immanent to halakhic thinking. While Salo Baron sees in the ahistoricism of Maimonides the influence of Hellenism; I rather see in it Jewish originality. Maimonides is unique among the Jewish mediaeval philosophers in that he was principally a halakhist. In this respect there is no absurdity in contending that Maimonides was less of a philosopher than Gersonides or Crescas, and in a sense also less of a philosopher than Judah Halevi.[1] His world was the world of Halakhah, and precisely for this reason history was irrelevant to him. Judaism was for him the service of God by man, not the theory of man, whether individual or collective—neither anthropology nor ethnology, and not even history.

To consider history as the foundation of faith is to deplete religion of all religious significance. It is to place man at the center—as against what is customarily inscribed on the lectern before the ark in the synagogue: "I have set God always before me"(Ps.16:8). To perceive history as the pivot of all thought or awareness is to set man always before one. The Bible is not a book of meditations on man as a historic being. One book in the Hebrew Bible, the Book of Job, is devoted entirely to reflection on man's position before God. Most of the Bible, the Pentateuch, the prophets, and the psalms also focus on this position. In God's response to Job, man is not mentioned, either directly or indirectly. Its intention is to disabuse Job and his friends of the idea that man is the center of creation and a being of supreme value. Maimonides, the thinker and preceptor who was the greatest of believers in Israel after the patriarchs and the prophets, devoted two pivotal chapters of his *Guide of the Perplexed* (III 13–14) to deny the notion of man's centrality in the world as the ultimate end of creation. He who sees in man a supreme value, and in humanity and its fate the meaning of divine creation, deifies man and turns the deity into a functionary of humanity, whether as the moving force of history or as the guarantor of the morality springing from the human heart. This deity is man's servant, and in this perspective serving God by observing Torah and Mitzvoth is utterly pointless. This is precisely where the ways of Judaism and Christianity diverge completely.

In contrast to the prevalent opinions, I do not think that the view of history as religiously significant is of Jewish origin. It stems rather from Christianity. And, indeed, in Christianity it is not man who serves God but rather God serves man. Human history acquires a divine meaning since God was incarnated in man. Judaism consisted in the service of God, in Torah and Mitzvoth, which alone constituted its persisting identity. All the other phenomena of Judaism, including the Kabbalah, which Gershom Scholem sets on a par with Halakhah, were merely episodic. The service of God as crystallized in the Halakhah is an ahistoric reality. Historical vicissitudes and changes have no bearing on man's posture before God.

Much has been said in the literature of a "biblical conception of history." I deny its existence, despite the abundance of historical material in Scripture and of references to historical circumstances and events; more pointedly, despite divine intervention in the course of history as depicted in Scripture. The language of Scripture is the language of religious faith, and one must distinguish between the essential significance of the words and its unavoidable linguistic expression, whether oral or written. "The Torah spoke in the language spoken by men"—and the language of men is incapable of expressing divine matters. No expressions in ordinary language are adequate for speaking of God and of the position of mankind before God. Our Sages of blessed memory already maintained that we would not have dared even to say "the great, the valiant, and the terrible God," had not Moses and Nehemiah used these words.[2] Utterances on divine matters require careful scrutiny if one is to distinguish intended sense from literal meaning. Words may seem simple and unambiguous, such as "and God descended upon Mount Sinai." Yet we require even of a child studying the Pentateuch that he understand that God does not dwell on the top story of a cosmic skyscraper from which he descends in an elevator or lands in a helicopter on top of the mountain. The same applies to all that is said in the so-called "historical books" of the Bible.

One may object, however, that the words of the prophets, even when they are delivering the word of God, calling Israel to the service of God, and admonishing the transgressors, hinge principally on historical events and draw conclusions from past history or forecast future history. This calls for a twofold reply.

First: is prophecy—its content and form—the constitutive element of faith and religion in Judaism? It is a favorite ploy of Christian thinkers, and of Jews who follow in their footsteps, to reduce "pure" Judaism to prophecy, out of contempt for the Torah and scorn for the Mitzvoth—in calculated and deliberate opposition to empirical Judaism. Our Sages of blessed memory said that were it not for the sins of Israel, they would have been given only the five books of Moses (the Pentateuch) and the Book of Joshua. The books of the prophets are the result of a historical "mishap," Israel's lapse into idolatry. Primarily, Judaism is the system of religious praxis the content of which—in the form given in the written Torah and in the Halakhah of the oral Torah—is atemporal and super-temporal.

Second, I deny the prevalent view that there is a specific biblical philosophy of history and that the prophets present a specific conception of the revelation of God in history in general and in Jewish history in particular. One must of course acknowledge that prophecy actually existed in Israel, and that the messages of the prophets are included in the Holy Scriptures and have become integral to the heritage of Jewish faith and consciousness. But it was not the vision of "the finger of God" in history that determined the attitude of the prophets toward historical events. It was rather their judgment of the actions, in the historical context, of individuals and of the nation by the criterion of fearing and serving God. The prophets do not regard historical events as possessing an inherent religious meaning. Rather, their judgment of historical reality—whether past, contemporary, or visionary—derives in each and every case from the desire or the necessity to present to the individual and to the nation the great demand to fear God and to serve Him in a manner appropriate to the level of faith which the people at that time had attained. This judgment may change, and does in fact change with the alterations of religious spiritual life. In other words, the prophets deals with history not from the standpoint of a religious philosophy of history, but from a religious opportunistic standpoint— and here this term is being used approvingly.

This point is illustrated in the Bible by the attitude of the two "political" prophets par excellence, Isaiah and Jeremiah, to the historical circumstances of their day, in which they were involved both personally and by way of their prophetic mission. On the face of it they seem to represent two divergent religious conceptions of the meaning of history and the question of national and political independence. Pivotal to Isaiah's historical prophecies is the belief that Jerusalem is unlike any other city in the world and its fate will not resemble theirs. Assyria conquers Damascus, Arphad, and Hamath, but will never conquer Jerusalem, the city of God. Therefore one must not surrender to Assyrian and should resist its cohorts, confident of God's deliverance. Jeremiah's position seems to be the opposite. He denies the uniqueness of Jerusalem relative to all other cities and does not envision a special historical fate for her. The great conqueror Nebukhadnezzar will conquer Jerusalem too. Judea must relinquish independence and surrender to him.

Do Isaiah and Jeremiah really express divergent viewpoints on history as a religious phenomenon? By no means! They express no religious view of history. Both are prophets of God, not philosophers of history. The core of their religious message is not the survival or destruction of Jerusalem, but God-fearingness and service of God. Neither he who "saw the Lord sitting upon a throne high and lifted up" (Isa. 6:1) nor he who was ordained a prophet in the womb (Jer. 1:5) are "religious historiosophers" because neither viewed the historical situation as possessing intrinsic religious significance. They regarded it from the standpoint of the religious-spiritual situation of their generation and accounted for it with arguments that do not apply to the situation of another generation. Invariably, the argument is aimed at rooting out pagan beliefs and practices and reinforcing the belief in God. Isaiah fought in his day against the pagan conception that the God of Israel is one of the territorial-national gods whose power is territorially limited, and that if Assyria prevailed over the land, it will also prevail over the God of Israel. That was the notion of Ahaz the wicked, who introduced the Assyrian idols into the Temple in Jerusalem. Against this Isaiah advances the great principle that all the gods of the nations are idols, and the Lord God of Israel, He alone is God. Consequently he interprets history in a way which accords Jerusalem, *qua* city of God, a unique significance and assigns it a special historical destiny.

A hundred years later the religious attitudes had changed, and Jeremiah turned the religious struggle in the opposite direction. Isaiah's very principle, which was accepted by the people, had become the idolatrous faith in the intrinsic holiness of Jerusalem as "The temple of God, the temple of God, the temple of God" (Jer. 7:4), a belief in a magical immunity conferred on the city by this status that was unrelated to the observance of the Torah and the fulfillment of its Mitzvoth. Therefore Jeremiah insisted that neither the city nor the temple had any intrinsic holiness or special immunity. There is no holiness save in serving God. When the people violated God's Torah, "the temple of the Lord" turned into "a den of robbers," and the singularity of Jerusalem and its historical destiny ceased. It was no different from any other city. The great power on its way to conquering the world will conquer Jerusalem too.

Thus the prophets do not present specific historical conceptions as essential to faith and to religion. They convey only the absolute demand to serve God, while the attitude toward history may change according to the changing implications of the historic situations for the observance of the Torah and the Mitzvoth. There is no philosophy of history that can be defined as "the religious attitude of Judaism toward history." In Judaism each historical situation, every historical vicissitude and change, and even the historical process as a whole are treated not from the point of view of a specific religious-historical conception but from the perspective of the religious interest. In the postbiblical era too this "religious opportunism" was reflected in the perplexities of the Hassidim, the Pharisees, and the Tanna'im when they judged the historical significance of their times and events such as the wars of the first Hasmonaites, the conquest of the later Hasmonaites, the Herodian dynasty, the Roman domination, and the rebellion against it. This "religious opportunism" is the stance of great believers, for whom the service of God is the supreme value and all human affairs are mere means and instruments for the service of God. These affairs include human history in its entirety and the history of the Jews in particular.

I was amazed to hear from some of my predecessors in this discussion that the "historical books" of the Bible are entirely devoted to a description of a process of profound religious significance, directed by providence to lead the Jews (or humanity as a whole) toward a preassigned goal: redemption in the End of Days. This is in line with the Christian exegesis, which presents the biblical narrative not as the chronicle of events in the history of the people of Israel but as *Heilsgeschichte* whose meaning lies beyond human history. This view has no foundation in Scripture itself, and it is nothing but a tendentious rendering of the biblical narrative, deriving from the interpreters' preconception as to what the biblical story ought to convey. An unbiased examination of the history of humankind and of the Jews as related in the Bible will not reveal in the entire process, commencing with the deluge (or the patriarchs, or the Exodus from Egypt) and going to the beginning of the second commonwealth (or a few generations after it), any design or definite direction, or gradual approach to a specific goal. In its sequence of changes and transformations, rises and falls, achievements and failures in a repetitive cycle, events succeed each other without any indication that a predetermined plan is being carried out. Ultimately the world remains as it was in its beginning, and the occasional divine interventions did not change it fundamentally. "All flesh had corrupted his way", "and the earth was filled with violence," and, several thousands years later, all of Europe was under the sway of a band of rogues. Yet man is required to serve God in the world as it is. This view accords with the description of Gibbon—that history is nothing but the story of crimes, follies, and calamities afflicting mankind. The anticipated "redemption," the rehabilitation of the world at the end of days, is presented not as the final link in a chain of events succeeding one another in history, but precisely as a transformation brought about from without, as a divine intervention which disrupts the continuity of history. The vision of the end of days is incapable of conferring meaning on the history of the period preceding it.

Some remarks are in order concerning the messianic idea (or vision) and its role in the Judaic religious consciousness, at least since the second commonwealth. There is a widespread opinion that this idea introduces into Jewish religious faith a specific conception of history as a preparation or education for the messianic era. Although some sources support such a view, there is good reason for doubting its authenticity.

As has already been emphasized, nothing in the history narrated in Jewish sources confirms such a construal. Moreover, the messianic idea can in no way be considered a conception of history, because the images of the messianic era break through the bounds of history. Even the depiction of messianic times by Maimonides, who endeavors to refrain from all that is miraculous and conceives of the messianic epoch as one in which "the earth shall be full of the knowledge of God, as the waters cover the sea," is no less supernatural than its description as a time when cakes and finely woven woolen cloths will sprout from the soil of the land of Israel. Attainment of knowledge of God by humanity in its entirety goes beyond history, the gist of which is the struggle for the knowledge of God in a world wherein it is absent.

At the conclusion of his Code, after discussing messianic redemption and the reign of the Messiah-king according to the talmudic-midrashic sources, which Maimonides interprets in his own manner, he goes out of his way to make a comment unlike anything in all the fourteen books: "And never should a man preoccupy himself with Aggadah, nor should one dwell on the Midrash pertaining to these matters and the like, and one should not make them central, for they do not lead to fear or to love."[3] Maimonides sensed the danger involved in immersing oneself in historical (or meta-historical) reflection on the future redemption. A person obsessed with the idea of the better world of the end of the days might come to despise the world of ahistorical Halakhah, which is the program of the service of God in the present, in the world as it is. The intention to serve God is essentially ahistorical. With respect to the service of God all periods and all situations are alike. The believer undertakes this service wherever and whenever he may be located, that is, in his present. The yearning for messianic redemption lures one into contemplating an alternative reality which will replace one's present. True, there have been important Jewish thinkers and multitudes of true believers for whom devotion to the Halakhah and adherence to the messianic idea were conjoined. But behind the messianic idea lurks the danger of antinomianism, the denial of the value and significance of the practical Mitzvoth of the Halakhah for the here and now. History teaches us that whenever a wave of messianic enthusiasm swept the nation, and the vision of redemption became central to the religious consciousness, disaster followed for the Judaism of Torah and Mitzvoth. From among the "messianic" Jews in one period sprang Christianity, and from messianic Jews in another period, Sabbateanism. Both led to the casting off of the yoke of Torah and Mitzvoth. Nowadays, too, the opponents of the centrality of Mitzvoth in Judaism tend to exalt the messianic idea as the supreme value and the principal content of the Jewish religion.

Perhaps it is against the background of this concern about the consequences of the idea of messianic redemption—a concern apparent also in the words of Maimonides—that one can understand the purport of the remarkable midrashic saying variously attributed to an obscure Sage, Rabbi Hiya Bar Nehemiah, and to Rabbi Akiba(!):"'and the years draw near, when you shall say, I have no pleasure in them'(Eccles. 12:1)—those are the days of the Messiah, wherein there is no merit and no liability." This statement implies that, in the religious sense, there is no meaning and value except in our world, where a deliberate effort ("pleasure") is required in the struggle for the service of God. The effort and the struggle—that is the Halakhah.

I am in no way disregarding the fact, which no one can well ignore, that the relation of religion to history forms one of the central motifs of Jewish thought and faith, or, at any rate, of important trends in Judaism. Much of Judaism is incomprehensible except in the light of this relatedness, be it to past history or to the (anticipated or envisioned) future history. The assessment of the historical situation, of the historical changes and transformations, and of the direction and purpose attributed to the historical process—all of these colored religious beliefs, opinions, and values. What I do reject is the prevalent view that the attribution of religious meaning to the historical process characterizes "Judaism" as such. I have endeavored to point out distinctive ahistorical elements in the thought and practice of Judaism, and it is my view that precisely these elements constitute its most profound and most significant stratum. "You were the same before the world was created, and the same since its creation." The very existence of the world—history as well as nature—is irrelevant for the cognizance of God and his service.

Judaism in its actual embodiment as the service of God in the form of halakhic practice is ahistorical. This ahistoric character remains unaffected by the changes and transformations of the Halakhah corresponding to the historical changes and transformations in the course of time. If halakhic rules and regulations changed—or were even deliberately modified—in accordance with changes and innovations in historical conditions, that does not indicate that history is constitutive of Halakhah or a determining factor. The changes reflect forced submission to irresistible external pressure. After the destruction of the Temple and the exile from the land of Israel, most of the Mitzvoth became practically inoperative. This meant that a greater part of *Seder Zera'im* (except for *Berakhoth*), *Kodashim* (except the Tractate *Hulin*), and *Tahoroth* (except the Tractate *Niddah*), and even a central part of *Nezikin* were no longer applicable.[4] Moreover, changes in the economic system within which the Jews were compelled to operate forced a reformulation of many of the halakhic laws relating to business transactions. These facts, however, attest to no change in perception of the meaning and the purpose of the Halakhah as such. They rather represent efforts to circumvent the new situation. In other words, there was no programmatic change or revaluation of the faith and its halakhic embodiment. It is by no accident that the greatest man of Halakhah in post-talmudic Judaism, Maimonides, is also the foremost exponent of ahistorical religious thought, in contrast to other great figures in Jewish religious thought and creativity who set history as the cornerstone of their faith. One of them was Rabbi Judah Halevi, who in this respect may be regarded as antithetical to Maimonides. But on this point one must take into account the amazing duality in Halevi's personality and work. The contrast with Maimonides is valid only with respect to the author of the *Kuzari,* whereas the divine poet of the *Selihoth* and the prayers is very different. The sacred poetry of Halevi expresses, with unsurpassed profundity and force, pure faith—the awareness of the position of man in the presence of God, and of serving God in heart and in deed, without any reference to past or future historical situations and the fate of the Jews. In these works Halevi reaches heights of faith that are not unlike those of Maimonides in the last chapter of his *Hilkhoth Teshuvah* and in the last chapters of *The Guide of the Perplexed*.

Some scholars "explain" Maimonides' ahistorical approach as resulting from the influence of the ahistoric Greek philosophy, which is opposed, as it were, to the historical essence of the faith of "Judaism." Yet Maimonides, who does use Aristotelian conceptual tools and categories, draws the content of his thought from the same authentic Jewish sources as does Halevi. Both represent legitimate aspects of faith in Judaism.

CHAPTER 10

The Religious and Moral Significance of the Redemption of Israel

(1977)

L et me object, at the outset, to any attempt to explain anyone's views by where he comes from or who he is. I object as well to any attempt to distinguish between those who come from a milieu shaped by Western culture and others whose cultural and spiritual origins lie in Eastern Europe. I, too, belong to the Western world although, geographically speaking, I come from the east. I spent my childhood in Russia, but am familiar with Western science, philosophy, literature, and society no less than are the "Westerners." I recall a public debate more than thirty years ago between myself and the late Dr. Isaac Breuer, one of the most interesting thinkers among religious Jews in the generation preceding ours, for whom I had great respect despite the considerable differences between our respective views. In that debate we drifted off to general philosophical problems, and although they were relevant to the issues that were close to our hearts, Judaism, Torah, and faith, they were fundamentally ontological and epistemological problems. Since Breuer argued persistently from the Jewish viewpoint, I said to him: "Dr. Breuer, why should we deceive ourselves? You know as well as I that in our treatment of philosophical questions both of us—who consider ourselves believing Jews, whose intention is to assume the yoke of the Kingdom of Heaven and the yoke of Torah and Mitzvoth—do not draw upon Jewish sources but upon the atheistic antisemite Kant. We cannot do otherwise!" Breuer conceded at once that it would be impossible—even he could not do it—to discuss philosophical problems without recourse to Kant. Today, too, it is not the lack of familiarity with various aspects of European culture that created the rift between us. We are all equally steeped in Western culture.

Severe criticism has been voiced against our attitude—the attitude of Judaism—to the Gentile world. Some accused us of attaching no human value to Gentiles, and of ignoring the image of God in *every* person. To this my reply is far more radical. A few days ago we concluded the Day of Atonement saying: "man has no preeminence over the beast: for all is vanity", and "You have distinguished man from the first and acknowledged him to stand before You." The question is not whether the Gentile is of value but whether *man* has any value, be he Jew or Gentile. About "God created man in His own image, in the image of God created He him," Rabbi Se'adiah Gaon said: "and in respect of this image everyone is equal, the righteous as well as the wicked, the one is a man and the other is a man."[1] Those who would ground morality on the image of God in man may remember that Adolf Hitler and Adolf Eichmann were created in God's image like you and me, and also every rapist and murderer, as well as the most righteous of men. The ultimate message of the Day of Atonement is that man, as such, has no intrinsic value; he acquires value insofar as he stands before God. In the last verse of Jonah, which is also read on the Day of Atonement, man and beast are on the same plane: "more than six score thousand persons . . . and also much cattle." Man—any man—is by nature beastlike; it is only the service of God that raises him from nullity to significance and confers value on him. "Let not the wise man glory in his wisdom, neither let the mighty man glory in his might, let not the rich man glory in his riches. But let him that glorifies glory in this, that he understands and knows me" (Jer. 9:22–23). Neither the essence nor the nature of man, his attributes or peculiar capacities, not even his achievements are of inherent importance. In God's reply to Jonah there is no mention of the fact that the people of Nineveh repented. Why? Because even man's great attainment, repentance, can only lead to expiation, but does not change human nature. In this respect there is no difference between Jew and Gentile.

In the course of discussion (the topic was "The Jewish People and the Nations of the World") the expression "a light to the nations" was frequently brought up. The use of this expression by Ben-Gurion and others to indicate the vocation of the Jewish people departs considerably from its original biblical meaning. The expression is borrowed from the Book of Isaiah, where it refers expressly to the prophet himself, charged with the mission "to bring Jacob again" to God, and beyond that, to be a "light to the nations"—much as Jeremiah was ordained to be "a prophet unto the nations."[2] The idea that the people of Israel has been endowed with a capacity for instructing and guiding all of humanity has no basis in authentic Jewish sources, and played no role—at least no more then a marginal one—in the consciousness of generations of Jews who assumed the yoke of the Kingdom of Heaven in the form of the yoke of Torah and Mitzvoth. This idea was fabricated by the heretics—from the Apostle Paul to Ben-Gurion—who meant to cast off the yoke of Torah by substituting for it a faith in an abstract "vocation."

The Jewish people were not given a mission; it was rather charged with a task—the task of being servants of God ("A Kingdom of Priests and a holy nation"). To transform religion and religious faith from a task and obligation into an endowment and a destiny is to degrade them. In the Ne'ilah prayer, and in that most sublime of prayers, Alenu, we give thanks to God for the good fortune to be His servants, while the elevation of the world through the Kingdom of God is assigned to Him and not to us. Similarly, in the prayer of the Days of Awe, we beseech God to impose fear of Him on all His creatures so that they may unite for compliance with His will. No mention is made of any role which Israel is called upon to play in realizing this vision.

The obligation imposed on the people of Israel was never met by the Jews, and they do not fulfill it today. The law-giver of Israel said on the day of his death: "behold while I am yet alive with you this day you have been rebellious against God and how much more after my death? . . . for I know that after my death you will surely be corrupted" (Deut. 31:27–29). More than three thousand years have elapsed since then—and the words of Moses remain true. It would seem that my predecessors in this debate have confused the vision of the prophets of Israel about the deeds of God with a vision of what the Jews will do, as if the God of Israel were a Jew like the God of the Christians.

The so-called messianic vision, the redemption of humanity and of the world, is depicted in the sources as the act of God, not as the enterprise of the people of Israel, which requires rehabilitation like all of mankind. In this respect there is no difference between Jews and other human beings. "The earth also was corrupt before God and the earth was filled with violence"—this holds for Jews and Gentiles alike. Furthermore then entire notion of the re-forming of the world and the redemption of humanity is peripheral, not central, to the religious thought, feeling, and faith of Judaism, not to mention its religious practice. Frequent repetition of the five verses opening the second chapter of Isaiah, while ignoring their location between chapter 1, which is read as the Haftarah of the Sabbath preceding the ninth of Av (the anniversary of the destruction of the Temple), and the strong exhortation following them, offers an escape from the severity of the demand made of man by the Bible. Were we to group together all the verses in the Bible which, literally or by interpretation, refer to the redemption of the world and the rehabilitation of mankind in days to come, we would see how few they are by comparison to the main body of prophetic discourse, which conveys the austere demand to serve God *in the world as it is.*

My construal of biblical prophecy does not rest on the authority of philosophers or theologians, but rather on the Tossafist annotators, who seem remote from philosophy and theology, and who express a "simple" faith in God and His Torah.[3] In connection with a statement in the Talmud about prophecy, the Tossafists comment that "the prophet only prophesies *what ought to be.*"[4] Here we have presented to us in full force the pure faith as opposed to the faith in magic and oracles. If prophecy were a statement of what will happen, it would have no religious significance. What is the distinction between the meteorological forecast and a prophetic oracle about tomorrow's weather? Both of them oblige me to do nothing, they are irrelevant to the service of God. One of the Tanna'im already said "'and the years draw near, when you shall say, I have no pleasure in them' (Eccles. 12:1)—those are the days of the Messiah, wherein there is no merit and no liability," which implies that there is no meaning and value in the religious sense, except in our world, where a deliberate effort ("pleasure") is required in the struggle to serve God. The conditions and circumstances in which man serves God are, in a religious sense, immaterial. Even if we extend the reference from the individual to the collective, to the larger Jewish collective, or even to all of humankind— it is all simply the world taking its natural course. Possibly this course of the world also includes the redemption at the end of days. Yet religious fulfillment does not attach specifically to this state of affairs, but rather to the service of God in *any* state of affairs. And so we return to the meaning of the end of Ne'ilah: "man has no preeminence over the beast: for all is vanity," on the one hand, and "you have distinguished man from the first and acknowledged him to stand before you" on the other. Man's standing before God is not contingent upon objective circumstances, whether these pertain to the world or to man. His faith is not affected by such circumstances, if the man is a true believer. Faith which is thus affected is not true faith.

The religious participants in this debate made ample use of the pronoun "we" when they spoke of "Judaism," "Jewish people," and "faith." I would like to ask: who are "we"? Does "we" mean all of the contemporary Jews? Some contrasted "us" with "the infidels." I presume there is no human group in which religious disbelief is as widespread today as among Jews. It is doubtful whether there is a human group in which the community of believers has dwindled as it has among Jews. This is hardly surprising, for the faith demanded in Judaism requires very great fortitude. Not in vain did the psalmist exclaim: "you mighty ones that do His bidding" (Ps. 103:20). What is surprising is not the prevailing lack of faith among Jews, bur rather the dominance of faith among them for so many generations. It is in conflict with human nature. It requires of one to subdue his inclinations and even suppress his human sensibilities. Let me remind you of Abravanel's comment relating to the Aqedah: "'And Abraham rose up early in the morning, and saddled his ass'—he overcame his materiality." To this he added a remark that is quite amazing if we recall that messianic redemption *in the future* is pivotal to Abravanel's thought, as the antithesis to Christian messianic redemption. He continues: "And that is the ass to be ridden by the Messiah—king." We may infer, then, that even for Abravanel the vision of messianic redemption is not simply the expectation of a future historical event, but chiefly the expectation that the faith of Abraham the Patriarch, of whom it was said that he believed in God, shall be the faith of the entire world. This is the very opinion of Maimonides on messianic redemption, which he expresses at the conclusion of his code with the verse: "for the earth shall be full of the knowledge of God as the waters cover the sea" (Isa. 12:9). As for the vision of messianic redemption as a future event in history—a belief that Maimonides enumerates as one of the fundamental articles of faith in the Jewish tradition—his real attitude is suggested to the discerning reader in his scathing comments on the aggadic redemption stories: "And never should one preoccupy oneself with the Aggadoth, nor should one dwell on the Midrashim that deal with these matters and their cognates, *and one should not make them principal,* for they do not lead to fear or to love." Consider the consequences for Judaism of every historical development in which messianic redemption became central to Jewish faith. Such situations brought forth Christianity, led to Sabbateanism and to Frankism, and in our day this focus has become a stumbling block to the disciples of Rabbi Kook, who were not intellectually equipped to understand his teaching.[5] Maimonides was aware of the danger of the ascendency of the messianic idea as a substitute for the authentic faith in God, which consists in assuming the obligation to observe Torah and Mitzvoth.

Of the two great distortions of Jewish faith, the first was the Kabbalah, which converted the obligation imposed upon the Jewish people into a vocation affecting the cosmos and God Himself. The Mitzvoth were interpreted as a method for mending disruptions in the world of divinity and rectifying the world's disorders. In that way man himself is elevated, as it were, to a divine level. This is the very opposite of the idea of Ne'ilah on the Day of Atonement. The Kabbalah transformed the Judaism of the service of God into a mythology about God, the world, humanity, and the Jewish people. The actual Jewish people, which under natural conditions is bound by Torah and practical Mitzvoth was identified with the mystical notion of Knesseth Israel (the "soul of the nation," in Rabbi Kook's words), which is identical with the Shekhinah, kabbalistically identified with the last Sefirah, that of Malkhuth (kingdom). Now, the Sephirah Malkhuth is related to the sixth Sephirah, Tifereth (splendor), which is represented by the Patriarch Jacob, who is Israel. Thence derives the pagan trinity of the Hold-Blessed-be-He, the Torah, and Israel. The contrast between regarding Torah and Mitzvoth as the service of God *for its own sake* and regarding them as magical means *for the sake of something else* (the redemption of Israel, the rehabilitation of the world, or for God's own need) is not confined to the medieval context; it is still meaningful in our days. The great dispute among Yemenite Jews between the Darda'im (the followers of Maimonides) and the Akashim (adherents of the *Zohar*) at the beginning of the twentieth (!) century is proof enough. This split in

Jewish religious thought is interestingly documented by the articles
and proclamations of Rabbi Yahieh Qafah of San'a and his colleagues
("Those Who Pray to a Long-Nosed Idol and to a Short-Nosed
Idol," and "Those Who Believe in a Decemy"); it is countered by awk-
ward, stammering reactions of the Jerusalem rabbis (including Rabbi
Kook).[6]

I was never a follower of Rabbi Kook, and the dangers inherent in
his doctrine impressed me more than its lofty aspects. I am cognizant
of his greatness as a scholar and a man of faith and not only through
his writing and published talks, for I had the great privilege of meeting
him and speaking face to face. I shall always remember a long conversation, in the course of which he graciously answered my queries about
Maimonides and the Kabbalah. It revealed his greatness,—but also his
limitations.

It was a mark of his stature that he made no attempt whatsoever to
bridge the enormous gulf separating what, in his view and deepest
conviction, was *Torath He'emeth* (Doctrine of the Truth, meaning the
Kabbalah), from the conceptual world of Maimonides—to Kook, as
to any Jew versed in Torah but especially to a great scholar, "the Great
Eagle," "the Right-Hand Pillar," "the Mighty Hammer" of the Halak-
hàh, whose work has been basic for halakhic learning and ruling for
seven hundred years.[7] The rift between Maimonides and the Kabbalah
was for him a stern fact, which, unlike many other kabbalists, he made
no attempt to blur. Some of them passed over this in embarrassed
silence. Others reacted to it by fabricating the silly legend that toward
the end of his life Maimonides studied the Kabbalah and accepted it.
Still others, who realized and admitted the bitter truth, came to the
point of maligning him, occasionally in a very harsh manner.[8] That was
not the way of Rabbi Kook. No one knew better than he what Maimonides was to Judaism. In his conversation with me he insisted most
emphatically on the validity of the Doctrine, which Maimonides did
not know or at least did not acknowledge. Nevertheless he stated that
it was Providence that gave Maimonides to the Jewish people to safeguard them against the danger of falling into idolatry, a danger particularly threatening to the adherent of the Doctrine of the Truth. Even
as "the greater the person, the greater his evil inclination," the greater
the measure of truth in one's faith, the greater is the danger of its
distortion.[9] "Between paradise and hell there is a partition two fingers

thick." Precisely the ardor of faith in God may cause those of feeble character or mind to stumble. The golden calf ("these by your gods O Israel") was made by the generation to which the Shekhinah revealed itself, and the evil inclination of idolatry capered among the Israelites all the while the Shakhinah was present in the Temple. The role of Maimonides in combating idolatry was like that of the prophets and of the men of the Great Assembly, (who shaped rabbinic Judaism early in the second commonwealth).

Maimonides did not introduce the "alien corn" of Greek wisdom into Judaism, as many naïve people believe. The extreme form of his doctrine of divine unity, which is the absolute denial of all the attributes to the point of ignoring or spurning the Doctrine of Truth, established a bulwark against the danger of gross anthropomorphism inherent in that doctrine, making of the service of God a worship of mediators.

At the time of my encounter with Rabbi Kook I was young and did not dare to tell the great old man to his face that even the enormous influence Maimonides had over believing Jews of all subsequent generations was incapable of saving many of them from being tripped by Kabbalah into Sabbateanism, Frankism, or apostasy; that he was incapable of preventing multitudes of genuine believers from lapsing into worshiping "divine names" and angels owing to Kabbalah. Today one can add that even the Doctrine of Truth of Rabbi Kook himself, which involves a confusion of the actual people of Israel with a mystical Israel, has become, in the hands of his disciples and their disciples, a deification of the nation and a fetishism of the land.

Reform Judaism is the second historical distortion of the Jewish religion. For the service of God through Torah and Mitzvoth as the end of religion, the Reform movement substitutes an end the Jewish people is destined to attain. And, paradoxically, in this respect Reform resembles the Kabbalah, except that the Kabbalah assigns to the Jewish people and Judaism a cosmic-metaphysical vocation, namely the rehabilitation of the world, the rectification, as it were, of a breach in the divine realm itself. Moreover, the Kabbalah endeavors to maintain the halakhic system as it is, ascribing to the practice of Mitzvoth a magical efficacy toward fulfilling this religious function. Reform, by contrast, assigns to Judaism a human-mundane vocation, "to be a light to the nations." Accordingly, it adapts the Mitzvoth in ways that seem most appropriate to this end, or even abrogates them when they seem superfluous or dysfunctional to that vocation. What is common to Kabbalah and Reform is the dissolution of faith lishmah, Torah lishmah, and worship lishmah, which are the very essence of the historical halakhic Judaism. These are then replaced by faith, Torah, and service for the sake of "redemption," the redemption of the Jewish people, of the world, of humanity. Reform Judaism empties Judaism of its religious content and reduces it to ethical humanism.

At this point some comments on Jewish Ethics cannot be avoided. There is no Hebrew word for "ethics," and the term "Mussar" in the sense of ethics is a neologism. In biblical Hebrew "Mussar" means teaching. Neither in Scripture nor in the language of the Sages is there a word for ethics, even as there is no biblical term for the concept "conscience." Indeed, only the ethical atheist follows his conscience, which is his inclination, whereas the believer who fears God is not guided by his heart or eyes.

Ethics is not a program of behavior. In itself an act is morally indifferent. A person loads and cocks a rifle and releases the safety catch; aims at someone and presses the trigger. In one instance, as a result of this action, the agent may be called an abominable murderer; in another instance, he may be regarded as a heroic soldier defending the fatherland. Clearly, it is not the act that is being judged but the intention. Moral judgment pertains to the intention of the actor. Ethics, then, is not the doctrine of correct behavior, but the doctrine of man's right intention. The intention does not guarantee the "goodness" of the action. The person may err, and the consequence of a good intention may be very bad. But moral judgment does not pertain to the result but to the intention.

Opinions differ, however, with respect to what is meant by "pure intention" and "the good." Western thought elaborated two major answers to this question, neither of Jewish origin.

The first maintains that man's moral judgment consists in the guidance of his will in accordance with apprehension of the truth about the world, not by his interests, feelings, drives, or passions. This is the great idea of Socrates, who believed in the Olympian gods.

According to the second, man's moral judgment consists in the guidance of his will, not by his inclinations or interests nor by knowledge and understanding of the world, but by recognition of his duty, a recognition which is imposed by conscience, by the self-awareness of a rational being. This is the great idea of Kant. But the text of Shema says: "And that you may not go astray after your own heart and after your own eyes." The Prohibition of following "your own heart" is a negation of Kant's great principle; the prohibition of following "your own eyes" is the rejection of the great principle of Socrates. And the reason for the two negations is: "I am the Lord your God." The believing man is guided by his consciousness of his standing before God, not before man. His judgment is not moral. Morality is an atheistic category.

Some of my predecessors in this debate seem to enjoy the pleasant illusion that the establishment of the state of Israel and its existence enhance the prestige of Judaism in a religious sense, both among the Jews and among the nations. I have written and said much about the status of Judaism in the Israeli state. This time I shall confine myself to recounting a conversation I had with Ben-Gurion some twenty years ago. He then said to me: "I well understand why you demand so insistently the separation of religion and state. Your object is that the Jewish religion reinstate itself as an independent factor so the political authority will be compelled to deal with it. I will never agree to the separation of religion from the State. I want the state to hold religion in the palm of its hand." The status quo, which formally interweaves elements pretending to be religious with the secular executive and administrative system of the state—an integration which the representatives of "religious national" Judaism make every effort to perpetuate—reflects the cast of mind of a man who entertained a bitter hatred of Judaism. It was to this conversation with Ben-Gurion that I alluded when I once wrote: "The status of Jewish religion in the state of Israel is that of a kept mistress of the secular government—therefore it is contemptible." The state of Israel does not radiate the light of Judaism to the nations, not even to the Jews.

I vehemently oppose the view that Zionist theory and practice are necessarily or essentially connected with the idea of "light to the nations." It seems to me that those who find allusions to this idea in the works of Ahad Ha'am and Herzl are mistaken. But even if such allusions existed, they would not turn a wild misconception into the truth. I reject the attempts to adorn the state of Zionism with a religious aura. Rather than exalt Zionism and the state, these efforts devaluate religion, turning it from the service of God into the fulfillment of human needs and aspirations. As to the meaning of Zionism—here is an account of a conversation I had some time ago with an important non-Jewish foreign journalist. He asked: "What is the meaning of Zionism?" He had previously posed this question to several Israeli public figures and received various answers. One was that Zionism is an endeavor to build a model society. My reaction was that this is the goal of many people of all nations and cultures, Jews and non-Jews, and striving to achieve this end does not necessitate the existence of a separate Jewish nation and state. Another answer identified Zionism with freeing the Jews from their state of alienation among the nations that regard them as foreigners and do not permit them to integrate except in a formal-legal sense, so they lack a feeling of existential security. This reply was rejected by the journalist himself, who pointed out that in the post-Hitlerite generation the obstacles to full integration of Jews were removed in all Western societies. In these countries Jews were massively absorbed into the economy and into cultural life, business organizations, and the academies, and were active in science and literature and even in politics. The sense of alienation between Jews and Gentiles has vanished, and the rise of Jews to positions of influence does not evoke any resistance and does not draw the attention of the non-Jewish public. In the United States Jews have served as secretary of state, attorney general, and mayor of its largest city; in Austria a Jew was chancellor. Forty-seven British M.P.s were Jews, and the first woman ever to become a minister in France was Jewish. As for feelings of insecurity, nowhere is Jewish existence so threatened as it is in the state of Israel. Some of the journalist's interlocutors identified Zionism as a mystical phenomenon, as the fulfillment of the prophetic vision and the messianic promises. Given the utter secularization of the great majority of the Jewish people, this is absurd.

My own answer to that non-Jew was that Zionism is the expression of our being fed up with being ruled by *Goyim*. I am aware that this "we" does not extend to all Jews. Still, it is the motive shared by Zionist Jews who differ widely in their human values and in their conceptions of Judaism. Zionism is best defined as the program for the attainment of political and national independence. Now that this has been attained in the form of a sovereign state, Zionism consists in the effort to maintain this independence. This is the function the state of Israel performs for the Jewish people, in addition to inspiring "the fear of authority" as does every system of government to maintain peace and tranquillity. More than that should not be expected from any state. The values people wish to realize, whether general humanistic ones like the idea of a "model society," or specifically Jewish such as the "prophetic vision and the messianic promises," or, most authentically, a condition in which "the earth shall be full of the knowledge of the Lord," are not the affair of the state. Their realization is a proper object for the aspirations and striving of individuals and groups *within* the state. It is outside the sphere of action of the executive and administrative apparatus of state coercion, which can never be the suitable instrument for the implementation of these values.

Zionism is not defined or determined by social, moral, or religious values. Moreover, the realization of Zionism affords no guarantee of the actualization of these values. Similarly, there is no congruence between Zionism and the concern for the well-being and physical safety of the Jews. True enough, the first two generations of Zionists—those of Herzl and Weizmann—believed that Zionism was a historical necessity because Jews were denied assimilation among the nations. The early Zionists believed that Jews in exile were eternally doomed to be aliens, either as tolerated foreigners or as outcast and oppressed strangers. They could only be delivered from this tragic situation by setting up a national home in their own land. This conception does not fit the contemporary scene. We are witnessing the accelerated assimilation of Jews and their complete integration in their host societies. The only ones resisting this process are Jews who do not want it. Zionism today is therefore a matter of a voluntary, deliberate decision made by Jews—a minority of them. It has also become evident that Jewish independence affords no guarantee to the well-being and security of the Jewish people, who are threatened in their land more than anywhere else. It follows that, in this respect too, the Jew is required to make a decision to accept (for himself and his wife and children) the risk involved in living under conditions of Jewish national independence.

Zionism has no connection to Judaism in its essential religious sense of the obligation to observe Torah and Mitzvoth; this is an absolute obligation imposed upon us regardless of particular historical circumstances or existential conditions. Zionism has no bearing on it whatsoever, since this task is binding on us in our land as in exile, in freedom as in bondage, and the effort to fulfill it continues and will continue so long as there are Jews who recognize it. Zionism as an aspiration to political-national independence is a legitimate Jewish aspiration, and the state is dear to us as its fulfillment. But it must not be given a religious aura. Only what is done for the sake of Heaven has religious significance. The category of holiness is inapplicable to the state. I deny that the establishment of the state of Israel and its very existence signal a beginning of the realization of the values of Judaism. Sovereignty is essential to the state, along with an executive apparats and the power and authority of coercion. The state fulfills an essential need of the individual and the national community, but it does not thereby acquire intrinsic value—except for a fascist who regards sovereignty, governmental authority, and power as the supreme values.

A state, as an instrument for satisfying certain needs, is not a vehicle for realizing values. Values are actualized only by human beings striving to that end, and not by an executive apparatus. Justice, equity, morality, or education, not to mention the religious values of fear of God, love of God, and the service of God, could never materialize with the mere attainment of sovereignty. Within the framework of the state men and women must fight for them. If Jews are not seen struggling for these values in the state of Israel, the state is not to blame. Equally, the great crisis of Judaism, "the hurt of my people," may not be attributed to the state as such. I do not expect our state to be a light to the nations. It is no light even to the people of Israel, who walk in darkness.

Some people contend that it is impossible to separate faith in God from moral-humanistic values. In God's words about Abraham, the "way of God" is defined as "righteousness and judgment," which is also the calling of his sons and their descendants. To this I reply that after God asserts that Abraham is a man of righteousness and judgment, and after He hearkens to Abraham on the issue of "doing right" to the men of Sodom, He still put Abraham to the test. To what end? What we learn about Abraham from the trial of the Aqedah that we did not know previously is the quality of Abraham's faith, what was meant when it was said of him that "he believed in God." Is it the kind of faith that is revealed in service of God for its own sake, or for the sake of such human desiderata as righteousness and judgment on earth? There are atheists and pagans who seek righteousness and judgment, and they instruct their children and household in their exercise. Even Avimelekh King of Gerar protested: "Will you slay also a righteous nation?" But Abraham is required to assume the service of God even when it is dissociated from all human needs, feelings, and values, even from the great historical ends which he was promised. For such service of God for His own sake reward or punishment are irrelevant. The Midrash already point out that Abraham could have presented forceful arguments: "Yesterday you said that through Isaac will be named your issue and today you tell me to bring him as an offering—yet he kept silent." Abraham (like Avimelekh) argues vigorously in his debate with God in His role of righteous judge, in analogy with a truthful human judge. But he refrains from all argument when God is revealed to him in His divinity. Contrary to what my predecessor in the debate said here, namely, that one cannot detach the service of God from human needs and values, the trial of the *Aqedah* conveys to us the essence of faith as man's ability to dissociate the consciousness of his standing before God from the problems of the individual, humanity, and the world. That is why Abraham is said to "fear God," and not because of his stand in the debate on justice, to which all those who wish to empty the Torah of its religious meaning and to reduce it to a "moral" principles love to allude.

(*From the audience:* It is possible to say that God has no interest in man and his world?)

I have no knowledge of the divine intentions. How could I answer your question? I only know of the interest man has, or should have, in God; on this point I draw your attention to the Ne'ilah prayer and to the first clause in Maimonides' *Hilkhoth Yessodei Hatorah*.[10] As for God's interest in the world, let us invoke the prayerbook: He "was before creation's teeming birth," as He "was when his fiat all ordained." ("You were ere yet the world was created, and are the same since its creation.") The meaning of this may be gleaned from the third clause of the above-mentioned chapter in Maimonides' Code.[11]

(*From the audience:* "You have completely ignored the notions of Israel as the chosen people and of the holiness of Israel—"a holy nation.")

These attributes are functional rather than essential. They do not describe a property that the people already possess, but refer to what they ought to be. In other words, these terms apply by virtue of a demand put to the people of Israel, directing it to strive toward that goal. As the object of this demand its status is lofty and sublime. The terms do not refer to properties Jews actually possess. This is put clearly and unequivocally in the benediction "Who has chosen us from among all peoples and given us His Torah"; "Who has chosen us from all nations . . . and sanctified us with His Mitzvoth."[12] The Pentateuch pronouncements are, "You will be holy" (Lev. 15:2) and "That you may remember and do all my commandments and be holy to your God"(Num. 15:40). This contradicts Qorah, according to whom "all the congregation are holy, every one of them"(Num. 16:3). The difference between the conception of election and sanctity as an eternal task, and their conception as indigenous characteristics of the people of Israel since the days of the Patriarchs until now, is the difference between belief in God and belief in nature. In the natural and human sphere there is only potential holiness—the intention to serve God, which brings man closer to God. Whoever ascribes holiness *in actu* to man, to nation, to an object, or to a country elevates that thing to divine rank, though God alone is Holy. Such a person has stumbled into idolatry.

(*From the audience:* Rabbi Judah Halevi attributes holiness to the Jewish people.)

Rabbi Judah Halevi, the divine poet, expresses in the prayers, in the *Selihoth,* and in the *Yotzeroth,* the pure faith in God. But as author of the *Kuzari* he entangled himself in religious polemics and stumbled into racist-nationalist chauvinism. Maharal and Rabbi Kook follow in his footsteps. Maimonides, in his celebrated reply to Rabbi Obadiah the proselyte, inveighs with extreme severity against any concept of biological holiness which is putatively ingrained in the Jewish race and peculiar to it.[13]

(*From the audience:* What about "a treasured people" (Am Segulah)?)

The singularity of the Jewish people consists in the Torah that was given to the people and the service imposed upon it. Without these the Jews are like all the others. The greatest believer among the Jews, Maimonides, does not at all mention the Jewish people in the first four chapters of his great Code, in which he discusses man's knowledge of God and His unity as well as man's knowledge of the world and of himself. "Israel" appears with striking suddenness at the beginning of chapter 5: "the entire house of Israel is enjoined to sanctify the Great Name." The Gentiles are not thus enjoined. The acknowledgment of God is universal: the trait that is peculiar to Israel is the service of God by observance of the Torah and its Mitzvoth. Consequently, Maimonides does not regard prophecy as singularly Jewish. "It is fundamental to religion that the Deity inspires *men* with prophecy."[14] This, of course, is in sharp contrast to Rabbi Judah Halevi's view.

It should however be noted that when Judah Halevi portrays the Hassid (*Kuzari* article 3), he succeeds in extricating himself from the racial-national and national-territorial elements of his doctrine and presents a figure of a servant of God that resembles the figure portrayed by Maimonides in the final chapters of his *Guide*.

(*From the audience:* What of the sanctity of the land of Israel?)

This term, too, refers to the service of God, namely to the Mitzvoth which obtain only in the land of Israel. The country has no intrinsic holiness and the Mitzvoth do not derive from its holiness. Rather, it is the Mitzvoth, when observed, that confer sanctity upon the land. This is well brought out by the Mishnah in Tractate *Kelim,* which describes ten degrees of sanctity attaching to certain locations and ascribes each of them to certain Mitzvoth which are in force at the specific location.[15]

Faith in the "holy God" ought to prevent man from ascribing intrinsic holiness to anything in the world. It ascribes holiness in the world only to the service of God. The appellation "God's estate" applied to the land of Israel does not refer to any special quality of this country, for "The earth is the Lord's and the fullness thereof, the world and they that dwell therein." And in respect of this relation to God, Paraguay and Cambodia and their peoples are equal to the land of Israel and its people. But there are special Mitzvoth in the service of God that are binding on the people of Israel only in their land, and it is these that confer its peculiar virtue upon this country. Possibly it was his concern lest the Torah be conceived as the Torah of the land of Israel that prevented Maimonides from including the settling of the land of Israel among the Mitzvoth.

I can find no statement more fitting to sum up my view on the nature of sanctity than the following words of Rabbi Meir Simhah Cohen of Dwinsk:

> The Torah and faith are the very principles of the Jewish nation, and all the sanctities—the Land of Israel, Jerusalem, etc.—derive from the Torah, and are sanctified by the holiness of the Torah . . . Don't imagine that the Temple or the Tabernacle are holy, in themselves, God forbid. The Exalted One "dwells" among his children, and if they desecrated the covenant, their sacredness is removed from the Temple and Tabernacle and they are like profane vessels . . . In sum, there is nothing holy in the world save the Exalted One in His necessary existence . . . All the sanctities derive from the imperative of the Creator to build Him a tabernacle in which to offer sacrifices for His sake alone . . . There is no holiness or divine matter whatsoever save the Being of the Creator may His Name be exalted.[16]

CHAPTER 11

Redemption and the Dawn
of Redemption
(1971)

B oth as memory of the past and as future expectation, the idea of redemption has been of major significance in Jewish religious life—in religious reflection, feeling, and action. In bygone generations as well as in our own time, among many pious Jews and among many of those who had cast off the yoke of Torah and Mitzvoth, this belief in redemption has been the mainstay of Judaism, the basis of the faith of Israel and its Torah. This attitude requires careful scrutiny.

In the Jewish tradition, the concept of redemption has had two distinct aspects: first, redemption as a fact, that is, the redemption which has already taken place; second, redemption as a vision, that is, the redemption that has yet to occur. Each of these aspects must be studied with an eye to its relevance for our position *vis-à-vis* the current situation.

The redemption which has already taken place was the Exodus from Egypt, the redemption referred to in the Torah, the Prophets, the Psalms, the Halakhah and Aggadah, and extolled in the prayerbook, the Passover Haggadah, and the Piyyutim. Moreover, some of the most important Mitzvoth are associated with the Exodus. Even the Sabbath is considered a reminder of the Exodus, though it is ostensibly an affirmation of the Creation.[1] Nevertheless, in view of the evidence of history and theological considerations, it would be quite erroneous to base faith in the Giver of the Torah and in the Torah upon this miraculous redemption.

The historical evidence indicates that the generation which experienced a miraculous redemption was lacking in faith. Their superficial faith, fruit of passing experience, did not pass a single one of the tests to which it was put. The redeemed people failed so completely that they caused the "first redeemer," Moses, to fail along with them. If such was the case with that generation, what could be expected of later ones? According to Maimonides, "all miracles are certain in the opinion of those who have seen them, however, at a future time, their story becomes a mere traditional narrative and there is a possibility for the hearer to consider it untrue."[2] If even the witnesses to the miracle did not believe, what could be its weight "at a subsequent time"? Moreover, "whoever believes because of signs has doubts in his heart."[3] It is no faith at all. The Exodus from Egypt was a redemption in the sense of a divine act of deliverance. It came short of being redemption in the true sense because it was ineffective in the hearts of men. In the "four terms for redemption" included in the promise of deliverance from Egyptian bondage (Exod. 6) a clear distinction is already drawn between redemption as an act of God and redemption as a human response: "I will bring you out . . . I will redeem you . . . I will take you to me for a people—and you shall know that I am the Lord your God." The first three actions are in the hands of God, but the last one must be performed by man. No act of deliverance becomes a redemption unless he who is delivered participates in the act with a religious intention. If he is merely passive, the deliverance is not truly a redemption. The people who regarded the golden calf as their god who had brought them out of Egypt were not redeemed. Only many generations later, when the people of Israel committed themselves truly to observance of the Torah, could the Exodus acquire the nature of redemption.

The order of prayers for Passover contains a symbolic intimation that the deliverance of Israel from Egypt fell short of being a complete redemption. The full depth of the sense of having been redeemed has been given appropriate expression in the halakhic tradition in the recitation of the Hallel (that is, the "Egyptian Hallel," which is read at the Passover Seder service.)[4] Yet the Hallel is read only on the first day of the feast commemorating the Exodus. It is not recited on the other days of the feast, not even on the seventh day, the day of deliverance on which the mighty hand of God was revealed on the sea—for deliverance did not involve true redemption. Deliverance becomes redemption only if Israel, upon deliverance and liberation, regards its freedom as freedom to observe the Torah. This is why Hallel is not recited in its entirety during the week of Passover after the first day. What transpired after the Exodus revealed that, even while they were being taken out of Egypt, the hearts of the children of Israel were not dedicated to constant service of God. On the other hand, the Sages saw fit to have the Hallel recited during the eight days of Hannukah, since, at that time, Israel experienced miracles, salvation, and deliverance in a war for the sake of the Torah.

The vision of redemption is the subject of the prophecies of consolation in the Book of Isaiah and is also to be found in the words of the prophets of wrath and destruction, Jeremiah and Ezekiel. This vision is often related to the return to Zion from the Babylonian exile, but the great promises of that vision were not realized then, and the return to Zion was never decisively established as a redemption. Crescas and Abravanel went so far as to regard the exile and bondage as extending without break from the destruction of the first Temple into their own time, since, in their opinion, during the period of the second Temple the Jews were in bondage in their own land. Therefore, at an early period, the prophecies of consolation were already interpreted as referring to an unknown future and became a "messianic vision," which some of the prophecies of redemption may have been predicting originally. How is this ultimate messianic redemption to be understood?

In one view the messianic redemption will be a temporal event like the redemption from Egypt that will come to pass at some future time. Thus the prophecies of redemption forecast what will come to pass, like oracles.

The second view is of messianic redemption as a direction and goal toward which we must strive, the attainment of which is an eternal task assigned to man. It is in this sense that we must understand the words of the Tossafists: "No prophet prophesies anything other than what ought to be."[5]

The expectation of a temporal redemption is a distinct article of faith without any link to the world of Torah and commandments, which are valid in the unredeemed world. The redeemed world is seen as an alternative to the world to which the Mitzvoth apply. The view of redemption as a goal is the idea which guides and stimulates the service of God by observance of the Torah, an idea which makes the Mitzvoth an everlasting task and duty. The redemption is regarded as a reality that always transcends any existing state, which one never reaches but toward which one must always strive. The first conception necessarily creates a tension between the world of Halakhah and messianic faith. Insofar as messianic redemption becomes the axis of the religious life, acceptance of the yoke of Torah and Mitzvoth becomes subsidiary to it. Maimonides was aware of this when, in the final chapter of his Code, which is devoted to the vision of messianic redemption, he cautions: "One should never occupy himself with aggadic themes or spend much time on midrashic statements bearing on this and like subjects, since they lead neither to fear of God nor to love of Him."[6]

From the tension between "fear and love" expressed by the service of God in the observance of the Torah on the one hand, and the "messianic vision" on the other, arose Christianity and later Sabbateanism, both of which abrogated the Mitzvoth. According to the second view, the Messiah is he for whose coming we shall ever yearn. A Messiah who actually comes is a false Messiah.

The four terms of redemption, when unaccompanied by the consummation demanded by the biblical verse: "And you shall know that I am the Lord your God" (Exod. 6:7), represent a false redemption, and a false redemption did greater harm to Israel than loss of faith in redemption. The fall of Jerusalem and the destruction of the Temple by Titus, even Hadrian's decrees outlawing the Torah and its Mitzvoth, failed to uproot Judaism even from the hearts of those who despaired of redemption. The Sabbatean upheaval, on the other hand, shattered the Judaism of the followers of Sabbatai Tsevi (the false messiah of the seventeenth century) and set the stage for the undermining of religion among the Jewish people as a whole. All of us, therefore, having no insight into the designs of Providence, must exercise utmost caution before proclaiming events of the nature of military victory or national political deliverance as the "dawn of redemption" or "the sprouting of our redemption."[7] There is no hope for a Jewish religion which places a messianic halo above a king who "did not depart from all the sins of Yorav'am the son of Ne'vat which he made Israel to sin," only because he "restored the border of Israel from the entrance to Hamath as far as the sea of the Aravah" (2 Kings 14:23–25). It is religious blindness not to distinguish the liberation of the Temple Mount by the Maccabbees from its liberation by Hellenizing Jews. Vigilance is in order lest a religious and spiritual collapse among the faithful of Israel follow in the wake of the new Sabbateanism.

CHAPTER 12

The Status of Women: Halakhah and Meta-Halakhah

(1980)

The question of Women and Judaism is more crucial today than all the political problems of the people and its state. Failure to deal with it seriously threatens the viability of the Judaism of Torah and Mitzvoth in the contemporary world.

Many people, religious women among them, perceive the problem in terms of the existence of a set of prescriptions which apply to men only. The most popular examples are Tsisith and phylacteries, or the Mitzvah of *Sukkah*.[1] They regard the exemption of women from these prescriptions as a humiliation or deprivation; at the least, as downgrading the status of women within the religious context, distancing them, as it were, from the worship of God. This is a totally erroneous view. These Mitzvoth do not prescribe certain acts because they are of intrinsic importance. Their entire significance derives solely from the fact that the Torah prescribed them. Were it not for this, they would be meaningless. In other words, these acts do not constitute worship of God except insofar as man is instructed by the Torah to perform them. If a person who is not obliged to do so performs them of his own accord, he is not thereby worshiping God but engaging in something like a sport or hobby. If Tsitsith, phylacteries, and Sukkah were valuable in themselves, then deterring women from observing them would be discriminatory. Conversely, women's performance of these acts of their own accord—even if their sincere intention is to do so for the sake of God, and even if this is accepted throughout the entire religious community—would be religiously pointless, and would achieve nothing by way of bringing women closer to the life of Torah.

In these instances, the position of women as compared to men is precisely like that of laymen compared to priests, who must obey certain laws which apply only to them, such as the proscriptions of touching the dead or of marrying a divorcee. Such discrimination does not detract from the worship of God by those who are not priests. Should the Israelites voluntarily begin observing the prohibitions applying to priests, this would not imply greater fear of God, love of God, or service of God. It would be totally pointless.

The issue of *Talmud Torah,* the study of Torah in its most inclusive sense, is an entirely different matter.

This too is a Mitzvah, one of utmost importance. The upshot of discussions throughout halakhic history was the general acceptance of the principle that women are barred from study of Torah at its higher level.[2] This is a grievous error and is likely to prove disastrous for historical Judaism. For besides its significance as the performance of a Mitzvah, Talmud Torah enables the Jewish person to share the Jewish cultural heritage and its spiritual content. One might almost say that is makes the student party to the presence of the Shekhinah in Israel.[3] Keeping women away from Talmud Torah is not to exempt them from a duty (as is the case with some other Mitzvoth) but is rather to deprive them of a basic Jewish right.

This deprivation renders their "Jewishness" inferior to that of men. The assumption, axiomatic in all cultures almost up to our own generation, was that spiritual matters pertain to men and not to humankind at large. Even the accepted Halakhah, which assigns women a very high status (much higher than they had in Classical Greece, for example) and holds their functions in the home and within the family in the highest esteem, does not grant women equal partnership in sustaining spiritual life. This is common to Judaism and the historical non-Jewish cultures, even modern secular culture. Only in the nineteenth century were secondary schools for girls established in the enlightened Western world, and until the end of the nineteenth century women did not set foot in the academic milieu.

The perpetuation of this attitude within Judaism and the Jewish religion is intolerable in the Jewish world of today. The religious Jewish public to whom these remarks are addressed belongs to a society whose culture is common to both men and women. Such is our mode of Jewish existence as well. Therefore, barring women today from Talmud

Torah segregates Judaism from the spiritual reality shared by Jews of both sexes. This is likely to break up our religious community. A step towards rectifying this situation is the attempt to establish a Women's *Beth Midrash* (a place for study of Torah), the like of which already exists in the United States in affiliation with Yeshivah University, and in Israel in the form of Ulpanoth. But the goal ought to be a Beth midrash for both men and women. To the contention that women do not intend to devote themselves to Talmud Torah to the desirable extent and are unable to do so, one may reply that even most men, who are under the halakhic obligation to study Torah, do not devote themselves to it, even though their participation in the community of Torah-observant Jews is beyond doubt. What is really important is that Talmud Torah should be available to the entire religious community, the duty and privilege of both men and women.

The same applies to the halakhic status of women in the public-political sphere. The prohibitions against appointing women to positions in government, the administration, or the military, and especially the judiciary, reflected a worldwide sociocultural understanding of the place of women based on their nature; they were not perceived as mere rules established by legislation and amenable to legislative alteration. On this view, public and political life are naturally the exclusive domain of men and it is inconceivable that women should take part in them. After all, even modern enlightened and secular countries had no women judges or members of Parliament and, needless to say, no Cabinet ministers, before the twentieth century. The very idea was considered outlandish even among the educated and progressive. Even suffrage was not granted to European and American women until after World War I, that is, no more than two generations ago! The halakhic decisions in Judaism barring women from public office tell us more about *what actually was the case* than about *what ought to be*. It is not coincidence that many of the regulations in this connection are introduced by the words: "It is not the way of women to . . ." or "It does not reflect favorably upon a woman . . ." (for example, to sit in the courtroom, or be a "*parnass* over the community" that is, to head, by appointment or election, any governmental or administrative position).

This situation has changed completely. Nowadays even our religious society is part of a world in which all political and public issues are shared by men and women. Thus it is "the way of women" to partici-pate in public affairs. Jewish religious society will not be able to survive if, for pseudo-religious reasons, we continue to deprive women of their due rights. This is the point at which we—those of us resolved to prac-tice Torah—cannot perpetuate the halakhic decisions of our fathers dating from a social reality which differed radically from our own.[4]

Certain conclusions follow concerning social forms and manners. A religious community of Jewish men and women that undertakes to practice Torah in our day must not confuse its acceptance of the "yoke of Torah and Mitzvoth," of absolute demands reflecting acceptance of the "yoke of the Kingdom of Heaven" that are not amenable to adjust-ment to natural or social factors, with practices which reflect given circumstances and the views shaped by them; in other words, between unconditional prescriptions and proscriptions and norms reflecting a given sociocultural milieu and its prejudices. The first category includes the laws of incest, family purity, and so on; the latter includes whatever pertains to the broad concept of "modesty" and has implications with respect to dress (what is "man's dress" and what is "woman's dress"), coeducation, military service, specialization in the different profes-sions, and so on.

All these considerations point to the need for discretion in halakhic decision—discretion, which would reflect our own deliberation rather than conformity with anything found in a literary source. In such mat-ters, no literary source of the past could possibly apply to our situation and none ever has applied.

CHAPTER 13

Religion and Science in the Middle Ages and in the Modern Era

(1976)

Are medieval discussions of the contacts and interactions between religion and science relevant to similar discussions today? Two distinct factors argue against it. The first is historic—the basic change which the conception of science has undergone. The second is the difference, which always existed and still exists, between two sets of religious attitudes toward knowledge.

The decisive difference between what was called "science" in ancient times and what is called "science" today is the change which has taken place in the conception of the relation between the cognitive and evaluative elements of the knowledge of reality; that is, between perception of reality and perception of its meaning. I shall concentrate mainly on the natural sciences, with only a few words about the humanities and social sciences at the end.

Ancient science, whose greatest figure was Aristotle, was further deepened by the Stoics and developed in the Middle Ages. Because it attributed meaning to the reality which it investigated, research itself was influenced by this putative meaningfulness. Its most characteristic aspects were the concepts of "formal" and "final" cause (of the four "causes" Aristotle postulated), now excluded from the scientific method as we understand it. Aristotle was a determinist, but his determinism was teleological. His notion of causality and ours are completely different. Our natural sciences are formulated in terms of natural laws, whereas the concepts of ancient and medieval science were formulated as principles of nature. So deep is this difference, that a student of scientific methodology today wonders sometimes whether science, in our sense, existed before the seventeenth century. This feeling is not mitigated by the important discoveries made in earlier times.

The conception of nature and the world in terms of meanings made the ancient researcher look at natural data as indicating and expressing something, and if this meaning was not obvious and clear at first sight, science was expected to reveal it ("to save the phenomena"). Therefore, there was no clear distinction in the Middle Ages between the sciences, as the term is used today, and the humanities, or between science and philosophy, or between science and theology. Since nature itself was understood as expressing something—a purpose, meaning, or value embodied in the phenomena—natural sciences were conceived in the ways we nowadays conceive the humanities and the social sciences.

The first four chapters of Maimonides' *Book of Knowledge,* which is a summary of fifteen hundred years of thought, do not give any sense of transition from theology and philosophy to natural science. The worlds of the "separate intellects," of the celestial spheres, and of the four elements are parts of a single continuum, since spherical and elemental phenomena themselves express certain meanings, and meaning is the constitutive element of the world of "intellects." The change that took place in the scientific outlook since the beginning of the seventeenth century was the introduction of the concept of the functional relation between the phenomena investigated by science. Functional relations do not harbor "meaning."

Modern scientific outlook attaches quite a different interpretation to the maxim: "the world keeps to its course" (or "the regularity of the world-order is constant") than did the Sages of Israel or Aristotelian science. Of course constancy and regularity in the natural processes were known in ancient times too, as we see from ancient, pre-Greek astronomy. This constancy and regularity is expressed in Genesis 8:22: "Sowing and harvest, heat and cold, summer and winter, day and night, will cease no more." Since Thales they are elements of philosophical (and scientific) thought. Yet the ideas of constancy and regularity were not derived from objective knowledge of the world, but from the meaning attributed to it: "the world keeps its course" not because this is its course, but because some meaning is embodied and expressed in this course.

The Aristotelian-Ptolemaic notion of the celestial bodies revolving with uniform velocities in circular orbits was not derived from observation. The observable facts, which prove all these movements to be neither circular nor uniform, were well known to the ancient Greeks. But because circular and uniform movement was deemed the "perfect movement," they forced themselves, by a tremendous intellectual effort, to devise an astronomy which ran counter to their observations in order "to save the phenomena."[1] It should be noted that in this respect Copernicus belongs to medieval, not modern science; Kepler was the forerunner of the modern approach, as he looked to movement itself, and not to a "perfect movement." The difference will become clearer if we consider a section of modern science in which the matter has not yet been entirely clarified and elucidated, such as biology.

Modern physical sciences have met with success by looking solely for functional relations between factual data. But biology still harbors a deep controversy between two approaches: one tries to base the science exclusively on the same foundations as physics, while another insists that life phenomena—capable of being exhaustively described in terms of the categories of physical science—differ, nevertheless, from physical phenomena by the conceptual necessity of perceiving them as an expression of "life." The outstanding modern representatives of these two approaches are Jacques Monod and Adolf Portmann. Experimental research in biology tends gradually to refrain from dealing with the problems of life itself and to focus upon its active mechanisms. These mechanisms may be described by the functional relations between the phenomena. Yet the question remains, whether these mechanisms constitute life itself or are no more than mechanisms active in life.

Generally speaking, then, ancient science, as well as medieval science, did not differentiate between the mechanisms functioning in nature (or in the world) and nature (or the world) itself. This is the background of the confrontation of "faith" and "science" in the Middle Ages. If the content and conclusions about natural phenomena bear a specific meaning and are expressions of this meaning, then matters of science are on the same plane as matters of man's stance before God. In either case, we are dealing with questions of meaning.

Whether faith and science were intertwined, antagonistic, or supplementary, there was no doubt that they met on the same plane—that of perception of meaning. But if science is no more than a matter of functional relationships which we succeeded in discovering in factual data, the world it describes does not express any specific meaning. When we now say "the world keeps its course," we intend this to be taken literally. In the modern period there is no common plane for natural sciences and for those spheres of human thought which are concerned with meaning. Our science is indifferent to values, hence its objective force. Our science is single, uniform, and common for all who understand it. In no way does it depend on their different outlooks and values.

In effect, there is no direct confrontation today between natural science and philosophy, between natural science and history, and, least of all, between natural science and religion. The process of emptying scientific knowledge of all meaning-content goes on. In the physics of the generation preceding ours it reached a peak in the revolution created by the relativity theory, which is considered a philosophical revolution by the broader lay public but which is really the liberation of physics from a partly unconscious burden of metaphysical categories, which were part of classical physics between the seventeenth and nineteenth centuries. Relativity is not a philosophy of space and time but an inquiry into the methods of observation and measurement of space and time. It is free from philosophical assumptions, which were still embodied in Newtonian physics. Newton could still say, in a very obscure expression, that space was God's sensorium. The contemporary scientist does not deal with the quality of space and time, but he does know something his predecessors did not know about the problems in fixing the parameters of distance and time, which appear in the mathematical formulations of functional relationships investigated in physics.

Again, speaking generally, modern science is not concerned with philosophic problems, and its progress in extending knowledge and deepening understanding of the data is associated with its gradual and progressive liberation from the task of discovering the meaning of reality. Hence its objectivity: it is shared by men of different outlooks.

Socrates and his followers strove to free the knowledge of truth (*epistémé*) from the different "opinions" (*doxai*) about truth. Modern science takes this same path in regard to the knowledge of nature.

We may ask whether religion and science are anywhere still brought into contact. While in the Middle Ages religious thought and scientific thought met on a common plane, today points of contact between them can be found, if at all, only in the restricted area of the cognitive elements in religion. For the vast realms of religious thought and practice, science has become indifferent. But it may very well be doubted whether cognitive elements are essential to religion. This is perhaps the most interesting topic of contemporary religious philosophy.

Does religion supply information? Medieval man took this for granted, since he did not distinguish between information and its meaning. The meaning he conferred upon reality was embodied in the information he had, or believed he had, about the world. In the example of the problem of the movement of the celestial bodies, the solution of the ancient scientists did not emerge from observation or from observation-based calculations, but from their conviction that this movement was perfect and therefore circular and uniform. The movement was not deemed perfect because of its circularity and uniformity, but because it was deemed perfect, it was thought to be circular and uniform. Meaning and value were constitutive of the information. Today we extract meaningless information from science and do not have to attribute cognitive content to religious thought.

Our source of information is science. To the extent that we possess any real knowledge it is by way of scientific cognition. Psychologically, the information it supplies is forced upon the consciousness of all who understand it, for a human being is unable not to know what he knows. But the constitutive element of religious feeling and consciousness is not information which is derivable from religion. The essence of religion is not the information it provides but the demand made of man to worship God. Undoubtedly this aspect of religious faith has always been the essence of Judaism, but today it is likely to be more conspicuous than in the Middle Ages, when informative significance was attached to religion.

While science provides information concerning the nature of the world, (including man's own nature), which does not make any difference to faith and values, the religious consciousness is focused on the acknowledgment of the consequence of man's stance before God: to worship and serve God, which is to accept "the yoke of Torah and *Mitzvoth*." Religious faith is not knowledge that such and such is the case. It is a decision made by the man of faith.

These two different approaches to faith in Judaism are hinted at or symbolized, by way of creative interpretation, in the opening passages of Maimonides' *Book of Knowledge* and in part of "Orah Hayyim" of the *Shulhan Arukh*. The former reads: "The most basic fundamental and the pillar of wisdom is to know, that . . ."; the latter: "Gird up strength like a lion, to rise in the morning to the service of God."

To forestall any misunderstanding, we must here emphasize that by the word "knowledge" Maimonides does not refer to scientific information but to the "knowledge of God," in the sense of "understanding and knowing me"(Jer. 9:23). The glossarist of the *Shulhan Arukh* rightly understood this "knowledge" in the sense of Maimonides' *Guide of the Perplexed* (III 52).

Contemporary scientific and religious thought do not meet on a common plane, as they did in the Middle Ages. The world as it is and man's obligations in it must be viewed from entirely different perspectives. "The world keeps its course," and something of the "course" is revealed to us by science. Scientists know very well how little we do know and that every new piece of information opens before us new horizons of ignorance. But the little we know, we know, and this cannot be denied by noncognitive factors. But the world we grasp by scientific knowledge does not make any difference for faith and tells us nothing in regard to values. For the believer, the problem of meaning or value is posed by the consciousness of his stance before God.

What has been said in this context about religious faith holds equally for other spheres of human thought; history, psychology, or sociology, for example, have meaningful actions as their subject and are therefore not amenable to the methods of inquiry of modern natural science. Religion differs from them all in its direct normative signification. It obliges man to worship God. As for the reductionist trends in the philosophies of science, which strive to base the realms of value and meaning on necessary functional relations—to date, their failure is absolute. There is neither a "unified science" encompassing natural and social sciences and the humanities, nor, among the natural sciences themselves, can biology be reduced to physics-chemistry.

Man's consciousness of standing before God has nothing to do with his knowledge of the world, which is understood scientifically. This great idea is articulated in the mighty conclusion of Yom Kippur, the Ne'ilah prayer, by the verse: "and there is no pre-eminence of man over beast, for all is vanity." Man, as part of nature and object of scientific research, is part of the web of indifferent functional relationships obtaining throughout nature. He acquires significance from the fact that "from the beginning You have set man apart and recognized him to stand before You."

It is not likely that the medieval thinker, while he recited the Yom Kippur prayer, could easily and wholeheartedly accept that "there is no pre-eminence of man over beast." Only the great believer, Maimonides, was able to extract the deepest meaning of the verse, to go beyond the "scientific knowledge" of his time and be able to deny the conception of man as "the crown of creation" (*Guide*, III 13–14). Most of the religious philosophers deduced from their "science" that the whole of natural reality bears some meaning, and that this meaning was orientation toward man.

In contemporary science, man—both as natural object and animal—is the object of scientific research, conducted by a method which excludes all reference to values and meanings, and which does not expect the scientist to discover values and meanings in the natural reality of man. If man—as a sensing and feeling, inquiring and thinking, striving and intending creature—is unable to cease considering values and meanings, he cannot appeal to science for relief but must necessarily turn either to atheistic metaphysics or to a religious faith.

Today we have no "science" in the medieval sense, in which religion and science meet, either as mutually supportive or as conflicting. They are entirely alien to each other. Hence the profound difference between the significance of the term "truth" in scientific research and its significance in metaphysical and religious contexts.

The concept of truth has two meanings: instrumental truth and truth as a value. The truth of science is instrumental. Here "truth" and "accordance with scientific method" are synonymous. I can integrate a differential equation only by applying "correct" mathematics. I cannot compute the distance of the sun from the earth using a fallacious trigonometry. The method of scientific research determines the truth about reality even against the will of the scientist. A machine can only operate in conformity with the truth of mechanics, not on the basis of a false mechanical theory. The correct deployment of a machine does not reflect the striving of the mechanic for "truth" but rather the necessity of "truth" for success in using the machine. Similarly, scientific research does not necessarily represent the striving for truth. Here, too, the truth imposes itself upon the investigator if he wants to achieve any theoretical or practical results. Moreover, intentional deceit is difficult because the scientist's work is open to the critical scrutiny of his colleagues. Any falsification will be found out sooner or later. This contrasts sharply with false declarations of faith or opinion, political and social slogans, metaphysical theories, and so on. In these cases one can only controvert falsehood; the deception involved cannot be demonstrated. "Truth" in science is a necessary means to scientific activity as such.

But there is also truth in a completely different sense, truth as a value, the value of *truthfulness,* which is not imposed, which one can ignore, and by which one need not abide. Such is truth in the relations between man and his fellows, between man and wife, between a man and the task he has undertaken, between man and his nation and state. Here deceit is always possible. Success in all these areas does not depend upon one's truthfulness. One can be a hypocrite, liar, or traitor, for dishonesty can rarely be proved. A person may have a successful political career advocating principles which, in the depth of his heart, he knows to be false, and only He who can probe the depths of his heart can establish that the man is lying.

There need not be any correlation between the instrumental truth of science and the truthfulness of a man's behavior. The truth of science is not a "value"; it is a datum within science. Values are not anchored in reality. They are what a man aspires to impose upon reality, including the reality of his self. That which is anchored in reality is value-free. It is simply that which is the case, not a model to which one seeks to make reality conform.

The value of truthfulness is not a cognitive attribute, but rather a conative one, a matter of intention. A man intends to be truthful. The investigator bent on scientific achievement is of necessity a man of truth.

A question which appears in an entirely new light as a result of the shift in the conception of science concerns the cognitive content of Scripture. Do the Holy Writings convey, or intend to convey, scientific information?

It is highly questionable whether we may attribute to the Torah—even to its narrative portions—a cognitive import similar to that found in history books or in scientific texts; rather, it is necessary to redefine the distinction between holy and profane. From the standpoint of religious faith, the Torah and the entirety of Holy Scripture must be conceived as a demand which transcends the range of human cognition—the demand to know God and serve Him—a demand conveyed in various forms of human expression: prescriptions, vision, poetry, prayer, thought, and narrative. The first verse of the Torah does not communicate information concerning what came to pass, since the reader is unable to derive from it any factual data which his mind is capable of grasping. If the reader were to try to impute to it a meaning, he would willy-nilly become involved in the ancient metaphysical problem of the beginning of time, a problem fraught with antinomies and paralogisms.[2] The second word, as well, cannot be rendered by any term which might indicate an act, or an event, or a process which the reader is capable of cognizing.[3] What I learn from these verses is the great principle of faith, that the world is not God—the negation of atheism and pantheism. Likewise, when we read, "God descended upon Mount Sinai"—five words in simple Hebrew—we teach a seven-year-old studying the Pentateuch to appreciate that God does not dwell up on high or descend therefrom; in other words, the human language in which the Torah is written may not be construed literally.

If the Holy Scriptures were sources of information, it would be difficult to see where their sacredness resided. Any information which satisfies the need of man for knowledge if profane. Information is obtained from historical, philological, physical, chemical, or biological inquiry. I convey information to my students within the framework of these disciplines. The idea that the Shekhinah descended on Mount Sinai (in any sense which may be accorded these words) in order to compete with the professor who teaches history or physics is ludicrous, if not blasphemous.

The writings of the medieval philosopher Ibn Ezra show a discernible tendency to detach religion from science.[4] In the preface to his commentary on the Torah, he criticizes the kind of exegesis which would introduce scientific matters into the meaning of the text as loading upon Scripture more than it can bear. More surprising is that more than a hint of this attitude can be found in the writing of Maimonides. What he has to say penetrates to the very foundations of faith, since it refers not only to scientific knowledge but also to metaphysics. At first reading the *Guide of the Perplexed* appears to be primarily an attempt to lay bare the metaphysical content embodied in Scripture. Yet when Maimonides interprets the Book of Job, his approach seems to undergo a radical change. He points out that in God's answer to Job's plaints "there is no going beyond the description of natural matters—namely, description of the elements or description of the meteorological phenomena, or description of the nature of the various species of animals, but of nothing else"—without any explanation of these "natural matters."[5] Yet his answer satisfies Job, because he came to understand that "the notion of His providence is not the same as the notion of our providence; nor is the notion of His governance of the things created by Him the same as the notion of our governance of that which we govern . . . so that you should not fall into error and seek to affirm in your imagination that His knowledge is like our knowledge, or that His purpose and His Providence and His governance are like our purpose and our providence and our governance."[6] When a man attains knowledge of this truth, which is the essence of faith, he ceases to expect from God information relevant to metaphysical problems, "whether He does or does not know and whether He exercises providence or manifests neglect." The quest for information is succeeded by "love." At the end of his Code Maimonides goes so far as to dismiss the significance of knowledge concerning messianic redemption, since it promotes neither fear of God nor love of Him. Religion, which is concerned with "fear" and "love," regards scientific knowledge, whether of nature or of history, with indifference.

PART II

RELIGION, PEOPLE, STATE

CHAPTER 14

The Social Order as a Religious Problem
(1947)

The problem of religion and state has been widely discussed, but most of the discussion is conducted from a sociological rather than a religious standpoint. The question usually posed is: what is the place of religion in society? What is the social function of religion? The so-called religious position in this debate is, in most cases, either an attempt to prove the necessity of religion as a condition for maintaining a just social order, or an exercise in tracing the cultural desolation and sociopolitical catastrophe of our times to the absence of religious content in modern culture. It appears as a modern gloss upon such verses as: "Is it not because God is not in me that these misfortunes have come upon me"(Deut. 31:17), or "Truly, there is no fear of God in this place and they will kill me"(Gen. 20:11). Conversely, the "secular" or antireligious argument denies the sociopolitical need for religion, which may even be regarded as an obstacle to the emergence of a desirable sociopolitical system.

Common to both parties is the lack of concern with religion as such. Instead they focus on the utility of religion for the furthering of sociopolitical functions, to which both sides attribute the highest value. Hence the conclusion of the debate is religiously irrelevant, unless religion is considered to be no more than a means or instrument to achieve other goals. This view is basically nonreligious. Once we appreciate this, we realize that the "religious" position in this debate lacks validity, not because of the answers it tries to give to the question under discussion, but because it agrees to discuss the question in a form that debases religion to the level of an *ancilla* of the political function.

We shall here examine the religious significance of society rather than the social importance of religion. This reversal of the question points up the difference between a sociological interest and a religious one. Illumination of the question of religion and society requires demarcation of the religious categories from the social ones. In our social organization, characterized by the hegemony of the labor movement in the *Yishuv*—and within our cultural-educational problematic—the question assumes a specific form, that of the relation of socialism and religion.[1]

In one approach to this question, a number of our best men of thought and the educational theorists of important sections of the religious labor organizations and religious youth movements raise the vision (or is it perhaps only a slogan?) of religious socialism. The ambiguity of the two concepts intertwined in this slogan makes it difficult to understand or to criticize it. Socialism is a cognitive category, since it involves a conception of the factors that determine the nature of a society. It is also a category of will, since it encompasses programs for a specific social system. Furthermore, it is also an historical category— for "socialism" denotes movements and activities in the past, in the present, and in an anticipated future. In each of these categories we encounter variety and dispute: Saint-Simonism; Marxism in all its forms; Fabianism; Soviet Communism; English trade unionism; labor settlements in Palestine, and so on. Each differs from the others. What is common to all? As for the concept "religion"—it is impossible to estimate the many phenomena it has covered. We have here two perspectives, different and remote from each other, and there is no way of relating them other than from an axiological viewpoint, that is, from a standpoint in which things are evaluated as ends or means. What all conceptions called "socialism" have in common is the setting of social values as ultimate, regard for the improvement of society as the highest end, and evaluation of everything by the standard of efficacy as a means to attain that goal. However, "religion" is also totalitarian in the realm of values. The common denominator of all manifestations of the religious consciousness is regard for knowledge of God and being close to Him as the supreme end. All man's activities are evaluated accordingly as good, bad, or indifferent means to attain this end.

It may, of course, be the case that a person will consider the religious consciousness to be a factor leading to socialism or even a necessary condition for its realization. However, this reflects a socialist and not a religious orientation, since the value of religion derives from its utility to socialism. It is likewise possible to view socialism as a realization of the command "To walk in His ways," and the reformation of the earthly kingdom as a condition for attaining the Kingdom of Heaven. Such a position is religious, not socialistic. This inverse relation of the scale of values precludes the synthesis of religion and socialism. Two men, affirming the desirability of the same good and working to further its realization, may nevertheless differ radically because each assesses his end by a different axiological standard. Socialism has one meaning for the "socialist" and a completely different meaning for the "believer." What matters is the goal he sets for himself or for mankind at large, not his judgment concerning the usefulness of particular means to attain it. From an axiological standpoint, the two components coupled in the concept of "religious socialism" cannot be equal. One must be the end, the other subservient to it as a means. Consequently, "religious socialism" cannot be the solution to the problem of religion and society; on the contrary—it is the very problem.

Is society a religious concern? Are the needs and the tasks of organizing society religious functions? Do the religious consciousness and imperative commit one to adopting a specific position on issues pertaining to society and the state? Good reasons can be adduced for both positive and negative answers and, undoubtedly, in some religions both opposing attitudes may be found. One can argue that religion is only nearness to God ("As for me, my good is nearness to God"; "they desire nearness of God") and that all religious manifestations are either symbolic representations of this nearness or methods of attaining it. Hence the religious situation is not conditioned or affected by the social reality. Even when religion and its precepts extend to broad areas of life, it is possible to agree that some matters are indifferent from a religious point of view. Neither the decision as to the appropriate medical treatment of a given disease nor the choice of technique for building a bridge have any religious significance. Both must be judged by purely instrumental criteria.

Can the manner of organizing relationships among men and between the individual and the community have an aspect that escapes utilitarian considerations and elevates it to the level of a religious task?

This is indeed the case. The social question does have dimensions which transcend the domain of utility. The prophet describes the goal of "those who seek the nearness of God" in terms of social justice (Isa. 48). But what is the sociological significance of this demand for social justice? Does it imply affirmation of a specific social order and the rejection of others? Again we remember the prophet who defined religious "good" and "God's demand of man" as "doing justice and loving mercy" (Mic. 5:8). However, "doing justice and loving mercy" have the same importance, the same value, and the same force in the case of relations between a master and his slave in a society based on slavery ("if I did despise the cause of my slave!"(Job 31:13), relations between the employer and his worker in a capitalistic society, and between comrades at work and rights in a socialistic system. Hence this religious-moral teaching offers no ground for preference of any specific socio-political program.

Among Jewish thinkers, we find Maimonides vigorously asserting the necessity for sociopolitical well-being as a condition for religious perfection: "For a person cannot understand the truth nor do good when he is sick or hungry or fleeing his enemies." Yet the author of "Duties of the Heart" undoubtedly represents a legitimate strain of Jewish religiosity, and sees the very essence of man precisely in the ability to understand the truth and do good even when he is sick or hungry or fleeing from his enemies.[2]

However, we are not concerned with the question of society as viewed from the perspective of an abstract religiosity, but rather with the question of its place in the Torah, in a religion encapsulated in a well-defined system of precepts and specific requirements of action. On the face of it, it would seem that the answer to our question is self-evident. After all, the Torah orders and determines a sociopolitical system, beginning with explicit Mitzvoth in the written Torah and concluding with the entire system of laws collected in the books *Possession, Litigations,* and *Judges* in Maimonides' Code and in part of *Hoshen Mishpat* of the *Shulhan Arukh*.[3] This answer, usually heard in Orthodox circles, merely evades the issue. On the contrary, the Torah, for all its explicit Mitzvoth, leaves us stranded with the problem of taking a definite political stand on concrete issues. We still do not know whether the Torah, for all its detailed and ramified social and political provisions, deals with society and the state as they ought to be or as they

really are. It is the intention of the Torah to create a specific sociopolitical system, defined by its Mitzvoth, or were the laws given to be
applied within an existing system? Consider the proscription of
ploughing with an ox and an ass yoked together. Does this imply a
duty to base agriculture on animal power and to create the opportunity
for fulfilling the prohibition? Reversing the terms, is mechanized agriculture, which obviates the use of animals as a source of energy, forbidden because it removes all opportunity for observing this Mitzvah?
Or is it permissible to assume a hypothetical imperative: in the event
that animals are used, avoid ploughing with an ox and ass yoked
together?

In this instance, every intelligent person will no doubt understand
the proscription in accordance with the second alternative. However,
adoption of this alternative is not so simple in relation to the corpus
of civil law in the Torah, which assumes that a specific sociopolitical
system already exists. The Torah, in the relevant chapters of the Book
of Exodus, assumes the existence of the institution of slavery and regulates it. The labor legislation assumes the institution of hired labor
and regulates it as well. Laws of fraud assume private commerce and
regulate its profits.

Our own historic situation is radically different. The sociopolitical
system is not already given. As participants in the shaping of a new
Jewish sovereignty we face the task of creating such a framework from
scratch. Our socioreligious problem takes the form of choosing among
three alternatives. In the first, it is our religious duty, the religious duty
of those who accept the yoke of Torah and Mitzvoth, to strive to create
the kind of system in which the sociopolitical legislation of the existing
Halakhah may be applied. We may, in the second alternative, surmise
that the relevant parts of the Halakhah were only used by the Torah as
a paradigm to exemplify realization of its social goal within an historically given situation. Our task is to clarify the nature of this goal and
seek a social order most adapted to its attainment in our situation as
we understand it. The third possible view is that the sociopolitical legislation of the Torah was intended only for the specific sociopolitical
reality that existed then. With its passing, social and political life and
the Torah were sundered, and we are free today to choose a social order
as we please. All that is required of us is the realization of "justice and
righteousness" in a form applicable to the framework we have chosen.

We shall discuss the three alternatives in the light of the social situation of religious Jewry today. In contrast to our forefathers, we are free from a predetermined social fabric that is shaped either by immanent law or by decree of a foreign ruler, both beyond our influence and responsibility. To a certain extent we have become masters of our fate. We are participants in the restoration of Jewish sovereignty by our own efforts and confront the task of establishing our own sociopolitical framework. We shall bear full responsibility for its character and worth. Today, the Jew who considers the Torah a life program—or pretends to do so—cannot evade the issue of Torah and society by claiming that the regime is forced upon him from outside. He must decide whether his religious stance includes an explicit and mandatory program for the sociopolitical order, or whether his religion is only a personal matter and "private affair," in conformity with the principle governing the legal system of contemporary secular liberal regimes. If the Torah does prescribe a sociopolitical order, what is it?

The three alternatives just formulated address these issues each in its own way, and all three have vocal or tacit adherents in the religious community. The first and the third appear to represent two extremes of religious thought on the matter and two contrasting approaches. However, in effect they have an important implication in common—both free the contemporary Jew from any religious duty with respect to ongoing social and political functions. It would not be amiss to claim that the third alternative reflects the position of religious Jewry on sociopolitical issues. This shows up in the public behavior of the large majority of religious Jews, and in the politics of the official institutions of the religious community and most of its parties, organizations, spokesmen, and proponents. They appear to regard the problems of state and society, national organization and international relations, economic system and economic activity and the like as indifferent from a religious standpoint and having no relation to Torah and Halakhah. Consequently, with respect to these issues, a religious person may conduct himself as he pleases. He may continue the behavior pattern of his fathers without recognizing a need for social criticism from a religious perspective. He may equally order his action by habit, by considerations of comfort, personal interest, or the appeal of some political or social ideology. This will not in the least discredit his religious status.

This position is not the result of conscious deliberation. It stems from a subconscious feeling that, indeed, there is no relation between social problems and religion. There is general agreement to regard the butcher shop where one buys meat as a criterion of one's piety, but not one's attitude to Zionism or anti-Zionism, to war and peace, to an economy based on private enterprise and hired labor as against an economy based on common ownership and collective labor. Clear and explicit religious teaching and guidance regulate personal matters and those between man and God, but not political and social affairs. A religious Jew does not generally feel that decision according to the Torah is called for in this area. Authoritative institutions, groups, and individuals who are considered legitimate representatives of religious Judaism exert much effort on matters of kosher slaughtering and little, if any, on the question of the draft in wartime or the vital problem of the relation between nation and state and the individual as a member of the nation and a citizen of the state. Religious Jewry, if not in ideology then in its everyday reality, recognizes the Torah as intended for the Jewish person but not as governing the life of the Jewish nation.

The historical background of this attitude is familiar and understandable. The separation of the circumscribed world of the individual, which can be regulated by Halakhah, and his political and social ambience, which cannot, was at first imposed on the Jew from without and gradually internalized. During many hundreds of years, lack of facilities and instruments for conducting an independent political and social existence limited the expressions of religious life mainly to the private sphere. The habit forced upon us became second nature, so that even today, when we have emerged from the confines of privacy, have gained a modicum of control over the factors that shape state and society, and are creating a regime of our own, religious Jews who participate in these activities are still wont to limit their religious horizon to private and personal matters and to deal with politics and social needs as though prescriptions and proscriptions of the Torah did not apply to them.

It is possible to find a religious-moral justification for this stand of official religious Jewry and its leadership, if we interpret it as an expression—perhaps an unconscious expression—of the approach that was described as our third alternative. It may well be that the Torah deals with the state and society as something given, and all its detailed political and social legislation was only meant to apply to a specific social reality and to specific economic conditions which once existed but no longer obtain: a king who consulted the *Urim* and *Tumim,* a Sanhedrin whose members were ordained in a continuous line going back to Moses and sat in the *Lishkath Hagazith,*[4] the distribution of the land among the tribes, a patriarchal agricultural economy, primitive economic relations (moneylending only for carrying the needy over a bad season), and so on. Perhaps only against this background is the political and social legislation of the Torah mandatory. Because we are not commanded to create such a framework, and in the absence of these conditions today, no prescription and no prohibition applies to any social system that exists or may come into existence. The positions taken in the present on social and political issues have no religious implications and cannot be determined by halakhic decision.

We do not presume to offer a definitive answer to the great theological questions of the purpose of the Mitzvoth—whether they are directed to the individual or to the community, whether the organization of society is a religious problem, whether the social legislation of the Torah is law *a priori* or law *a posteriori,* and so on. There are arguments pro and con, and in the framework of legitimate historical Judaism we can uncover lines of thought inclining toward both views. Therefore we have no right to deny the religious integrity of a person or a community which does not draw from the Torah any political or social conclusions in the form of halakhic instruction for the contemporary world. In other words, a person can be a pious Jew without adhering to a religious political and social program.

But this admission applies only under certain conditions. The persons or community in question must be consistent in their practice and theory and meticulous in maintaining the boundary between religious reality as a spiritual experience and a system of personal norms, on the one hand, and political and social reality with its problems and challenges on the other. Both logically and morally there is no more blatant contradiction than an organized presence on the political scene purporting to set forth "religious demands" for a state "according to the Torah," and the absence of an obligatory program for a social system which would accord with the Torah. The result is not a religious struggle but clerical politics.

Some time ago we were privileged to see a delegation of the official leadership and communal representatives of religious Jewry appear before the British Commission for the Partition of Palestine to voice the demand that the projected Jewish state be based on the Torah. Let us imagine that the Gentile members of this commission were to take that delegation and to its proposal seriously and to ask questions about it. What do you mean by a state according to the Torah, and what will its legal system be? Will this be a democratic state, in which political authority derives ultimately from the people who confer it upon their leadership, or will it be a state in which political authority flows down from the apex of a political pyramid? Will office holders be elected or appointed, and by whom? Will this be a state that maintains an army and weaponry and includes the conduct of war, when necessary, among its legitimate functions, or will it be a neutral and pacifist state that does not acknowledge war at all as an instrument of policy? Will the economy of the state be based on private enterprise, each person doing as he pleases with his own property, with production based on the institution of hired labor, or will it be a socialist or communist economy? Such questions might have been asked by the commission in reacting to the demand for a state formed according to the Torah, and only a delegation that had considered these questions and concluded that it could give clear and binding answers derived from its understanding of the Torah and Halakhah had a right to appear with such a religious-political demand. Actually, however, this delegation represented a religious community and religious institutions whose religiosity involves exemption of the political and social spheres from the criticism and guidance of the Halakhah. The Torah, as they conceive it, is limited to the *Shulhan Arukh,* which does not and could not deal with even one of the political and social questions of an independent Jewish society in the present, since none of these questions were relevant either in Safed where Rabbi Joseph Caro resided, or in Cracow, the home of Rabbi Moses Isserles.[5] Had the delegation been asked such questions, it would have become evident that it had no answers and that its demand for a Jewish state according to the Torah was only a verbal slogan without real political content.

A religious public that actively participates in the nation's effort to build a homeland and to gain political independence coined the slogan,

"The Land of Israel for the People of Israel according to the Torah of Israel."[6] However, during a generation and a half, no person, institution, or movement has succeeded in clarifying for themselves and to others what was meant by the "Torah of Israel" for the present people of Israel in the land of Israel, when the Halakhah is a mandate only for the individual Jew in his personal life. In truth, we have neither understanding for the need of new halakhic legislation in matters of society and state nor the wish to institute such legislation. The fact that the sector of the religious public organized as a political movement lacks a religious program for the conduct of the state deprives its religious struggle of all value and significance. The secular public preceives it not as a struggle for a distinct and encompassing conception of public life, but rather as a series of petty assaults upon the freedom of the individual. This is the great failure of religious Jewry in our generation. It is the consequence of its following the third alternative described above.

To avoid the widespread misunderstanding infecting religious propaganda, especially in the youth organizations and the workers' movement, we must insist that the *Hoshen Mishpat* has nothing to contribute to the issues we are here discussing. *Hoshen Mishpat* is a code of civil law which deals with relations within a given social system. It does not deal at all with the social order as such. The code cannot determine whether the socioeconomic system presupposed by it is obligatory according to the Torah, or whether we are free to build our own social order on completely different foundations, which would be more effective, in the contemporary situation, in realizing the judicial and moral ideals animating the Halakhah. We have no guidance in the *Hoshen Mishpat* on pressing issues of the structure of society and state: of the rights and duties of a person not to his fellow man, but to the great anonymities—state, society, nation, country. Its Halakhah offers no applicable precedents. Only new legislation can deal adequately with these matters. Rabbinic decisions in our days are based on the *Shulhan Arukh* and are therefore restricted to the subjects it deals with. The rabbinate refrains from engaging in new legislation—thus evading its duty to render decision in matters which cannot be referred to the *Shulhan Arukh*. This explains the moral weakness and helplessness of the rabbinate when it comes to dealing with such issues as Jewish labor, the draft, and similar matters that arise in the unique circumstances of our day: the absence of an externally given political-social framework, and the dedication of Jewish efforts to build a political and social order from the ground up. In all the decisive questions facing it, the religious community remains without religious guidance.

Much clearer is the significance of the first extreme alternative, which considers the political and social legislation of the Torah as unconditional. According to this approach, accepting the yoke of Torah and Mitzvoth commits one to the political-social arrangements presupposed in the books of Exodus, Leviticus, and Deuteronomy and all the oral Torah deriving therefrom, and obliges us to strive to establish precisely that system and those conditions which enable the literal realization of the Torah. When these conditions do not exist and we are unable to create them, we are forbidden to undertake all independent political activity "till a spirit inspires us from above." A fitting analogy may be the sacrifices, which are conditioned upon the rebuilt Temple, pedigreed priesthood, purity of the Temple, its utensils and those who serve, and so on. In the absence of these conditions, not only are the laws of the sacrifices not in force, but the very offering of sacrifices is forbidden. Similarly, we might be forbidden today to create political and social frameworks of our own, since they violate religious law. It would be our duty to continue our social existence in the interstices of Gentile society, for which we are not responsible, and where—until the coming of the Messiah—each Jew in his private sphere could perform the obligatory Mitzvoth. It is difficult to impugn such an approach from a religious or moral standpoint, provided that its proponents are consistent in both their practice and their theory. It is not difficult to find sources and precedents for this individualistic religiosity in historic Judaism. However, those who participate in the modern national-political movement, in the upbuilding of the land and development of the institutions of political and social independence of the Yishuv, have indicated, in effect, that they reject this approach. Few who adopt it do so consciously and explicitly, but even if not explicitly asserted, it is implicit in behavior. This confusion echoes in the words of one halakhic authority in Israel. When Jewish farmers in the land of Israel approached him for halakhic guidance in dealing with questions that arose in the modern settlements, he answered, "Why must you be farmers? Why not be shopkeepers like your pious fathers?"

It remains to inquire where the second of the three alternative approaches leads. What are the answers it gives, or could eventually give, to the fateful questions that today confront the Jew who sees in the Torah a program of life?

According to this approach, the Halakhah is only a paradigm offered by the Torah, to indicate its intention. It is necessary to clarify this purpose and to strive for that sociopolitical order which, according to our understanding, is most appropriate for the attainment of this eternal goal in our historical circumstances.

This approach involves a great difficulty. We have spoken of the appropriate order according to our understanding. Whose understanding? It is clear that different people can understand and imagine the "appropriate order" in very different ways, and consequently espouse different systems. Obviously, religious workers, Halutzim (settlers), and soldiers, all of whom share responsibility for the state and the maintenance of its services and functions, will have social concepts and aspirations very different from those of the previous generations, which did not enjoy national independence and lacked political responsibility and whose characteristic representatives were either the lay-members in the local Jewish communities, or men whose occupation was the study of Torah. Even in the past traditional Judaism offered varying conceptions—even opposed ones—of "the spirit of the Torah," its intentions, and the purpose of its Mitzvoth. All of them, despite their mutual contradictions, were sanctified over the generations and are considered legitimate expressions and manifestations of Judaism. It will suffice to mention the seemingly unbridgeable gulf which separates those who, like some of our medieval philosophers, regard the Mitzvoth as pedagogic means for the education of man, from those who consider them, as did the Kabbalists, to be mystical and even magical symbols, performance of which affects the supernal worlds. Yet in the history of the Jewish religion legitimacy has been conferred upon both views. Today we cannot decide either, *a priori*, which conception is legitimate. Is it more legitimate to consider society and the state as categories belonging to the sphere of religious concern to be subjected to the Torah and Halakhah, or is it better to envision a society for which the Halakhah, in the form which has taken shape over the centuries and which excludes problems of state and society from its governance, is the absolute manifestation of the Torah, and hence requires that we avoid dealing with the religious problematic of political existence? Between these two approaches there can be no theoretical compromise. Their practical implications are incompatible. The division will, in all likelihood, bring about a decisive split in religious Jewry.

Whoever acquiesces in the restatement of Halakhah for application to the problems of contemporary society and state in the spirit of the written Torah and the tradition, and in the light of the halakhic paradigm which was formulated in circumstances other than our own, has no alternative to being guided by his understanding of the spirit of the Torah and the intention and purpose of its Mitzvoth. Together with others who share this view, in collective struggle with doubt and uncertainty, he will strive to apply the practical conclusions which may be reached by this approach.

CHAPTER 15

The Crisis of Religion in the State of Israel

(1952)

I t is one of the great paradoxes of Jewish history that two antithetic events, centuries apart, should have had the same effect on
Judaism. The reestablishment of Jewish independence and the
ingathering of exiles have proven as catastrophic for the Jewish religion
as were, in their day, the destruction of the Jewish state and the dis-
persion of the people. After the Roman conquest of 70 C.E., the generation of Yohanan ben Zakai was confronted with the fateful question: can a valid Judaism survive the loss of the sacrificial system? The
revolutionary turn of events that has now produced the state of Israel
confronts our own generation with an equally fateful question: can a
valid Judaism survive the emergence from the conditions of Diaspora
and political subservience in which it has subsisted for so long? The
Jewish religion in the state of Israel now faces a crisis unprecedented
since the destruction of the second Temple. This chapter will attempt
a fundamental analysis of the ideational roots of that crisis—an analysis
which must precede any attempt to deal with specific halakhic problems.

One approach to the question of religion and the state is sociopolitical, dealing with the role of religion in organized society. Another is
religious, dealing with the role of society, state, and nation as means
toward achieving an awareness of God and the fulfillment of His will.
My approach here is the religious one. In other words, the Torah is
here regarded as the primary and eternal datum of which the history
of the Jewish people is the variable framework. This, of course, is a

denial of the view that considers the historical Jewish people as the reality, of which the Torah is but one manifestation.

The current formulation of the question, even on the part of religious groups, is the sociopolitical one. The "religious" position in this formulation usually attempts to prove the indispensability of religion for the maintenance of a decent social order in general, and among the Jewish people in particular. Its proponents argue that the great political, social, and cultural debacle of our time has resulted from the elimination of religious content and religious values from the institutions of state and society.

This justification of religion is, in effect, its vulgarization. To be sure, it has its uses for didactic purposes. Even the Patriarch Abraham used this line of reasoning when he had to make a point with the pagan King Avimelekh. "I thought the people here might kill me, since there is no fear of God in this place" (Gen. 20:1). Four thousand years later, that old cynic, Voltaire, posited this quite simply as the real basis for religion. "If there were no God," he said, "we should have to invent Him." It was his custom to implore his guests not to express their doubts about God and immortality in the presence of his servants. He was afraid that the latter, once deprived of their faith, might murder him in his bed!

The secularist or antireligious position on this issue usually denies that the social order needs religion. Social and national ideals can be achieved, it is argued, without religious beliefs or practices. In a more extreme form, the antireligious argument presents religion as an obstacle to the achievement of the "good society."

It will be readily apparent that neither party represents a truly religious point of view, since both measure the value of religion by its contribution to the welfare of the body-politic. But from the truly religious viewpoint religion is the end in itself, against which all other human aspirations and goals are to be measured. The crucial evaluations in every field of life and thought involve the differentiation of ends and means. This is especially true in the area of religion. A person may be convinced that the avowal of religious principles and a religious way of life are indispensable prerequisites for the achievement of his social, political, or national ideals. His perception is that of a socialist, nationalist, or what you will, but certainly not of a religious person.

For his "religiosity" is subject to a higher criterion, and thus falls under the category of "conditional love."

True devotion to religious value is totalitarian. "To know God and cleave to Him" is the ultimate value. All human activities which are not religiously indifferent are to be judged by their contribution to the realization of this end. In the section of Genesis cited above, the term "God-fearing" is defined quite differently in reference to Abraham's own fear of God. "Now do I know that you are God-fearing, in that you did not withhold your only son from Me" (Gen. 22:12). In this context of the Aqedah, the highest expression of religious devotion, the fear of God no longer appears as a condition for the realization of other human values, but is itself the supreme value before which all human considerations must be set aside. In the light of this definition, it becomes irrelevant to argue that religion serves the needs of society, or the nation, or the state. In the words of Maimonides: "The ultimate requires no further justification." From a Jewish religious point of view, therefore, the theory that the Torah was given to Israel merely as an instrument of national survival cannot be accorded validity. A religious Jew must reject the idea that it is the function of the Sabbath to preserve the Jewish people; rather, it is the mission of the Jewish people to observe the Sabbath.

The religious person is capable of being completely objective in considering the political effectiveness of religion. He need not distort or ignore the facts in order to defend any specific thesis relating to this much disputed question. At the empirical-historical level, we have no proof whatsoever that the religious consciousness and the practice instigated by it have ever been effective in the solution of social, political, and national problems. There is no indication, either in the history of Israel or in that of other peoples, that a sociopolitical organization dedicated to religious values and conducted by religious agencies has been better ordered, less subject to internal contradictions, conflict and crises, exploitation, oppression and bloodshed, or manifestations of hatred, lust for prestige, or sheer folly than were sociopolitical organizations which lacked any religious basis. Where there is no "fear of God," men commit murder, but murder is committed as well with fear of God. Only a shallow perfectibility will believe that there is a faith or teaching, a regime or constitution, a human or divine enactment or arrangement which is capable of redeeming individual or collective man from the influence and effects of his destructive drives and tendencies. The religious Jew, in particular, should know that even revelation of the Shekhinah at Sinai and Israel's response, "We will do and obey," did nothing to alter the human and social substance of "the generation of the wilderness." The wilderness is perennial.

In the new state of Israel, with its desiderata of strong defense, vigorous economy, honest administration, and the like, it is perfectly clear that religion, so far from being an aid to the state, is one of its most severe hindrances—a veritable stumbling block. In Israel today the Jewish religion does not unite us; it divides us. From a purely national sociopolitical point of view, it complicates no end the task of the young state. Recognition of these facts, however, need in no wise trouble the conscience of the religious Jew—provided always that he approaches the problem from a really religious point of view. The central question is whether such a genuinely religious viewpoint exists in Israel today.

Does the very existence of the state affect religion in theory and in practice? As for the Jewish religion, embodied as it is in Torah and Mitzvoth—action imperatives—what role does it assign to the Mitzvoth covering the relationship between man and his state? And if there be such Mitzvoth, how shall we reconcile them to those defining relations between man and his Maker? Or even between man and his fellow man?

On the face of it, the answer to these questions seems obvious—simply consult the sources of Jewish law, from Torah and Talmud through Maimonides to Caro's *Hoshen Mishpat*. This is the usual answer given by religious Jews. But it is totally inadequate. So far from being a solution, it points up the problem in its sharpest form. For we find that the corpus of Jewish law does not ordain social forms; it accepts them as given and regulates them. Exodus 21 finds the institution of slavery in existence and proceeds to humanize it. Similarly, institutions like private trade and wage-labor are not created by the law, but rather regulated by it. What is more telling, the Halakhah accepts the absence of Jewish statehood as axiomatic, or one might even say, as a prior condition for the fulfillment of its prescriptions. This is true, at any rate, insofar as the corpus of traditional Jewish law deals with actual conditions rather than with a utopian society in some hypothetical future. Here lies the crux of the problem facing religious

Jewry today, when it finds itself a participant in the creation of a Jewish state in the here and now.

A frank acceptance of the discrepancy between the social-political realities of the present state of Israel, and those taken for granted by the historic Halakhah, does not clash with a belief in the theological principles underlying that same Halakhah. Those principles the writer accepts as common ground among religious Jews. To say that the whole detailed development of Jewish law represents a historical process is not to challenge a metaphysical view of the Torah. A person may adhere to this concept, rejecting pseudo-historical theories of naturalistic historiography and the secular mythology which views the Torah as an expression of the "spirit of Judaism," or "the national genius at work"—and still not fail to realize that the Halakhah has not developed in a social vacuum, but within the framework of very specific historical conditions.

To be sure, the Halakhah nowhere makes explicit its assumption that Jews live in exile, or in a Palestine ruled by Gentiles. Yet these were the circumstances under which Jewish law did develop, not only after the year 70 C.E., but even to a decisive degree during the second commonwealth. This latter was the very period of Soferim and early Tann-a'im, who left their stamp so tellingly on the Halakhah. Admittedly, the conditions in which they lived did contradict the theoretic basis of the Halakhah—but they were the actual conditions in which the Halakhah was put to practice, and their influence on it is everywhere apparent.

The regime of the Torah as it has come down to us constituted a way of life for a community free of responsibility for internal and external security, for foreign relations, for national economy, for administration of the body politic, and even for a judicial system operating with state sanctions. Yet no community and no individual can get along without all these public functions, unless they are provided by some outside agent. Jewish community life as guided by the Halakhah depended historically on Gentiles, who provided the matrix of public law and order within which the Halakhah functioned. Take, for example, the sixteenth-century code of Joseph Caro, the *Shulhan Arukh*— still cited as authoritative. It begins on a truly inspiring religious note, with these words: "I have placed God before me always; let a man gird up strength like a lion to rise in the morning, to serve his Creator."

Now Caro was perfectly aware that no one can rise in the morning, much less sleep safely through the night, unless the prior conditions of public safety and social order have been provided. Properly speaking, our codifier ought to have prefaced chapter I of his *Orah Hayyim* with a complete code of public law, providing the framework within which it becomes possible to live in accordance with the "Regulations for Rising in the Morning," as well as all the other regulations of the four parts of the *Shulhan Arukh*.

Caro did not do so for a very simple reason. He had a silent partner to whom he could leave the entire sector of life called government, the Turkish governor in Acre, who had jurisdiction over Safed where Caro lived. It makes no difference whether the Turkish system was one of justice or of *baksheesh* (bribery), of integrity or of intrigue. The point is, it was there, and it freed Caro and his contemporary Jews from political and administrative duties, so that they could undertake quite different responsibilities in that sector of life which was within their control. Had Caro not been able to take for granted an existing system of law and order, he would have had to write a very different *Shulhan Arukh*.

It scarcely needs to be said that the position of religious Jewry in Israel today is not what it was in sixteenth-century Galilee. It shares responsibility for the conduct of every sector of life. Nevertheless, it still professes to view Caro's *Shulhan Arukh* as a program for our times, although this code applies only to certain areas of life and neglects the others. These Jews seem to entertain the principle, "I have set the non-religious Jew before me always," since, in the last analysis, they depend on the latter to do their work for them in many sectors of life, leaving them free to serve God as heretofore. This state of affairs is scarcely worthy of being called "fulfillment of the Torah." It is rather a distortion of Torah—a veritable profanation of the divine Name!

What has been said of the *Shulhan Arukh* applies equally to all the classic sources of Halakhah, from the Mishnah to Maimonides. None of these provide us with a religious-halakhic approach to the present Jewish state. The state described in the Mishnah and Gemara of Tractate *Sanhedrin* or delineated in Maimonides' Code under the rubric "Laws of Kings and Their Wars" never existed, and never will exist within the framework of historic reality. It is a metaphysical entity, belonging to a world in which physical nature will undergo a metamorphosis, if we follow the aggadic line, or in which human nature will be fundamentally different, as Maimonides seems to imply. Only two forms of the "state of Israel" are known to the Halakhah—the prehistoric and the posthistoric. One is the Kingdom of David and Solomon, from an idealized semi-mythical past. The other is the Kingdom of the Messiah—a vision of the end of days.

What the Halakhah never envisaged was the emergence of the state of Israel in real history, in the year 1948, unaccompanied by any theophany (as pictured in popular tradition), or even by the emergence of the perfected human type (as depicted by Maimonides). The ineffectiveness of religious Jewry today in dealing with the real phenomenon of the state of Israel is rooted in an incoherent attempt to view it through the prism of a system which never reckoned with the possibility that such a phenomenon would exist!

Religious thinking must make the transition from the fantasy of a hypothetical ideal state to the realities of the state of Israel. It cannot do so without introducing innovation into the religious way of life, into the Halakhah itself. Authority for this step inheres in the Torah itself. Concern for Torah makes it obligatory. That religious segment of Jewry which has been integrated into the new historic situation of the Jewish people can no longer avoid making decisions, not merely in the capacity of "students (men) of the Torah," but also in the capacity of "builders of the Torah." The religious daring involved in this step cannot be evaded in our generation, for it cannot solve these problems by looking to the past, whether distant or proximate. It is a mistake to believe that the crisis of Torah in our times is merely the product of recent history, and that the way out is, in the words of Scripture, to "seek out days of yore." It has been argued, to be sure, that the figure of King David, as aggadically depicted, in which the ruler and military commander are blended with the religious leader and law-maker, is proof that the tradition sees no dichotomy between the two aspects of life; thus we have a fulcrum on which to balance past and present. But the Aggadah also shows David conducting military operations by consulting the Urim and Tumim. It is difficult to envisage a religious Defense Minister or Chief of Staff in our day making use of this method!

A more important example is the Great Covenant of Ezra and Nehemiah and the men of the Great Assembly, the founders of the second commonwealth. Their document deals with separation from the Gentiles, with Sabbath and the priesthood, and the like. If Ezra and Nehemiah had been asked how they could expect their religious community to function without sociopolitical instruments, they would have answered simply and honestly that government was the business of the Persian Emperor in Susa, or of his local satrap. There was nothing wrong with this; it was realistic statesmanship. But today the same attitude becomes a distortion, freezing the eternal Torah into a halakhic mold which has practical application only under foreign rule, or in an unrealized utopia.

Political subservience played a similar role in the halakhic teachings of the Soferim and the Tanna'im, for they too lived and worked under foreign domination of the Greeks and the Romans. In those sections of the Mishnah which do not deal with man's own conduct, with his relation to God, or with his relations among individuals but with social and political man, there is quite apparently no intention to create a system of public law for a world in which human nature and physical nature remain what they are. Thus the Mishnah is no guide for conducting the present-day state of Israel. The whole magnificent structure of sovereignty, the judiciary, and procedural law laid down in the talmudic Tractate *Sanhedrin* was never intended to function under historical conditions, but was rather the result of a series of projections backward, to an idealized past, and forward, to the "end of days." This, clearly, applies to the cases which, according to Tannaitic sources, "never happened and never will happen," like the law of the rebellious son, or the law of the apostate city, which are discussed nevertheless in great detail.[1] It also applies to the whole of mishnaic public law, which never functioned and never will until human nature is radically transformed. In the "real" world, or for the "time being," so to speak, the Torah entrusts the security and welfare of man and society to quite other agencies. In order to ensure the public order, the halakhic powers of the judiciary must be supplemented by the extra-halakhic ones of the king.[2] Apparently then, the whole edifice of courts, from the High Court of 71 judges in the Lishkath Hagazith through the courts of 23 in each tribe and every city, along with all the procedural details and limitations of their jurisdiction, is not sufficient to "break the power of the wicked" and not intended as a realistic system. Tractate *Sanhedrin* is apparently theoretical-messianic. For practical purposes, it would seem, the Torah itself leaves things to the sovereign, who is free of these limitations and empowered to rule in accordance with the "needs of the hour."

The halakhists themselves, in their great creative period, were well aware of the conditions and circumstances which affected their application of halakhic precepts. This is reflected in the innovations introduced with the words: "On that occasion they said." It is not by chance that this formula is most often employed in the areas of public law, which are functions of changing circumstances, rather than in the domain of private law and the regulation of religious conduct, which are oriented to the unchanging nature of humankind.

During the 500-year period when the monarchy had lapsed in Israel (586–104 B.C.E.), the Halakhah envisaged a type of perfect king who would obey the Torah and be subject to legal proceedings like any Jew. But when the monarchy became a reality again, after the Maccabean revolt, it became clear that the laws relating to kings were not compatible with the flesh-and-blood king of the contemporary reality, and that any attempt to reconcile them was doomed to failure; witness the attempt of Simeon ben Shetah and King Jannaeus. It was then that a new principle was established: "At that time they said: the king may not act as judge and may not be brought before a court; he may not testify, and testimony may not be brought against him."[3]

For 420 years (586–187 B.C.E.) the Jews had waged no wars, but lived peacefully and observed the Torah under the aegis of benevolent Persian and Greek monarchs. At the outbreak of war, some pious communities believed that war could not be conducted on the Sabbath, which for all practical purposes meant that war simply could not be waged by observing Jews. Only the actuality of war forced a reexamination of the question of Sabbath-observance in warfare.[4] Similarly, a Tannaitic source reports changes in the procedure for storing weapons on the Sabbath upon returning from action against enemies outside the town walls. The changes were introduced after some bad experiences with procedures which were intended to minimize desecration of the Sabbath.[5]

The Judaism of a later age likewise recognized the halakhic force of political and social realities. Don Isaac Abravanel is the one religious thinker who dealt with political theory in terms close to our modern concepts. Unlike his predecessors, he did not identify the idea of the state with either aggadic idealization, or with the mediaeval type of suzerainty. He was acquainted at first hand with such states as fifteenth-century Portugal, then engaged in creating the first overseas colonial empire. He knew Ferdinand of Aragon in Spain, the first European power; he was familiar with Naples, and the Italian principalities and republics of Machiavelli's day (*Il Principe* was written only a few years after Abravanel's death). Small wonder that this conservative theologian utterly rejected the halakhic views of his predecessors (for instance, Maimonides) to the effect that "You shall surely appoint a king" is a positive commandment. On the contrary, says Abravanel, "This is no obligation at all."

In this light, how tragic, or perhaps tragicomic, was the debate in the Knesseth on capital punishment. Certain deputies of the religious parties attempted to make out a case based on the Tannaitic dispute in Tractate *Makkoth:* "Had we been in the Sanhedrin, no man would ever have been executed," as against "You would thereby have increased bloodshed in Israel."[6] These deputies did not apparently sense how devoid of meaning were their arguments in the current situation. Back in the first century, rabbis Aqiba and Tarphon argued with R. Gamliel as to what they would have done in theory if they had ever had capital jurisdiction—which in fact was, and had been for a long time, in the hand of the Roman Procurator. The rabbis knew that their dialectics were not a matter of life or death, as when Gamliel chided Aqiba: "Shall this one be executed just because you read meanings into similar terms *'bat'* and *'u-bat?'*" But a present-day member of the Knesseth does not find himself in the position of Aqiba in Bnei Brak, nor of Tarphon in Lydda, nor of Gamliel in Yavneh, but rather of the Roman Procurator in Caesaria! If our member of the Knesseth is religious, he must ask himself a question that the Halakhah could never even dream of: How shall the Roman Procurator govern in accordance with the Torah?

The religious question arising in the contemporary state of Israel is how to conduct affairs of state according to the Torah and the needs of the hour. The Halakhah, as we know it, never envisaged this "hour." The philosophy of history on which it was based dealt with three possibilities only: Jewish independence and sovereignty in an ideal past; exile and subservience in the real present; independence and sovereignty in an ideal future. But God shapes history independently of our theories, and He has seen fit to bring about a fourth possibility—Jewish independence and sovereignty in an unredeemed world, a world in which humanity, Jewish and Gentile alike, is still unperfected. Religious Jews will have to stop facing both ways—trying to base a positive attitude to the Jewish state on a system of thought which does not admit of the possibility of such a state. The contradiction is both logical and moral; it is the source of untold trouble for organized religious Jewry, whose spiritual and political leadership wants to integrate the Jewish religion into the Jewish state, yet tries to tackle the problems of that state by means of a system of religious law whose basic assumption is that there is no such state.

Now that the scope of Jewish life in the state of Israel has been broadened to encompass political and social functions—government, legislation, economics, technology, communications, foreign and international affairs, internal and external security—it immediately becomes apparent that the traditional regime of the Torah, once an all-embracing way of life for generations of Jews who lived in the Diaspora, suffers from both excess and deficiency; excess in that many of its provisions prevent the citizen of Israel from performing his duties as a soldier, policeman, public official, or just plain citizen who must participate in meeting the needs of the state "according to the needs of the hour"; deficiency, in that this tradition gives no direction to the needs of the state, which "the hour"—*this* hour—requires.

Religious Jewry must, of necessity, choose between two contradictory approaches, each of which can be grounded in the literary sources, traditions, and historic realities of Judaism. The choice will have fateful consequences for the future of the Jewish religion.

One approach takes the traditional halakhic way of life as crystallized over two-and-a-half millennia, to represent the obligatory demand of the Torah. The Torah is indeed intended to encompass human existence in its entirety, but only in a utopian world of the past or the future. In the present, that all-encompassing Torah cannot lay down the fundamental institutional bases for human existence, those of state and society. Until the messianic age, the Torah requires us to erect a superstructure of Jewish life upon an independently existing substructure. The Torah enjoins the people of Israel to carry on its existence in the interstices of Gentile society. The creation of the Jewish state is a forbidden act, a rebellion against Torah. This, in essence, is the standpoint of the Neturei Karta, who deny the validity of the state of Israel and seek to separate themselves from it in all its manifestations.[7]

Against this approach others claim that the achievement of national liberation and political independence for the people of Israel is a religious duty, precisely because these conditions are indispensable for the actualization of the Torah as an all-encompassing way of life. Adherents to this view are unwilling to confine the way of life in accordance with the Torah to the private sphere or local community, if they are not forced to do so by inescapable external compulsion. An independent state in our national homeland is an authentic state of Israel, whatever its faults or its defects. Hence, also, the individual Jew has a religious obligation to help advance the security and welfare of this state.

The second of these viewpoints alone provides any logical, moral or religious justification for the existence of religious parties on the political scene. Yet officially organized religious Jewry refuses to take a clear-cut stand on the fundamental issue. On the one hand it affirms the religious validity of the state; on the other, it refuses to accept full responsibility for the public services of the state. On the one hand it participates in government and public life; on the other, it casts aspersions on the secular nature of the state. At no time have the religious leaders ever offered a concrete program for operating the existing state in accordance with the Torah.

The religious community has adopted a position lacking both clarity and honesty. There seems to be no desire to formulate a religious code of public law. On the contrary, the religious bloc prefers to have the state remain secular in form and essence. Their only concern is that the traditional form of the Halakhah antedating the state remain intact in all its details. They are satisfied to have it preserved by a religious sect within the framework of a secular state. This robs the so-called *Kulturkampf* of any real religious significance, and reduces it to a series of petty quarrels over individual rights.

None of this impugns in any way the sincerity and devotion of those Jews who regard their Judaism as a matter of purely personal belief and observance. This is a perfectly legitimate school of thought within Judaism. When it is maintained consistently, this point of view establishes a sharp line of demarcation between religion on the one hand, and social and political programs on the other. There can be no greater logical and moral incoherence, however, than the appearance on the political scene of a religious bloc of parties demanding "a state in accordance with the Torah" but lacking any concrete program for administering that state in accordance with halakhic norms. The result is mere clerical politics.

This sort of attitude can only discredit religion, even in the eyes of religious Jews, particularly the younger generation. It will, of necessity, be regarded as parasitic, in that a sectarian Judaism depends upon the secularity of the state and the non-observance of Halakhah by those who run the state. Let other Jews keep electric current and water supply running on the Sabbath, they seem to say, so long as our group is exempted from that duty. Of course there must be police at work on the Sabbath; let its functions be performed by other Jews. There must be a navy; let nonreligious Jews be sailors. They assent to military service for women; only let their daughters be exempt. In the Knesseth the religious bloc voted in favor of equal status for women in matters of testimony and inheritance; but they made it a condition that these same laws must not apply to the rabbinic courts! They demanded and were granted exemption from military service for Torah students, on the assumption that the army would be maintained by those who do not study Torah! One sector of religious Jewry, which prides itself upon being more exacting in its halakhic observance than others, found a way of enabling several hundred farmers to observe the restrictions of the Sabbatical year without even raising the question about what would happen if that kind of observance were adopted by the entire agricultural community in Israel.[8] But, clearly, a halakhic policy for observing the laws of the Sabbatical year must be feasible for the agricultural community as a whole. If the Jewish religion in the state of Israel is to be saved from a process of spiritual and social decay, certain clear-cut and explicit decisions must be made. The issues cannot be glossed over by verbal parries. A specific and detailed halakhic code for administering the full panoply of state functions is called for. Religious Jewry must clarify these matters first to itself, and then to Jewry as a whole. The result would be a clear picture of how the religious parties would run the state if and when they came to power. Without such clarification, the religious bloc as a contender for office has no right to ask the public for its confidence.

The spokesmen of religious Jewry claim that such a program already exist potentially, but can only be worked out in detail once they are entrusted with the reins of government. This is a sorry jest. It is also dishonest. Equally unworthy is the other excuse one hears from the religious parties: let the state and its organs first prove that they are willing to accept the authority of the Torah, only then shall we answer their questions. The Torah is not an oracle, which answers only those who seek it out. It is a way of life, an eternal challenge to the Jewish people. Let it be set before them; let arguments be advanced on its behalf. Whether or not the majority in the state at this moment accepts it or rejects it, such a program could at least rally the forces of religious Jewry, exert a mighty educational influence, and prepare the ground for the political entrenchment of religious Jewry on its way to attainment of political power.

An arid conservatism, not the means for the preservation of certain values, but an end in itself, will not promote the working out of such a platform. This requires creative initiative on the part of religious community, leading to new halakhic decisions in all those areas of public life which the traditional Halakhah did not handle, because it was not foreseen that they would have to be treated as part of Jewish existence. Today issues of public life must find their place on the halakhic agenda owing to the historic act of our bringing about a national-political renascence before the advent of a messianic redemption. There is no doubt that this will involve certain departures from the pattern of life before Jewish political independence. That pattern was halakhically legitimate and was hallowed by the usage of generations. But it was the reflection of the "needs of the hour." Truth to say, Halakhah in practice is normally the eternal Halakhah as applied to the shifting situation of Jewish existence. In converting forms of life which reflect specific historical conditions into models which must be strictly imitated under all conditions, one is confusing the eternal Torah, "inscribed in black fire against a background of white fire," with one of its transient exemplifications.

No action to change this can be expected from the official religious authorities of our day, for they are psychologically committed to methods which were adequate in the limited world to which Jewry was confined for centuries. Conditions then did not call for new religious legislation. It was enough to rely on analogy and precedent. These methods sufficed for an era in which the framework of social and political life was imposed on the Jews. But our generation has done something unprecedented in Jewish history by creating a Jewish state, and has thus altered one of the fundamental assumptions of the traditional Halakhah. The crucial problems of the present will not yield to rulings in accordance with existing precedents; they call for newly legislated Halakhah. The responsibility for decisive action now returns to the first instance in Jewish religious life; to that body from which the constituted religious authorities derive their power, to the collective body of Jews who believe in the Torah and want to observe it.

Religious Jews ought not to be fainthearted about approaching this problem with only their knowledge and conscience to guide them. In this generation of physical and spiritual confusion in Israel and in the world at large, we have had the audacity to free ourselves politically. We did this with our own resources, without divine intervention, without any intimations that the messianic age is here. Only the Neturei Karta, who reject this act of ours as sacrilegious, have a right to disclaim any responsibility for its consequences. The rest of us, who participated in this audacious venture and who share in the fruits of its success, are under a moral obligation to bear the responsibility for its religious consequences.

In the face of this tremendous responsibility, should the religious public not reconsider its participation in the achievement of political independence, and act to remove the protective confines set up about the life of Torah and tradition in conditions of exile and political subservience? Let me state emphatically that unless we do so, we will be shirking our historic task and ignoring the true religious significance of our national renascence. Liberation, independence, and political autonomy once more confront the religious Jew and the religious Jewish community with the need to perform decisive functions which were forgotten and lost sight of in exile and subjection. The Torah has been extracted from the artificial greenhouse environment in which it was cultivated, in which it was spiritually and psychologically convenient for the Jew to be Torah-observant, because he was exempt from the function of setting up the very framework and basic conditions of his existence in accordance with the Torah.

Whoever believes that the Torah was given to us so that we may shape the life of this world under its direction must accept the responsibility of applying it to society and to public life. Now, at long last, the Jewish religion will be put to the test. Is it to be "Torah of life" in the full sense of the word?

For many centuries the Jew has had to suffer for the sake of the Torah. From now on he faces the challenge to create for the sake of the Torah. Formerly he needed chiefly physical courage, so that he might, if need be, die for the Torah. Henceforward he must find the spiritual courage to live by the Torah.

Privileged is the generation that has been summoned to this, the greatest of all responsibilities.

CHAPTER 16

A Call for the Separation of Religion and State

(1959)

S eparation of religion and state" is a slogan heard from time to time in public debate in Israel. It is not, however, the actual policy of any party or political group. The slogan is raised as the expression of a theoretical position in "secular" circles, but its advocates do not regard it seriously as a political demand to be realized in the present. They do not attempt to clarify its meaning nor do they propose a plan for embodying it in law and government. Their struggle is limited to episodic clashes with religious or pseudo-religious aspects of administrative behavior or legislative action. At the same time, official religious Jewry, its spiritual leaders and political representatives, who rejected the idea of separation and supported the existing relation between state and religion, never accounted for their own position. It is doubtful whether they have ever critically examined it. A struggle over the relation of religion and the state has never really been conducted between the religious and secular in Israel. Out of sheer opportunism, both sides accept the reality of a secular state with a religious façade.

In these pages the demand for separation of religion and state will be presented from a religious viewpoint, from which the present relations between the state and the Torah appear as Hillul Hashem, contempt of the Torah, and a threat to religion.[1] Two prefatory remarks are necessary in order to clarify this position.

First, the religion with which we are concerned is traditional Judaism, embodied in Torah and Mitzvoth, which claims sovereignty over the life of the individual and the life of the community—not a religion which can be satisfied with formal arrangements grafted on to a secular reality.

Second, the state of which we speak is contemporary Israel, a state defined by its manner of coming into being in 1948 and its mode of existence from then onward—not the state as an ideal. In other words, the relation of religion and state is not discussed here as an article of faith. We shall not inquire as to what, in principle, should be the relation between "religion" (in general) and "state" (in general), nor seek to demarcate "the holy," "the secular," the historical, or the metaphysical essence of the Jewish people as the people of the Torah. We are concerned with determining what sort of political-social organization would be in the religious interest in the existing situation.

The state of Israel that came into being in 1948 by the common action, effort, and sacrifices of both religious and secular Jews was an essentially secular state. It has remained essentially secular and will necessarily continue to be such, unless a mighty spiritual and social upheaval occurs among the people living here. The secularity of this state is not incidental but essential. The motivation and incentive for its foundation were not derived from the Torah. Its founders did not act under the guidance of the Torah and its precepts. It is not conducted by the light of the Torah. That "the state of Israel is a state ruled by law and not a state governed by Halakhah" is recognized by all—including the religious—as the principle governing the activity and administration of this state, in which official religious Jewry has participated since its establishment.[2] Whether we are religious or secular, we brought this state about by dint of our common efforts as Jewish patriots, and Jewish patriotism—like all patriotism—is a secular human motive not imbued with sanctity. Holiness consists only in observance of the Torah and its Mitzvoth: "and you shall be holy to your God." We have no right to link the emergence of the state of Israel to the religious concept of messianic redemption, with its idea of religious regeneration of the world or at least of the Jewish people. There is no justification for enveloping this political-historical event in an aura of holiness. Certainly, there is little ground for regarding the mere existence of this state as a religiously significant phenomenon.

Even from the standpoint of religious awareness and faith, this Jewish state is in the same category as the kingdoms of Yarov'am, Ahab,

Menasseh, and Herod were in their time. A person does not and may not sever his connection with a criminal parent, nor may a parent repudiate a son who has gone astray. Likewise, the Jew, including the religious Jew, may not dissociate himself from this state. However, though we fully recognize its legitimacy, it is necessary to confront the secular state and society with the image of a religious society and state, that is of a state in which Torah is the sovereign authority. What is truly illegitimate is the surreptitious introduction, by administrative action, of religious items into the secular reality so as to disguise its essential secularity.

The demand for the separation of religion from the existing secular state derives from the vital religious need to prevent religion from becoming a political tool, a function of the governmental bureaucracy, which "keeps" religion and religious institutions not for religious reasons but as a concession to pressure groups in the interest of ephemeral power-considerations. Religion as an adjunct of a secular authority is the antithesis of true religion. It hinders religious education of the community at large and constricts the religious influence on its way of life. From a religious standpoint there is no greater abomination than an atheistic-clerical regime. At present we have a state—secular in essence and most of its manifestations—which recognizes religious institutions as state agencies, supports them with its funds, and, by administrative means, imposes, not religion, but certain religious provisions chosen arbitrarily by political negotiation. All the while, it emphasizes its rejection of guidance by Torah ("a state ruled by law, not by Halakhah"). We have a rabbinate invested by the state, which receives its appointment, authority, and pay from the secular government and confines itself, therefore, to the functions that this government allots to it. It is a religion whose position in the state parallels that of the police, the health authorities, the postal services, or customs. There is no greater degradation of religion than maintenance of its institutions by a secular state. Nothing restricts its influence or diminishes its persuasiveness more than investing secular functions with a religious aura; adopting sundry religious obligations and proscriptions as glaring exceptions into a system of secular laws; imposing an arbitrary selection of religious regulations on the community while refusing to obligate itself and the community to recognize the authority of religion; in short, making it serve not God but political utility.

This is a distortion of reality, a subversion of truth, both religious and social, and a source of intellectual and spiritual corruption. The secular state and society should be stripped of their false religious veneer. Only then will it become possible to discern whether or not they have any message as a Jewish state and society. Likewise, the Jewish religion should be forced into taking its stand without the shield of an administrative status. Only then will its strength be revealed, and only thus will it become capable of exerting an educational force and influencing the broader public.

Against this argument, religious circles claim that such separation would make the social and perhaps even physical existence of religious Jews within the secular state and society unbearable and compel Jews to forsake their religious way of life. These arguments stem, to some extent, from naïveté, from misunderstanding the implications of separation of religion and state for the conduct and administration of state and society. To some extent they only pretend naïveté and veil vested interests. In effect, such separation would not in the least narrow the possibilities open to religious Jews of living according to their wont. It would even foster the expressions of religious life in the community at large. Let us attempt to gain a realistic view of the consequences of separating religion and state.

The religious institutions will be conducted by the religious community with religious considerations in view; in the interest of religion and not in conformity with the dictates of a secular authority. Officials exercising religious functions will no longer be appointed by governmental authorities not subject to the Torah. Religious projects and institutions will not be administered by government agencies. Religious Jewry will have a rabbinate that is not an "official state rabbinate," an institution which had earned only contempt in Jewish history.[3] This rabbinate will constitute an authentic religious leadership rather than an arm of the secular state. It will be able to speak with the voice of the Torah and the Halakhah on every matter and every public issue in which there is something to be said, not only in the restricted domain allotted it by the secular authority. This would put an end to the intolerable situation in which the rabbinate—as a governmental agency—must refrain from public statements on what is the most urgent religious issue of the day, that of secular and religious education, and be silent when

Jewish children are seduced or forced into abandoning their religion.[4] The change would eliminate the disputes and clashes among religious functionaries of an atheistic government—between a Minister of Religions and a Chief Rabbi—whose squabbles concern not Torah issues or questions of halakhic import but distribution of the petty authority granted them by a secular regime.

Who will maintain the agencies required by the religious community? In the first place, the religious community will do so through its own funding, as was done at all times wherever an organized religious community existed. To be sure, this requires sacrifices. But the religious community has always and everywhere borne this burden as something to be taken for granted, an inseparable aspect of its religious existence. Even the poorest community in a remote village in Yemen or Libya maintained its rabbis, ritual slaughter, synagogues, and cemeteries, without the help of the United Jewish Appeal or an appropriation from the imam or the sultan—and never complained that this was beyond its capacity. Only in the state of Israel, which transformed religion into a function of the secular government, has the religious community been corrupted and become accustomed to financial dependence upon a secular authority. If the situation is reversed, there is no doubt that after a short period of confusion which will follow the separation of religion from the state, the self-respect of the religious community will be restored, and it will once again maintain and support its own agencies as religious institutions. In this respect we can learn from parallel developments in the Gentile world. In France during the nineteenth century, as a result of the Napoleonic Concordat that made the religious institutions functionaries of the state, the Catholic Church and clergy were subject to scorn and contempt. In the twentieth century, after the separation of church and state, when the church and its personnel had to be supported solely by contributions of the believers, its prestige grew and its influence increased.

It is necessary to ascertain whether, from a religious standpoint, the Jewish religious institutions should or may accept financial support from the secular state. This writer believes that religious Jewry should—in the interest of fostering respect for the Torah—refuse to accept such support. Should the religious community, upon due deliberation, decide otherwise, it could be entitled to such support even after the separation of religion and state by virtue of its status as tax-payers who share the burden of the state and its services.

The religious councils will be chosen by all religious Jews who are interested in their activities. They will cease to be affiliated with the Ministry of Religions. The abolition of the Ministry of Religions will free Judaism and religious Jews from a religious anomaly—now passed over in silence by the religious establishment—of supporting institutions of other religions (some of which are actually idolatrous, according to the strict law of the Torah) with the money of Jews.[5] Without a Ministry of Religions, and without state funding of Jewish religious institutions, our democratic state will be free of the obligation to support the institutions of other religions. Members of all religions will maintain their own clergy.

The Sabbath. In the present integration of religion and state, the Sabbath is desecrated by the state. The law recognizes the right of every person to desecrate the Sabbath publicly, for example by driving. The police and courts were called in more than once to protect this right—even when official religious Jewry, with all its parties, participated in the government and shared responsibility for the actions of the police. The prohibition of public transportation on the Sabbath is only a sop to religious Jewry, a face-saving device. The hypocrisy of this arrangement, which degrades religion and reveals the "religious" stand in a ridiculous light, attains its peak in Haifa. Religious Jewry, which is represented in the city council, shares responsibility for operating the bus transportation on Sabbath—in exchange for participating in the coalition governing the city council. Yet it is ready to fight against operating the subway on the Sabbath—presumably because of a political agreement on maintenance of a status quo in religious matters.

The existing law does not recognize the sanctity of the Sabbath. It removes the definition of "rest" from halakhic jurisdiction and vests it in the secular authority or in inter-party agreements. There is no basis for the fear that the state, after religion is separated from it, will make any change in the Sabbath law, which establishes the workers' right of rest and the obligation to close stores and work places on the Sabbath. The extent to which this Sabbath rest will correspond to the religious prescriptions concerning the Sabbath will depend on public opinion and the influence of religious Jewry in public matters. This influence will, in all likelihood, be increased upon separation of religion and state with the growth in prestige and educational effectiveness of religion.

Sabbath and Kashruth in the army. The Sabbath and Kashruth (dietary laws) are observed in the army, but not in consequence of the formal interlocking of religion with the laws of the state; rather, because so very many Jews could not serve in the army were they not assured of the Sabbath rest and kosher food. The state could not draft the entire Jewish population for defense of the state in one unified national army if it did not provide them. It cannot maintain a separate "religious army" alongside the general army.[6] These provisions of the army will not change even after the separation of religion and state. It should be noted that even now the religious prohibitions of desecrating the Sabbath and eating nonkosher food are not enforced in the army, because every soldier is permitted use of one mess-tin for meat and milk. The army only enables every soldier who so desires to rest on the Sabbath and to each kosher food.

Law of marriage and divorce. It is erroneous to argue that the institution of civil marriage by the state will divide the Jewish people into two nations which will not be able to intermarry. Civil marriage will not annul the institution of religious marriage. Whoever so argues overlooks—deliberately or out of ignorance—the hundreds of thousands of religious Jews in Western lands, who conduct their family life according to the Torah in states which recognize civil marriage and divorce (as in England) or even require them (as in Imperial or Weimar Germany). A Torah-observing Jew will continue to marry according to Jewish law and if, unfortunately, the couple divorce, they will do this according to the law of Moses and Israel. Those who rebel against religion will be content with registering their "marriage" or "divorce" in a government office in a form that will be determined by law. Here the two terms are put in quotation marks, because from a halakhic standpoint, no marriage took place. Consequently, upon separation there is no need of divorce. In the absence of halakhically recognized marriage there is no question of *Mamzeruth,* since a child born out of wedlock is not disqualified from marrying.[7] The rabbinical courts do not seem to have dealt seriously and pertinently with the halakhic significance of "civil marriage" for Jewish couples that explicitly refuse marriage according to the Torah. One may question whether such a marriage has any halakhic force.[8] This ruling, which would reduce the incidence of Mamzeruth to a minimum, would be a great improvement over the present situation under the Law of Marriage and Divorce which, given the sexual practices of considerable portions of the community, tends to aggravate the problem of Mamzeruth in Israel. Prohibition of adultery concerns only those involved and can hardly be grounded today in moral or social considerations; moreover, it is a purely religious proscription. Consequently, many sectors of the population where the authority of religious law has been undermined—and they include many very respectable people—do not consider adultery immoral. Hence those who force religious marriage on people who do not recognize its sanctity are violating the proscription of placing a stumbling block before the blind. Men and women are led into a far more serious halakhic transgression than that of living together without religious marriage.

In the face of these realities, the fear of dividing the nation as a result of rescinding the Law of Marriage and Divorce is ridiculous and perhaps insincere. Can a Jewish man and woman marry, if one of them sees himself bound by the laws of family purity, and the other does not accept them? These precepts are much more stringent than the prohibition of cohabitation with an unmarried woman. Furthermore, religious Jewry, more than any other sector of the nation, is committed to the view that the state of Israel is not merely the state of those now living in it but is the Jewish state, that is, the state of all Jews, who are all potential citizens. Did religious Jewry, in its fear of Mamzeruth on the one hand and concern for the unity of the nation on the other, think of the problems that will arise the moment—perhaps not so far away—when masses of Jews from the U.S.S.R. or the United States will stream to Israel? These Jews have conducted their lives for two generations, or even more, in accordance with the legal provisions and social patterns of their countries of residence. It will not prove possible to trace their precise family status. How does religious Jewry think it could assure the unity of the nation in those conditions?

*   *   *

The issue of the separation of religion and state also includes the problem of "who is a Jew"?—a problem which could arise only as a result of confused categories. Transient and changing interests of coalition governments have led them, on one occasion, to an attempt to abrogate the historical-traditional criteria of belonging to the Jewish people, and at other times to abandon this attempt. If the state of Israel were formally and legally recognized as secular, the problem would not arise at all, for a secular state does not determine the "Jewishness" or "non-Jewishness" of its citizens. It recognizes only "citizens" and "non-citizens," and the concept "Jew" would retain its historic-traditional connotation. The (momentary) retreat of the government from its position on this question—a retreat which the religious parties regard as their victory—shows that the status of religion in the state is determined more by the communal consciousness and the pressure of public opinion in Israel and abroad than by the organs of the state. Releasing religion from its integration in the political-secular system is the most effective way to strengthen religious consciousness and its influence on the public.

Religious education. There is no direct link between the status and extent of religious education on the one hand, and the legal position of religion in the state on the other. Such a connection exists necessarily only in the framework of a totalitarian regime. It does not obtain in a liberal polity, in which social reality is not identical with the official political order. Among well-ordered and enlightened states, all of which have compulsory education laws, educational systems differ considerably in uniformity and in degree of involvement of the government in the pedagogic process; compare, for example, England, France, Germany (of Weimar and Bonn), Holland, and the United States, in all of which religious education flourishes. In the United States, where the Constitution and the Supreme Court forbid support of religious education by the state, there is a network of thousands of Catholic elementary and high schools, numbering four million pupils, which are not inferior in level and achievement to the secular public schools of the states and cities. In other countries the policy of every school is determined by the parents' committee, and within the broad framework established by law, the education authority accedes to the parents' preferences. The common feature of all these systems is that the secular state is not in control of religious education and religious education is not one of its functions; it is set up and maintained by the religious community that desires it—whether this be a community with a ramified church organization or one represented by parents of a specific school. The extent of state support of these schools is determined by law. Their main support depends largely on the will of the religious community and the strength of its religious commitment.

In all these matters the state of Israel could emulate the best-governed nations, and, from a Jewish religious standpoint, it is most desirable that it do so. The fear that without governmental backing religious education could not support itself or would be curtailed—the fear of educational independence—reflects the moral failing of the religious community fostered by the dependence of religion on the state. In the past, religious Jews customarily devoted great efforts to educating their children and were prepared to pay the price. A condition for religious revitalization, without which there is no future for religious education in any of its forms, is the revival of initiative and readiness of religious Jews to undertake this burden.

Removal of religious education from control of the secular state and its transfer to the religious community—with or without financial support of the state—will open new prospects for expansion and enable it to reach broader strata of the population. The existing law, which purports to obligate the state to support religious schooling, is in reality a legal arrangement for confining such education within the limits the secular authority is prepared to tolerate, and to localities in which the secular authority is willing to forego its control in favor of the religious population. In return, the religious public refrains from serious struggle for expansion of religious education to include more children. Cases have even been recorded of explicit agreements over percentage quotas of pupils to be allotted to religious and to secular schools. Only by conducting independent religious schooling can Jewish religion appear on the public scene in its full potential, communicate its message in its entirety, and exert the influence of which it is capable.

The separation of religion and state would involve neither withdrawal of religion to a secluded niche nor removal of religious Jewry from the political scene. On the contrary, it would signify the beginning of the great confrontation between Judaism and secularism within Jewry and the Jewish state and initiate a genuine struggle between them over the hearts and minds of the citizens. Religion as an independent force will be the principal opposition to the regime of the secular state, an opposition which can present a clear and unambiguous alternative in all areas of life in the state and society.

CHAPTER 17

After Kibiyeh

(1953–54)

On October 13, 1953, Arab infiltrators from the region of Kibiyeh—an Arab village in Samaria—tossed a hand grenade into a Jewish home in the immigrant village of Yehud. A mother and two of her children were killed in their sleep. This act, which followed a continuous series of murderous attacks in the area, brought about a reprisal by the Israel Defense Force. On October 14, an Israeli force attacked Kibiyeh, which is a considerable distance past the truce line. In this action, more than fifty inhabitants of the village were killed and forty houses were destroyed.

This action caused a storm of protest in the world. Israel's explanation, that the attack was carried out because of the bitterness and wrath in Israel against the crimes of infiltrators from the region, was not accepted by public opinion in the world and the UN Security Council strongly condemned Israel.

Kibiyeh, its causes, implications, and the action itself are part of the great test to which we as a nation are put as a result of national liberation, political independence, and our military power—for we were bearers of a culture which, for many generations, derived certain spiritual benefits from conditions of exile, foreign rule, and political impotence. Our morality and conscience were conditioned by an insulated existence in which we could cultivate values and sensibilities that did not have to be tested in the crucible of reality. In our own eyes, and, to some extent in those of others as well, we appeared to have gained control over one of the terrible drives to which human nature is subject, and to abhor the atrocities to which it impels all human societies—the impulse to communal murder. While congratulating ourselves upon this, we ignored, or attempted to ignore, that in our historical situation such mass-murder was not one of the means at our disposal for self-defense or for the attainment of collective aspirations. From the standpoint of both moral vocation and religious action, exilic existence enabled us to evade the decisive test. Attachment to the *Galuth* (Diaspora) and the opposition of many of the best representatives of Judaism to political redemption within historic reality was, in no small measure, a form of escapism reflecting the unconscious fear of such a test—fear of the loss of religious-moral superiority, which is easy to maintain in the absence of temptation and easy to lose in other circumstances.

However, values are precious to the extent that their realization is difficult and easily frustrated. This is the true religious and moral significance of regaining political independence and the capacity to deploy force. We are now being put to the test. Are we capable not only of suffering for the sake of values we cherish but also of acting in accordance with them? It is easy to suffer physically and materially and even to sacrifice one's life for their sake. This requires only physical courage, which is abundant to a surprising degree in all human communities. It is much more difficult to forego, out of consideration for such values, actions which promote other prized ends—legitimate communal needs and interests. The moral problem becomes acute when two good inclinations clash. The overcoming of an evil inclination by a good one is difficult but not problematic.

It is very easy—and therefore hardly worthwhile—to express moral reservations about acts of violence and slaughter when one bears no responsibility for defending the community in whose cause such acts are perpetrated. Before the establishment of the state, the community included some adherents of "purist morality" who immigrated to Palestine against the wishes of the Arabs and conducted their lives here under the protection of British bayonets and the arms of the Hagganah (Jewish self-defense organization), but considered that the right of other Jews to immigrate depended on the consent of the Arabs. They declared *Aliyah* (immigration) without such consent to be immoral. Yet they did not oppose the creation and operation of the Jewish national-cultural center (the Hebrew University) in Al-Kuds (Jerusalem) against the angry objections of the Arabs, because this institution was dear to them. Nevertheless, they allowed themselves to denounce the institutions of the Yishuv which were responsible for bringing in Jews and settling them on the land, when, in the face of vigorous Arab opposition, they carried out these activities. Even after the establishment of our state, for which we alone are responsible and in which only we have the power to act, some of our intellectuals, pretending to represent Jewish teaching of mercy and charity, addressed themselves to the ruler of another state and petitioned him to pardon spies who had threatened the security of the state.[1] These self-righteous "saints" in Jerusalem failed to appreciate that since they were not responsible for the security of the United States and their actions and reactions had no influence for good or bad, it was easy for them to be the "righteous ones." The president of the United States, however, bore the responsibility for the welfare and security of 180 million fellow Americans, and his choice of justice or mercy could affect their fate; the "righteous ones" were not in this position.

Only the decision of one who is capable of acting and on whom rests the responsibility for acting or refraining from action can pass the genuine test of morality. We, the bearers of a morality which abominates the spilling of innocent blood, face our acid test only now that we have become capable of defending ourselves and responsible for our own security. Defense and security often appear to require the spilling of innocent blood.

This moral problem did not arise in connection with the war we conducted for our liberation and national restoration. True, we used to see war as the "craft of Esau," but it was repulsive only to the extent that it was made into a way of life in the sense of "by thy sword shall you live" (Gen. 27:40). But war, often enough, is one of the manifestations of the social reality, an inseparable part of it so long as messianic redemption has not occurred. We accept war—without enthusiasm or admiration, but also without bitterness or protest—just as we accept many repulsive manifestations of human biological reality. In declaring our will to live as a real historic nation—not a meta-historical and metaphysical one—we took upon ourselves the functions of national life we had shunned when we were not bound by the tasks and concerns of normal national existence. By the logic of history and of moral evaluation, our war of independence was a necessary consequence of our two-thousand year exile. Only one prepared to justify historically, religiously, or morally the continuation of the exilic existence could refuse to take upon himself the moral responsibility for using the sword to restore freedom.

Therefore, in our religious-moral stocktaking, we neither justify the bloodshed of the war (in which our blood was spilled no less than that of our enemies) nor do we apologize for it. The problematic issues concern the *manner* of conducting that war, which goes on to this very day, and what is to be done after this war will be over. It is a difficult and perplexing problem: Once the "craft of Esau" has been granted legitimacy, the distinction between the permissible and the forbidden, between the justified and the blameworthy, is very subtle—it is like that "handbreadth between heaven and hell."[2] We must constantly examine whether we have transgressed and crossed that fine dividing line.

We can, indeed, justify the action of Kibiyeh before "the world." Its spokesmen and leaders admonish us for having adopted the method of "reprisal"—cruel mass punishment of innocent people for the crimes of others in order to prevent their recurrence, a method which has been condemned by the conscience of the world. We could argue that we have not behaved differently than did the Americans, with the tacit agreement of the British, in deploying the atomic bomb: America saw herself in the fourth year of a war she had not initiated, and after the loss of a quarter of a million of her sons, facing the prospect of continued war in the style of Iwo Jima and Okinawa for an unforeseeable period of time. This fear led to the atrocity of Hiroshima, where 100,000 civilians, mostly women and children, were killed in one day to bring about the quick termination of this nightmare. We, too, are now in the sixth year of a war that was forced upon us and continues to inspire constant fear of plunder and murder. No wonder that border settlers and those responsible for their life and security overreacted and reciprocated with cruel slaughter and destruction.

It is therefore possible to justify this action, but let us not try to do so. Let us rather recognize its distressing nature. There is an instructive precedent for Kibiyeh: the story of Shekhem and Dinah.[3] The sons of Jacob did not act as they did out of pure wickedness and malice. They had a decisive justification: "Should one deal with our sister as with a harlot?!" The Torah, which narrates the actions of Simeon and Levi in Shekhem, adds to the description of the atrocity only three words (in the Hebrew text) in which apparently it conveyed the moral judgment of their behavior: "and came upon the city unawares, and slew all the males." "The sons of Jacob came upon the slain, and spoiled the city, *because they had defiled their sister*" (Gen. 34:25, 27). Nevertheless, because of this action, two tribes in Israel were cursed for generations by their father Jacob.[4]

Although there are good reasons and ethical justifications for the Shekhem-Kibiyeh action, there is also an ethical postulate which is not itself a matter of rationalization and which calls forth a curse upon all these justified and valid considerations. The Shekhem operation and the curse of Jacob when he told his children what would befall them in the "end of days" is an example of the frightening problematic ethical reality: there may well be actions which can be vindicated and even justified—and are nevertheless accursed.

Citation of this example from the Torah does not reflect belief in the uniqueness of the "morality of Judaism." It does not imply that the action is forbidden us as Jews. It is intended to indicate that the action is forbidden *per se*. "The morality of Judaism" is a most questionable concept—not only because morality does not admit a modifying attribute and cannot be "Jewish" or "not Jewish." The concept is self-contradictory for anyone who does not deliberately ignore its religious content.

There is, however, a specifically Jewish aspect to the Kibiyeh incident, not as a moral problem but an authentically religious one. We must ask ourselves: what produced this generation of youth, which felt no inhibition or inner compunction in performing the atrocity when given the inner urge and external occasion for retaliation? After all, these young people were not a wild mob but youth raised and nurtured on the values of a Zionist education, upon concepts of the dignity of man and human society. The answer is that the events at Kibiyeh were a consequence of applying the religious category of holiness to social, national, and political values and interests—a usage prevalent in the education of young people as well as in the dissemination of public information. The concept of holiness—the concept of the absolute which is beyond all categories of human thought and evaluation—is transferred to the profane. From a religious standpoint only God is holy, and only His imperative is absolute. All human values and all obligations and undertakings derived from them are profane and have no absolute validity. Country, state, and nation impose pressing obligations and tasks which are sometimes very difficult. They do not, on that account, acquire sanctity. They are always subject to judgment and criticism from a higher standpoint. For the sake of that which is holy—

and perhaps only for its sake—man is capable of acting without any restraint. In our discourse and practice we have uprooted the category of holiness from its authentic location and transferred it to inappropriate objects, thus incurring all the dangers involved in such a distorted use of the concept. This original sin of our education appears already in our Declaration of Independence. Its use of the expression "the Rock of Israel" in the concluding sentence reflects a fraudulent agreement between two sectors of the public, which is to the credit of neither. The secular nation and state adjusted the sense of this term at its convenience, and used it to bribe the religious minority. The latter did not refuse to accept the bribe, even though it recognized the hypocrisy implicit in the use of this sanctified epithet. The "Rock of Israel" invoked by King David and by the prophet Isaiah, and incorporated in the benediction following the reading of Shema in the morning prayer, is not an attribute of Israel but is above Israel and transcends all human values and manifestations, personal and collective. The "Rock of Israel" of the Declaration of Independence is immanent in Israel itself. It is the human essence and might of Israel; Israel as manifested in history. The use of the term from the Bible and the prayerbook to designate values of our consciousness, feeling, and the forces motivating our national-political activity leads people to transfer the connotations of holiness, the absolute normative force associated with this term, to these human values. If the nation and its welfare and the country and its security are holy, and if the sword is the "Rock of Israel"—then Kibiyeh is possible and permissible.

This is the terrible punishment for transgressing the stringent prohibition: "Thou shalt not take the name of the Lord thy God in vain." The transgression may cause our third commonwealth to incur the curse of our father Jacob.

CHAPTER 18

Jewish Identity and Israeli Silence

(1966)

This is a slightly abridged version of an interview by Ehud Ben Ezer in 1966. The last section was added in 1974.

Q. How would you define Zionist ideology?

A. Zionism is not an ideology but a complex of activities undertaken to restore independence to the Jewish nation in its own land. There are only anti-Zionist ideologies, for the purpose of denying that the Jewish nation is a nation. But anyone who thinks that Zionism is a solution to the problem of the Jewish people is mistaken; it is nothing more than the set of those activities on behalf of national sovereignty. It offers no solution to the essential problem of the Jewish people, that of the continuity of its historic spiritual and cultural being. The major problems of the Jewish people are not those of Zionism.

Q. Does that mean that from the Jewish standpoint you are disappointed with Zionism?

A. I am not disappointed with Zionism, because I never imagined that it would provide a solution to the problems of the Jewish people. Moreover, man's essential problems are not political ones. Any solution of social and political problems solves nothing but these problems, not the problems of man's essential being.

Q. Would it be correct to conclude that your main concern is with the Jewish people and the essence of Jewishness?

A. You ask if I am concerned with the Jewish people? I am concerned with nothing else but the Jewish people and Jewish man. The state of Israel interests me only insofar as it functions as the state of the Jewish people, for otherwise it is not only superfluous but is an irritant aggravating international problems. We are an element of unrest, a cause of conflict. In itself it has no positive value, but if it is the state of the Jewish people, I am not troubled by the strains it generates. The Galuth (Diaspora) was brought about by the Jewish people's uniqueness and, were this uniqueness to vanish, the Jewish people would cease to exist. This is as true of the Jews in Israel as it is of those in the Diaspora.

Disillusion with the kibbutz is a good example of disappointments which are not warranted. Who has been disappointed? He for whom the kibbutz has not provided what he foolishly expected—namely, the salvation of man. If anyone expected the kibbutz to bring this about, he is a fool and there is no sense arguing with him. Values can be realized only directly. If someone aspires to the moral improvement of man, he must engage in it directly and not imagine that it will be brought about by creating some projected social order. The kibbutz has fulfilled its objective. It constituted the form of settlement which made possible occupation of the country under conditions of an Arab majority and foreign rule. It makes no difference whether or not this was the conscious and original intention of the kibbutz founders. Obviously, it was not. Neither A. D. Gordon nor Shlomoh Lavi had this aim in mind.[1] Retrospectively, this stands out with surprising clarity, but I admit that at the time, even to me, it was not as obvious as it is today that the only way of gaining control of the country was by quasi-military settlement, like the colonies the Romans founded when the small Roman Republic took over all of Italy. One must not attribute to any social or political movement qualities that do not arise directly from its activities. The question is not what the people with the highest level of self-consciousness thought about their project, but what was in fact done. In the case of the kibbutz it was the creation of a framework that enabled a man to be a farmer and soldier at the same time. Considerable naïveté, bordering on folly, resides in the belief that altering social relationships would alter the nature of man. This notion is absurd.

To return now to your question. The essential problem of the Jewish people is that of Judaism, while Zionism is not a solution of the Jewish problem but rather, as we stated earlier, the means for the restoration of the Jewish people's national sovereignty.

Q. What is your view of the relationship between the state of Israel and the Jewish people?

A. The Jewish people as a whole will not gather in the state of Israel. They can do so only under the influence of a vital Judaism. Judaism has not become dependent on the existence of the state, but only genuine Jewish awareness can bring Jews to return to the land of Israel.

The great majority of the Jewish people today have lost any attachment to the substance of Judaism. Moreover, one may not disregard that the Jewish people today is a remnant. The majority have survived, but the vital center has been destroyed. The major question concerns the extent to which the state of Israel is capable of bringing about a revival of Judaism among Jews. Only thus can they be motivated to return to their own land.

The state has done nothing towards bringing about this revival; it has contributed nothing to Judaism. I am far from entertaining the naïve idea that the state will provide the answer to the problem of Judaism. On the other hand, it is obvious that the state should be the arena in which the struggle for Judaism takes place. It seems to me that this is the only possibility at present for bringing about a Jewish reawakening in the Diaspora. Unfortunately, a true struggle for Judaism is not taking place in the state of Israel. The state of Israel is a governmental and administrative apparatus that is devoid of all content.

Q. Isn't this true of every state?

A. An ordinary State is identified with the nation that resides in its territory. This is not true of the state of Israel if it is viewed as the state of the Jewish People. To consider the state as an entity in its own right, and its problems of survival and system of administrative and political relationships as intrinsically valuable, is of the essence of Canaanism.[2] Whether or not people use this term explicitly is immaterial. All the individuals and public bodies that share in governing the state will emphatically reject any association with Canaanism; the majority, quite sincerely. This does not alter the fact that the social reality before their eyes is not the Jewish people as represented by three thousand years of history but the territorial administrative framework we have erected in the past generation. I myself have no interest in this framework as such, and consider the idea that it possesses intrinsic value a clear-cut expression of chauvinism that is partly naïve, partly brutal, or to use a stronger term—an expression of fascistic mentality.

Q. Isn't there a danger that even the objective interests, which are of the Jewish essence of the state, will also lead to extreme manifestations of the kind you mentioned?

A. The question is, what do I want as a Jew, not what are the Jewish people's "objective" interests. There are no objective interests, because an interest is nothing other than what an interested party wants. We waged a war, we shed blood, we drove tens of thousands of refugees out of the country. None of these things is cause for rejoicing. But it was the war of the Jewish people. I know, this is no justification—no non-Jew will see it as such. But for a Jew it is a justification.

Q. The existence of this justification does not alter the feeling of siege in which we live and the heavy price we are paying, psychologically and morally, for our political situation.

A. A feeling of siege? On the contrary, it seems to me there is a general feeling of well-being, of self-satisfaction. And even those who see the danger are being corrupted by the comfort of the present situation into indifference to the need for changing things, even if they do understand that we are heading for catastrophe. The situation really is catastrophic, but, all the same, it is possible to derive a great many temporary gratifications from it, so that even those who understand its perils lack the motivation to do anything about it.

Consider the recent election campaign. Finance Minister Pinhas Sapir proclaimed that in 1969 the gap in our balance of payments would reach 800 million dollars. What is implied by the existence of such a gap? To my mind it is an index of the parasitic nature of the economy and its living standard, which are maintained only by foreign support. Who took any interest in the fact that the gap, which is now somewhere between four and five hundred million dollars, would double within the next four years? Moreover, recognition of this shocking fact, which reflects the corruption of the nation, does not prevent Mr. Sapir from continuing to be one of the pillars of the administration responsible for this state of affairs.

Consider an example from a different area. Five years ago Yig'al Allon stated publicly that the launching of the Israeli rocket Shavit 2 was damaging to the interests of the state and only in the interest of a certain party's election propaganda. This did not prevent him subsequently from joining a cabinet consisting of the very people who, in his opinion, had been ready to sacrifice national security for partisan interest. No less symptomatic is that these people did not refrain from bringing into their cabinet a man who had levelled such accusations against them.

Q. Let us go back to the basic question: will an essential Jewishness, a "Jewish content" of the state insure us against these dangers?

A. Jewish content insures Jewish content and nothing else. Just as solving a constitutional problem will not of itself solve any spiritual or moral problem, solving a spiritual or moral problem will not solve a strategic problem nor will the answer to a strategic need solve any economic problem. Only *charlatans* think there is an answer to a given problem that will resolve all other ones. This is the great psychological error of Marxism, for example. The notion that the solution of a social problem can resolve all human conflicts is a grave psychological error.

Q. Was not one of the tenets of the Zionist outlook and an integral part of its mythology, the belief that the establishment of a just, modern society in the land of Israel will bring us nearer to the Arabs, a "psychological error" of this sort?

A. Not everyone believed it. Weizmann and Brandeis certainly did not;[3] perhaps A. D. Gordon did believe in it—but that only goes to indicate the limitations of his intellectual acumen. One might say that, in general, the realization of any value is the source of new conflicts and tensions.

Q. In other words, Zionism has not solved the problem of assuring the Jewish people's survival?

A. There is no assurance of survival in the world. Perhaps there is assurance for the Chinese people, because it is almost impossible to wipe them out. But do the Poles have any assurance? A generation ago no one imagined it was possible to destroy a nation. But in a third world war—who knows? Perhaps in another generation, in the southern part of Africa—South Africa and the new Rhodesia—a "final solution" of the white problem will be effected, the physical destruction of men, women, and children in the way Hitler understood it. And, on the other hand, perhaps the white Afrikaaners will strike first, while they still have an overwhelming preponderance of power, and destroy the African population, just as the Spaniards destroyed the Indian population in the Antilles. There is no assurance today, therefore the entire problem is a theoretical one. Zionism's demand for a guarantee of security arises from the nineteenth-century outlook which considered security one of the normal characteristics of human life. But in our day we can see—even on the level of science fiction—that the human race feels its life to be hanging by a thread. Hence trends and aspirations today are not measured by the criterion of better or worse security. Perhaps life for a Jew in the state of Israel is more dangerous than in Brooklyn or New York, but I want to be a Jew in Israel and not in Brooklyn. Therefore, for me, the issue of security is irrelevant and cannot serve as a criterion.

Q. What do you think the attitude of Zionism was toward the Arab question from the outset?

A. One can say that Zionism harbored an almost mythological illusion. Herzl and even Jabotinsky and, needless to add, the creators of Socialist Zionism had the impression that the interest of the Jewish people and the Arab people could coalesce. And if this seems absurd today, it is not because we are wiser than the first generation of Zionists but because they, for obvious psychological reasons, did not want to see the truth and did not realize they were deluding themselves and their followers. The Jewish-Arab conflict was not brought about by incorrect tactics or even an incorrect policy; it is an expression of the essence of the Jewish people's historic tragedy. The fact is that the country which is our homeland became the homeland of another people; and neither side can nor will it be able—nor from its standpoint does it even have the right—to renounce its claim. It is not the problem of the Arab refugees that stands between us and them; it is that the state of Israel's very existence prejudices the historic estate of the Arab nation. There are nations that live in permanent conflict with their neighbors, and Israel may have to live generation upon generation in a permanent conflict. On the other hand, perhaps common interests will develop which will shift the essential historical contradiction aside. Perhaps in the mid-fifties—from 1954 to 1956—there was such a moment, and we deliberately let it slip by. Not everything is up to us, and solving the moral problem will not solve the political one, but, obviously, anything like the Kafr Kasm incident, aggravates matters which are difficult in any case.[4]

Here I must draw some distinctions. It may be that even an ideal government would not resolve the conflict or bring about peace. But I have no doubt that everything the present regime does runs counter to a peaceful resolution. It is obvious that the whole policy of the state of Israel, both internally and externally in keeping with the political interests of its leaders, has resulted only in an exacerbation of the situation.

The idea that making concessions to the Arab minority will endear us to them is an illusion. There is no reason why they should not be a fifth column in the state. Yet, all the same, it is obvious that the Military Government is merely a constant source of provocation.[5] It was not designed for the security of the State but for enforced dependence of the Arab citizens on the favors of the party in power.

This situation can best be described by way of a medical analogy. If a person has a bodily defect that cannot be remedied he has to live with it. It makes life difficult, but there is no alternative. The Arab minority in Israel, by the logic of its situation, has been and will be antagonistic to the state; it is a basic aspect

of our political situation. Like the water shortage, there is no
way to evade it. We cannot choose another country where water
is abundant. It is the same with regard to the twelve percent of
our citizens from whom we cannot expect unconditional loyalty
to the state.

The danger will increase if, after a generation, the twelve percent become twenty percent, and in two generations much more.
This will not be the result of the Jewish-Arab relationship, but
the consequence of the way of life that the Jew in our land has
adopted, one that is turning us into one of the biologically decadent islands of humanity. I refer to our low birthrate. Today,
throughout the world, there is a high rate of natural increase but
there are also islands of humanity which, biologically speaking,
are decadent, that is, have a low birth rate. The Jews of Israel are
one such island and within three generations the Arab minority
may become the majority in Israel.

Q. How do you picture Israel as a state whose chief concern would
be the question of Jewish identity?

A. I do not wish to suggest that the state give one answer or
another. My contention is that its entire justification (not from
the moral or political standpoint) would arise from its becoming
a framework within which the struggle over Jewish identity took
place. This would awaken something in the consciousness of
Jews throughout the world who have an interest in their Jewishness. My protest is aimed at every group in our midst, the
"right" and the "left," the "religious" and the "secular." Instead
of a struggle over religion, there is an agreement on all sides that
there shall be no such struggle—just as there is no struggle over
any other matter of consequence. We maintain a secular state
that is publicly thought to be religious and is run by a clerical-
atheistic coalition. If someone took the trouble to read all the
party platforms published before the last elections, he would
have seen that, except for the names, he would have no way of
knowing which party is which. A similar fluidity follows the
elections. All forms of coalitions are possible. There is no basic
reason for any party not to enter a coalition with any other, so
long as an agreement is reached regarding the distribution of
power.

Q. If so, what struggle is desirable?

A. There is a profound contradiction between the concept of Judaism derived from its historic being and the Canaanite conception. As an example, let us take the case of the abduction of Yossele Schuchmacher.[6] The law and the courts of the state, in accordance with the concept of justice prevailing in our society, accept the elementary right of the individual to educate his children as he pleases. From the standpoint of Judaism, however, parents have no right to determine what education their children shall receive. They must train them to the Torah and the observance of Mitzvoth. In the historical tradition of Judaism, the Jewish community of Mainz, Germany, at the time of the Crusades, is considered holy because parents slaughtered their children to prevent their forced apostasy. According to all the concepts prevailing in the present society of the state of Israel, this was a criminal and insane act. These two viewpoints cannot be bridged. If the debate of religion and state were about this, and if there were a religious Jewry in opposition to the entire regime (and not to a certain chance coalition)—it would give the state content, in the form of a struggle between the values of the world of Torah and Mitzvoth and the values of the Declaration of the Rights of Man and of the Citizen.

Not all of the Jewish people in exile have lost the desire to keep the Jewish tradition, but many have and are lost to Judaism, especially in the small Jewish communities that will disappear by intermarriage within one generation. But a large segment of the Jewish population still wishes for some specific Jewish content that makes demands upon them. A Jewish state *per se,* as a value in its own right, does not interest them because today the issue does not interest the modern man in the Western world. It interests the Zambesians and Tanganyikans. This is not to discredit the African peoples. They are now in their nationalist phase. But it does not interest the educated Frenchman or Dutchman or the like. The latter have readily surrendered their empires and are no longer moved by the desire that a large part of the world be printed on the map in the color of their state. The Jewish people in the West has become a nation of intellectuals whom nationalism does not excite. By its very nature nationalism cannot interest the intelligentsia in the West to which the majority of our people belong.

Not so long ago I talked with a group of young Jewish intellectuals from France and discovered how remote they were from every political and philosophical trend which seems important here in Israel, and how remote the issues that are important in their eyes are from our public awareness. The young Jewish intellectual is not excited by the fact that our ambassador is received in state ceremony by President de Gaulle. He will not consider the flag of the state of Israel a symbol of that which he is seeking, his Jewish identity. If we say to him that here we are creating an equitable social order (which is not true), this avowed accomplishment does not interest him either, because this is something that was and is being done by the Fourth and Fifth French republics, and the Labour government in England, and there is nothing specifically Jewish in it. But if he has any dim feeling that he belongs or wants to belong to the Jewish people, then we must show him that belonging to the Jewish people involves engagement in struggles over matters that are specifically Jewish and that are not part of the reality of the non-Jewish world. I am not maintaining that observance of Torah and Mitzvoth is the exclusive expression of Jewishness today. I am advocating a social and political condition in which the struggle over specific Jewish matters is a real struggle.

Q. How do you view the position of the Jewish intellectual in Israel? Can he maintain the position of a "stranger," an outsider? Does he have the capacity to develop a Jewish content that will present a challenge to the educated Jew in the Diaspora?

A. The Kafr Kasm incident could have happened anywhere in the world. Bloodshed has become a common occurrence today. But the shocking thing is that our public passed the matter over and those responsible for it have all remained in their posts. In any well-run state the Minister of Defense would have resigned immediately, and so would the Chief of Staff and the lower echelons who shared responsibility. The resignation would have been accepted by the entire nation as appropriate, for the simple reason that the action occurred at a time when they were in command. Yet here the public did not demand this. Our intelligentsia shows more signs of cravenness than its counterparts do in other countries. Stalin was able to rule only by executing and imprisoning millions of people; only thus could he silence the Russian intellectuals. Here all that is needed to silence a writer, professor, or member of an academy is the threat that he will not receive an invitation to lunch with the president or will fail to receive some other sign of honor.

Q. From the political and practical point of view, what do you think are the chances of the state of Israel becoming a Jewish state in essence and content?

A. This seems to be precluded by the parasitic quality of our dependence on the financial support of Jews outside Israel. For its vital requirements, every state today obtains support—assistance in development of agriculture and industry, and even military assistance. But we receive support to maintain a standard of living by virtue of which the regime can enjoy popular support. Our leading economists hold that the flow of free money inhibits the development of a healthy economy. To a layman like me this seems plausible. Free money distorts the normal process of development, to say nothing of additional undesirable phenomena which it entails, such as an ever increasing gap between the First and Second Israel.[7] Nor is the negative influence limited to internal effects. It is also distorting our entire relationship with the Jewish people in the Diaspora. The course we are following is not one that fosters the feeling of belonging to one people but divides us into givers and receivers of doles, which, more than anything else, deepens the chasm between us. It is the diametrical opposite of the feeling that we share a common fate.

Instead of inciting the Jewish youngster in the Diaspora to rebel against his parents, instead of arousing a critical attitude toward them and toward himself and enlivening the implicit, though barely conscious, conflict over their Jewish identity, we come to his parents appealing for funds, which become a surrogate for genuine participation in the life of Israel. And so, instead of a movement of rebellion in the interest of a renewal of Jewish life, Zionism, and with it the state of Israel, have become a tranquilizer relieving Jews of personal engagement with the problems of Jewish existence.

Let me give a specific example of how a state of Israel oriented to the needs of the Jewish people should, in my opinion, act, an example which would put the matter in sharp focus. From the outset, we should never have joined the United Nations. Switzerland, for example, has not joined because of a historic political tradition of neutrality, which is embodied in its constitution and which prevents it from participating in any proceedings which are tantamount to adopting a stand in international disputes or supporting a given state or bloc against another. This position has gained the esteem of the entire world, as expressive of Switzerland's unique historic and political experience. It is not accused on that account of isolationism or of apathy. Now if the state of Israel had a true "Jewish consciousness"—if it considered itself as representing the Jewish people and its unique historic destiny, and if it proclaimed to itself and to the entire world that, in accordance with this historic national uniqueness, it was responsible not only to its inhabitants but for the fate of Jews the world over, even those who did not recognize it as representing them—it would have announced as soon as it was created that it could not join the United Nations lest it be compelled on some occasions to vote in a way that might jeopardize Jews in some other country. Such a position would have strengthened the awareness of Jewish singularity among Jews throughout the world, and would also have been accepted with understanding and respect by the Gentile world, which at the time of the state's establishment clearly felt the uniqueness of the event. As a member of the United Nations, whether we like it or not, we are a satellite of the West. Were we neutral, it might have softened the attitude of the Soviet Union toward us and even toward its own Jews. Under such conditions, it might have been easier to achieve a rapprochement with the Arab world. All these opportunities have been squandered because of our insistence that the state be like any other, rather than the center of the historic Jewish people.

A glaring instance of this severance from Jewish history and the lack of consideration for the significance of the state of Israel in the continuum of that history is our relationship with Germany. If our leaders had had the slightest feeling for Jewish his-

tory or any concern for the shaping of Jewish national consciousness in the future, no consideration of present profit
would have brought them to accept a harlot's gift from Germany
and to establish normal diplomatic relations with it in this generation, thus exonerating it before humanity and history.

Q. Your point of departure is the religious one. But there are religious circles in Israel that consider the Six Days war, the conquest of the Western Wall, Old Jerusalem, and the other places
holy to Judaism, as the first act of our redemption. They tend to
regard the Jewish religion in a messianic light, to sanctify military power and to attach a religious value to the greater Israel
and the integrity of the homeland—in other words to Jewish
dominion over all the territories conquered in the last war.

A. This is latter-day Sabbateanism, a modern incarnation of false
prophecy, a prostitution of the Jewish religion in the interest of
chauvinism and lust for power.

Q. What do you think of the Knesseth's resolution of "who is a
Jew" issue—a resolution that is largely based on Jewish religious
law?

A. Who is a Jew? The entire issue is absolutely irrelevant. The state
of Israel does not represent Judaism and can make no decision
about Judaism. No state past, present, or future has, or will,
represent Judaism.

Therefore the Knesseth's decision is relevant only as regards
the state, not as regards Judaism. As regards Judaism, all that is
relevant is that a person who from the standpoint of the fundamental concepts and legal provisions of Judaism is a violator of
the covenant, a willful apostate, and an infidel is nonetheless
entitled to be an officer in the Israel Defence Forces and to command Jewish soldiers. And this right of his is unassailable, given
the nature of this state as agreed to by both the religious and the
irreligious. My Jewishness has nothing to do with the definition
in the law of the state of Israel. Therefore I do not care who is
or is not registered as a Jew in the lists of the state. There is no
copyright over the word "Jew" and anyone who wants to use it
can do so at will. The essential meaning of the word is known
to me and to those who share my outlook and opinion, and it
remains unaffected by the laws and regulations of the state. If

the Knesseth tomorrow should decide by a majority of sixty-one to fifty-nine that anyone who smears green paint on his nose is a Jew, it will be a law of the state. But for me it is not relevant. Anyone who accepts democracy must recognize the possibility that a piece of folly may be enacted by a majority vote.

Q. In your opinion what is the ideal, or utopian, image of the state of Israel? Would you be in favor of a halakhic state?

A. I am not able to answer this question. It is not I who establishes facts. The majority of the Jewish people think along lines that are completely different from mine. It is a hypothetical question and cannot be answered. There never has been and never will be a halakhic state. The struggle between religion and the secular nature of the state is eternal.

CHAPTER 19

The Jew in His Community, on His Land, and in the World

(1968)

This chapter consists of discussion at a symposium on "Judaism and Jewishness" at the Sixth Annual American-Israeli Dialogue held in 1968.

George Steiner opened this discussion with a description of Judaism and the Jewish person of our times. As an Anglo-American Jewish intellectual, he is deeply rooted in the social and intellectual world of the enlightened West, involved in its problems and dilemmas, and at the same time aware of belonging to the Jewish community, which, because of its "Judaism," has retained its separate identity in that world. Steiner regards the essence of Judaism as consisting in the vanguard position which Jews occupy in the struggle for social, moral, and intellectual progress. In this sense, he recognizes the existence of a Jewish nation and identifies with it.

In effect, George Steiner envisages the subject of this conference as a problem of his personal status as a Jew. He defines Jewish nationality in terms of a universalistic human role, associated with a culture and a set of values usually referred to as "humanism." In other words, Steiner characterizes the Jewish nation in terms of its relation to the non-Jewish world, which is his own environment. He does not acknowledge his own Jewishness. He does not recognize any content which is specific to Judaism in itself. Perhaps he deliberately ignores them. All the values which Steiner presents as constituting the essence of Judaism are identical with the values of the non-Jewish world, more precisely, the values which characterize movements and trends of which he approves.

One can extract from the history of Judaism and of the Jewish people various and even contradictory ideas, aspirations, and tendencies. Any such selection is arbitrary. Objective references to "Judaism" or "Jewish values" can be ascribed only on the basis of the realities of Jewish life over 100 generations. This empirico-historical Judaism was neither a set of specific ideas nor a hotchpotch of differing conceptions and values, but a distinct way of life determined by the Torah and its Mitzvoth as crystallized in the Halakhah. Jews like George Steiner, who do not assume the burden of this way of life and even reject it outright, have to face the question: what reason or justification is there for their demonstrated attachment to the Jewish people if this tie is not meaningful? It would seem that Steiner, the humanistic cosmopolite and extreme opponent of nationalism, perceives his belonging to the Jewish people in a purely formal nationalistic sense. What an ironic paradox!

What was the character of the empirical-historic life of Judaism? We have already stated that it consisted of a way of life embodying the Torah and its prescriptions. This does not mean that Jews did not participate in what went on outside the world of Torah. However, their achievement in the outside world cannot be considered specifically Jewish. They were agents in various domains of culture who happened to have been born Jews.

Thus it was most surprising to hear some speakers refer to Einstein and Freud as the great gifts of Judaism to the world. Einstein, a German physicist, belongs by birth to the Jewish people, and it is true that he regarded himself as a Jew. There is nothing in his work, however, that derives from a specifically Jewish source. It has no bearing either on the character or the future of the Jews or of Judaism. One may say of Einstein that he is the gift of the non-Jewish world to the Jewish people. Helmholtz and Mach founded the body of thought upon which Einstein built his theories; Poincaré was his mentor in mathematics; Fitzgerald and Lorentz were his predecessors in physics—yet Jews take pride in having produced Einstein. If we think of Einstein in a Jewish context, we owe the non-Jewish world our gratitude for his achievement. As for Freud, who gave the world a much publicized mythology, his work, too, in no way derives from Judaism and had no connection with Judaism.

Jewish creativity exists only in connection with Torah and Mitzvoth:

in the realm of praxis, a halakhic way of life; in the cultural sphere, religious thought in all its forms, Aggadah, religious poetry, philosophy, and Mussar. What is called Jewish philosophy is essentially a theology intended to establish rational grounds for observance of the Torah. The contribution of Jews, among them first-class intellects, outside the sphere of thought associated with Torah does not belong to the philosophy of Judaism. It did not spring from the soil of Judaism but from that of European philosophy, the context within which their thought developed. The same must be said with special emphasis regarding ethics, as against those who would secularize Judaism and reduce it to a "morality." Judaism as embodied in Torah and its precepts is a religion, not a moral code. In a deep sense, religion and ethics are antagonistic, and a religious personality cannot be identical with an ethical personality. This radical severance of the two, which many find outrageous, is grounded in the following consideration: moral descriptions are not descriptions of mere acts, which in themselves are morally indifferent. In the example of a man's firing a gun at another person, the act may be variously termed "murder," "self-defense," "heroism," or "defense of the homeland." Thus it is not the act which is moral or immoral, but its purpose and intent. Moral judgment deals with proper will and intention, rather than with acts divorced from their motivation.

In Western thought two great conceptions characterize the free moral agent: the Socratic view that man acts as a moral agent when his action is determined by knowledge of truth and reality, and the Kantian contention that only an action performed for the sake of one's duty is moral. Kant insisted that mere compliance with the morally demanded did not constitute morality. Religious praxis, in Judaism, invokes an entirely different motivation: performing the Mitzvoth of God and being holy to Him. Those who pray daily recite from the Shema, "and that you seek not after your own heart"—the negation of Kant. What follows, "and your own eyes," is a negation of Socrates. The reason is immediately provided: "For I am the Lord your God." To the extent that man is conscious of his position before God, he is not a free moral being. Judaism is not an ethic, and it is no coincidence that the great ethical thinkers were all atheists—Buddha in his world, Kant in ours.

I am not contending that Jews do not act as moral agents or could not legitimately contribute to ethical thought, but rather that their ethical ideas did not flow from specifically Jewish sources. Just as some matters are ethically indifferent or neutral, so some issues are religiously neutral but demand ethical judgment. Ethnic labels do not describe ethical evaluation, and in authentic Jewish sources there is no idea that Jews are singular because of their ethical values or their striving for reform, human advancement, and redemption—as though these values did not exist in the non-Jewish world. Jewish values are expressed in the Sabbath, Kashruth, family purity, study of the Torah. In these matters Jews were distinguished from the Gentiles, as were the Gentiles from them. This is what kept the Jew from assimilating, rather than specifically Jewish ideas of an ethical, social, humanistic, or philosophical nature.

In empirical Judaism there is no ground on which to base any values which lie beyond the world of the Mitzvoth. They determine the Jewish specificity. This fact cannot, in its turn, be a determinant of any man's evaluation. One individual might identify with it whereas another, precisely because of this, will turn his back on Judaism. But history cannot be revised. Only in the Soviet Union do they have the ability to revise history.

Some people do not accept the tradition of empirically historical Judaism but nonetheless wish to be Jews. We appreciate that Jews for whom the content of the Jewish experience has lost meaning persist in the wish to belong to the people of Israel, even to be concerned with its survival. Their Judaism can subsist only as a species of nationalism. This opens the great dilemma, which I would like briefly to consider again from two angles: first, from the axiological point of view; second, in its pragmatic aspect.

In terms of values, I am familiar with two basic conceptions of man's essential nature. Both are legitimate, though they differ greatly from each other. One is the theocentric view embodied by the Judaism of Torah, as expressed in the opening paragraph of the *Shulhan Arukh*: "Gird up strength like a lion to rise in the morning for the service of your Creator." Not, mind you, to serve man, reform society, redeem humanity, but to serve God. This is the entire meaning of Judaism of Torah and Mitzvoth. It is not mere chance that the supreme symbol of faith in Judaism, is the sacrifice of Isaac: "Take your son, your favored one, whom you love, and offer him there as a burnt offering . . . So early next morning Abraham saddled his ass . . . and took the firestone and the knife and his son Isaac. And the two of them walked on together." Because of this deed, for this alone, it was said that Abraham was a God-fearing man; that is to say, he suspended all human values for the sake of the service of God.

A second axiological conception is the anthropocentric one: the view of man as pivotal. In effect this is a view of man as God, and this is Kant's great idea—man as an end in himself. It is the ultimate logical consequence of atheism. Both conceptions are legitimate; the theocentric conception represented by Judaism of Torah, and the anthropocentric concept embodied in its highest form in the philosophy of Kant, and, less authentically, in Christianity.

But there is also a third conception, one that is vicious and despicable. In it man is judged from the standpoint of a deified collective, not in respect of his position before God or of his intrinsic worth. This is the ethnocentric view, which regards as central a particular human collective—a people or a race—rather than God or man. This idea has generated much evil and has been the source of great calamities. I am afraid that those who honestly cling to their relationship to the historic chain of the Jewish people, who hope it will be continued and look upon themselves as a link in this chain even though they have become alienated from the theocentric core of Judaism, unwittingly assume the ethnocentric position.

At this conference, strangely enough, the ethnocentric attitude was voiced by representatives of the official national religious establishment. From their statements it would appear that they have deified the nation, adopted patriotism as their faith, and made the state their religion. Their concern is not with the Jewish people as (potentially or in actuality) the People of the Torah, but with the Torah as serving the interests of the nation and the state.

From this perspective we can consider the dilemma of the state of Israel, a state which certainly does not embody Judaism. But can there be a state which embodies Judaism? I would like to offer a negative answer. I do not accept the foolish notion that the Torah reflects the genius of the Jewish people. If one rejects the folly of the Torah as the creation of the genius of the Jewish people and sees it instead as divine, one must appreciate that the Torah cannot be fulfilled. A divine Torah cannot be fulfilled by man. It requires a desperate struggle for its fulfillment, a struggle which constitutes a perennial task. If anything may be considered realization of the Torah, it is precisely this struggle.

Clearly, there can never be a state governed by the Torah. Such a state would be engaged in a constant struggle to fulfill it, and most likely without success. Still, the struggle would have to be waged, and this very effort would stamp the state with a religious character. Obviously, this picture does not fit the state of Israel. The state is not a religious entity; no reasonable person would challenge the fact that the state of Yarov'am was the kingdom of Israel. The prophet Elijah did not contest the fact that the kingdom of Ahab and Jezebel was the kingdom of Israel and that Ahab was the king of Israel; indeed, it was for this reason that Elijah denounced him. If he had been a foreign king there would have been no reason to oppose him. The state of Israel remains the state of Israel, but it is not identical with Judaism. Judaism cannot be reconstructed on the basis of this state without ceasing to be a religion.

The lecture which opened our discussion was entitled "The Function of Religion." The very title must arouse indignation. A religion which has a function, which serves as a means to some other end, is not religion. From the standpoint of Jewish faith, religion, that is to say, the service of God, is itself the ultimate end "and an ultimate end serves no further end" (Maimonides). If the service of God is not recognized as the human *telos*, religion is meaningless. It does not ground secular-humanistic values and, as far as national political interests are concerned, it is a bothersome hindrance. If one may talk of the function of religion in the political sphere, it is precisely in terms of its power to check the influence of political values and to restrain patriotism and nationalistic enthusiasm. Religion forbids regard for state and nation as absolute values.

If religion has a function, it is to place man's limited values in a true perspective. The state has no value; it is only an instrument serving man and his goals. I recognize that the state is a necessary framework for the realization of particular human goals. But man owes nothing to the instrument, the tool with which he works. To conceive of the state otherwise is to transgress the commandment, "thou shalt not take the name of God in vain," for the state is not sacred. I take exception to the claim that one cannot be completely Jewish outside the state of

Israel. It is a brute fact that the major portion of Jewish history has taken place in the absence of a Jewish state. I might add that it is possible to have a very highly refined Judaism outside of Israel. Still, I am a Zionist; which is to say that I do not wish to live a Jewish life within the framework of the Gentile world, subjected to its rule. I have had my fill of this rule. But important as the existence of the state is for me, I do not attribute to it any elements of sanctity and do not regard religion as functioning in its behalf, any more than I regard it as performing a function in behalf of the Jewish people.

The author of the *Shulhan Arukh* had good reason for his opening clause: "Gird up strength like a lion to rise in the morning for the service of your Creator." This act requires a maximal effort. It is not natural for Jews to observe the Torah. The opposite is true. The claim that the unique history of the Jewish people is due to "a religious factor indigenous to the soul of the Jewish nation" makes no sense. Jewish history has involved a perpetual struggle between Judaism and the Jewish people who resist it. Those to whom the divine presence (Shekhinah) was revealed, those who were at Mount Sinai, were the very ones who made the golden calf! The forty-eight prophets and seven prophetesses, as tradition counts them, through whom the Shekhinah addressed the people, did not reform a single soul. In the history of humanity there has been no failure as massive as that of Israel's prophets. Yet scores of generations of Jews, not single individuals but masses, were perfect in their faith and devoted their lives to Torah. Generations that saw no revelation of the divine presence, no prophets, and no miracles, were still educated and educated themselves to Torah and Mitzvoth.

Again and again, Jewish history demonstrates the insignificance of miracles from a religious point of view. Jews did not keep their faith because of the miracles they experienced. It was their faith which led them to interpret their historic experience as miraculous. Reference to the miracle of the Six Day war is idle prattle. The miracle is that we have built a modern army, whereas Arab societies are still not capable of doing so. One cannot extract a pacifist stand from the sources of Judaism, which recognize war as an element in human existence. But it is no less significant that these sources lack admiration for military prowess and make no religious assessment of victory and conquest. A wicked king is described as triumphant in his wars, and a righteous king lost his life in battle and dragged the entire nation to defeat. God is not revealed in history; He is not the gendarme of humanity. History can hardly be considered to manifest "the finger of God." "The earth is God's, and the fullness thereof," and this includes the entire course of history; its "normal" course no less than those events which appear extraordinary. In their religious significance, all events are equal. In other words, all are, religiously speaking, indifferent. Only those deeds which are performed for the sake of the worship of God are religiously meaningful. The world follows its regular course, and in that world it is incumbent upon man to serve God.

What ties the Jews who continue to accept the yoke of Torah and Mitzvoth with those who reject it? I do not refer to those who seem to have lost all sense of belonging to the Jewish people. Although I fear the majority of Jews belong in this category, they need not be considered in the present context. There still remain millions of Jews who, notwithstanding their deep ideological differences, are united by such a sense of belonging to the Jewish people and by their will to continue as a people and to maintain their link to it. Within this group, there is an existential abyss separating those who observe the Torah from those who have rejected its yoke. From the point of view of the Halakhah, there is actually no problem. The Halakhah does not define a Jew in terms of his conduct or beliefs. The son of a Jewish mother, or one who has converted to Judaism according to the prescribed procedures, is a Jew. If he is delinquent in fulfilling his halakhic obligation, he is a transgressor. He does not cease thereby to be a Jew. From this standpoint, the Jewish people are one. But what is the reality, in terms of the possibility of a common life? We in the state of Israel, are more aware of this problem than others. A Jew who observes the commandments cannot eat at the same table with one who does not. Sabbath observance is an obstacle to joint enterprise in business, in the trades, and, as I myself can attest, even in scientific research. Even marriage between observant and nonobservant is problematic, because of the laws of family purity. In effect, there is little contact between the observant Jews and those who reject the commandments. The situation is bitter. It is not new. From time immemorial, these factors have divided the people.

*   *   *

I must comment on the sacred cow known as national unity. I am not aware, in Jewish history or in any other history, of a worthwhile achievement of ethical, social, intellectual, or religious character, which was attained thanks to national unity. Whatever is of worth was achieved through difficult struggles, sometimes even bloody civil wars. It is clear that values are not a basis for unity. It is possible to unite on the basis of interests, and, even then, only the most commonplace interests lay the grounds of unity. Struggle among the people is a normal and healthy phenomenon. The very thing fools fear is what we desperately need, what in European political jargon is called *Kulturkampf*. This struggle is essential for intellectual and moral health. Value differences necessarily entail a struggle.

The Religious Significance of the State of Israel

(1975)

From a discussion at a meeting of the Movement for a Judaism of Torah.

I wish to introduce myself at the outset as one who hasn't been at all disappointed by the state of Israel. For me, the state of Israel has fulfilled all the hopes I had for it ever since my early youth. Of course, it is very difficult for a seventy-year-old man vividly to envision himself as he was in his youth. But it seems to me that ever since I reached maturity and became a Zionist, Zionism meant for me the endeavor to liberate Jews from being ruled by the Gentiles. The state of Israel completely satisfies the demand for freedom from domination by others. To the extent that I am able to recall my opinions of fifty years ago, I believe that it never occurred to me to assign to the state— any state, including Israel—the function of realizing values, whether educational, cultural, or moral; certainly not the religious values of Torah and Mitzvoth.

When the members of a movement for the advancement of a Judaism of Torah speak of values, I presume that all of us know what we are talking about. The struggle to realize these values is the problem of the Jewish people, not of the state of Israel. It seems to me, though, that the discussion that took place here, in which important statements were made, with many of which I agree, suffered for lack of a clear distinction between two things: between the Jewish people as the bearer of Judaism and the sovereign state instituted by this people as its instrument of self-government. The crucial religious problem is the problem of the Jewish people, the continued historic existence of which has become questionable ever since the identification of the Jewish people with Judaism ceased to be axiomatic. Until the end of the eighteenth century no one ever questioned this identification, neither Jew nor Gentile. Yet from the moment the conception of the Jewish people as the bearer of Judaism by definition ceased to be taken for granted, Jewish peoplehood itself became a problem. The question as to who is a Jew is not a formal question. It is now an essential question. In what sense are millions of persons who regard themselves as Jews, and are so regarded by others, members of the Jewish nation? For most of them it is merely a matter of sentiment and memory, which are indeed powerful historical forces. But if these are not anchored in elements specific to Jewish existence, it is hard to imagine the survival of such a Jewish national identity for any length of time.

The problem of the religious significance of the state of Israel is, in one respect, a theological-political problem. In another, it is a problem of the psychology of faith. One may ask whether historical facts as such have any religious meaning. How a religious person ought to react to historical occurrences and facts, regardless of their intrinsic meaning, is quite another matter. It seems to me that the first question should be answered in the negative, and that the religious problem which is our concern is the second one. In opposition to one of the earlier speakers here, I believe that no state whatsoever, in the past, present, or any foreseeable future, in any society, in any era, in any culture, including the Jewish culture, ever was or will ever be anything but a secular institution. The function of the state is essentially secular. It is not service of God. The very words of Maimonides that my predecessor adduced in support of his claim imply that the state has merely instrumental functions, and lacks any intrinsic value. Whenever the Jews had a state, the history of that state was that of a continuous struggle between religion and the political leadership. Even when the state was established in the name of Torah, for the sake of Torah, as the outcome of struggle for the Torah—I have in mind the Hasmonaean state—the sixty years of that state's existence witnessed a constant struggle between the bearers of the Torah and the secular regime. This struggle is logically and factually inevitable. Religion, that is, man's recognition of his duty to serve God, cannot be integrated with the machinery of government. The political organization, necessary as a condition of survival, merely sets the ground for the struggle for religion, which is by its very nature an eternal struggle that will never end in victory. The state of Israel of our day has no religious significance, because no such struggle is being conducted in it. It is simply the political framework which liberates us from subjection. The calamity of religious Jewry in this state consists in its voluntary dependence upon the political organization—a dependence which spells its doom. Golda Meir was quoted in this forum in this connection. I wish to cite someone greater. Some twenty years ago I had a lengthy conversation with Ben-Gurion, whose attitude toward Judaism is well known to you, about the problem of religion and the state. He said to me: "I understand very well why you demand the separation of religion from the state. You want the Jewish religion to be reinstated as an independent factor with which the political authority will have to contend. Therefore I shall never agree to the separation of state and religion. I want the state to hold religion under its control." The official representatives of Jewish religion are resigned to this state of affairs; even worse, they count on being "kept" by the secular government.

The state, as such, has no religious value. No state ever had. Political achievements, conquests, victories—none of these are religiously significant. Who "restored the border of Israel from the entering of Hamath to the sea of the Aravah," and "recovered Damascus and Hamath which had belonged to Judah in Israel" (2 Kings 14)? Who was the greatest of warriors and conquerors among the Israelites? "The King Yarov'am the son of Joash," who "did that which was evil in the sight of God and departed not from all the sins of Yarov'am the son of Nevat" (ibid.). What was the religious significance of these enormous conquests about which we know only from two verses of the Book of Kings? From the empirical religious point of view, from the standpoint of the religious tradition, from the mark that these deeds left upon religious consciousness—it was nil. Our Sages of blessed memory found some merit in Yarov'am in that he did not harm the prophet (Amos) who said: "Yarov'am shall die by the sword and Israel shall surely be led captive out of their own land" (Amos 8,11).[1] This is what counts in his favor, whereas the tremendous events summed up in those two verses left no mark in the religious consciousness of Israel.

I contend that it is not by accident that no festival or holiday commemorates the conquest of the Land of Israel by Joshua, the son of Nun, and that no festival or holiday marks the conquest of Jerusalem by King David. We do have the holiday of Hanukkah, in memory of a civil war between the Jews who observed the Torah and the Hellenized Jews.

From the standpoint of faith as well as from that of theology, the question whether history has any religious significance at all is one which cannot be avoided. The world follows its natural course, and historical events are included in this course. The Halakhah is a program for living within this fixed course. A historical event becomes an exception to the course of the world and acquires religious significance only if it is an act performed for the sake of Heaven, or suffering undergone for the sake of Heaven. In this sense the war of the first Maccabees, the martyrdom of 1096, and the slaughter in 1648—all events in which the Holy Name was sanctified—were religiously significant.[2] No religious significance attached to the triumphs and conquests of Yarov'am the son of Joash and of Alexander Jannaeus.[3] The Holocaust of our generation is religiously meaningless. The Holocaust belonged to the course of the world, it merely exemplified the lot of the helpless who fall prey to the wicked. What was not done for the sake of Heaven, or was not suffered for the sake of Heaven, is indifferent from a religious point of view. Since the establishment of the state of Israel was not inspired by the Torah nor undertaken for the sake of the Torah, religiously speaking, its existence is a matter of indifference.

The genuine religious problem is not the problem of the state, but rather that of the Jewish people, which for the last two hundred years or so, generation after generation, has progressively been losing its essential attributes. This process was not halted or even retarded by the establishment of the state.

The foregoing debate raised three separate questions. The first is a question of faith and theology: so far as Judaism is concerned, what is the meaning of the historic event of the establishment of the state of Israel, which restored political independence to the Jewish people? Here the term "Judaism" refers to the elements of the religious consciousness and sensibility which constitute its abiding basis and remained stable through all the changes of three thousand years of history.

Quite another question is the one regarding the psychological impact of this historical development—the establishment of the state—upon the believing Jew.

A third question relates to Halakhah in the state, the Halakhah within the new reality. I shall briefly tackle all three points.

Theologically speaking, as a man of faith, and without special reference to the state of Israel, I emphatically deny that a state might have any intrinsic value at all. Moreover, beyond any considerations of theology or of faith, but by general axiological criteria, a state is not a *value*. A state is needed in order to fulfill two needs. The first is the individual's need for survival, "for were it not for fear of the political ruler men would swallow one another alive."[4] "The impulse of man's heart is evil from his youth." (Gen. 8:21). Unlike Robinson Crusoe on his island, human beings in society cannot coexist unless a regime and government is imposed upon them, or they impose it on themselves. What that Sage said aphoristically was repeated in systematic fashion some one thousand and five hundred years later by one of the greatest social and political thinkers, Thomas Hobbes.

The state's role in assuring a nation's survival is far more problematic than its function of safeguarding the existence of the individual. We shall not, however, delve too deeply into the matter but will recognize both needs as legitimate. Since the point of the state's existence is the satisfaction of a need, it obviously is not concerned with *value*. A man's needs are imposed upon him. No choice, decision, or commitment is involved. Values are operative only in consequence of a person's commitment, decision, and choice in posing them as goals toward which he strives. This striving does not spring from human nature. Every man has to eat—hence eating, of course, is not a value. Even life is not a value because, willy nilly, you live. Most people, the vast majority, do not have the mental power to put an end to their lives deliberately and willingly. They are forced to live by the necessity of their nature. It follows that life, as such, cannot be a value.

Regarding the state as an intrinsic value is the essence of fascism. If this is true in general, it is all the more true when the values of "the Judaism of Torah" are attached to it. The state certainly has its place in the Halakhah, because the Halakhah concerns itself with mundane matters. It deals with man as flesh and blood, with his food and drink, with his copulation, his work, and so on. Political reality as a value is not accorded much prominence in Judaism. We saw how the exploits of the greatest victor and conqueror are buried in two verses in 2 Kings! Those who are not well versed in the Hebrew Bible are not aware of them even if they are religiously committed Jews.

I cannot ascribe religious significance to our having regained political independence. From the pronouncements of colleagues who preceded me in this evening's debate one might infer that they "hear the words of God and see the vision of the Almighty" (Num. 24:4); that in historical events they discern "the finger of God" and the final cause of the overflow descending from the upper to the lower world.[5] I have no reliable source for knowledge of the divine intentions and do not detect in the occurrences of the lower world any religious significance, unless they incorporate an intention in the lower world aimed at the upper world; in other words—insofar as human beings act for the sake of Heaven. Apart from this, history has no religious meaning. History belongs to the course of the world and it is this course which constitutes divine providence. Every historical event is an instance of divine providence, so no particular event has greater religious significance than others. The selective invocation of the "finger of God" regarding what is convenient or desirable is comparable to the use of the concept of "holiness," which is so often abused for national-political purposes. When the holiness of the Temple Mount is imputed to its being "God's estate," I ask: is not any plot of land equally the "estate of God"? After all, "the earth is God's and the fullness thereof"! (Ps. 24:1, a verse religious Jews repeat four times a week). The ingathering of exiles in itself is not yet a religious phenomenon; see the verse "but when you entered, you defiled my land, and made my heritage an abomination" (Jer. 2:7). Yet this consideration does not deter certain rabbis from the Sabbatean announcement of "the Dawn of Redemption."

The psychology of faith is, however, a different matter. Here we are exempt from theological and axiological analyses and can deal with phenomena amenable to observation. In this respect nothing has changed as a result of the events of the last twenty-five years. The establishment of the state of Israel did not alter the consciousness of believing Jews, and no one from the secular camp has been affected by it. I ought to correct myself: the creation of the state, and especially the Six Day War and the conquest of Jerusalem, did have an impact on part of the religious sector, a pernicious one. Some went so far as to identify the nation and the homeland with the Godhead, the military victory with realization of the Torah, the conquest with the enhancement of Judaism. The believers' religiosity was debased by patriotism and nationalism. This was the reaction of the disciples of Rabbi Kook. In no small measure, he himself was responsible. Though he might not have intended these consequences, he formulated his doctrine in a way that readily lends itself to such interpretation by disciples who did not take the trouble to inquire too deeply into his true intentions.

There is the additional problem of the Halakhah. We have established our independent state, and in so doing have raised questions that were not discussed and could not be discussed in the Halakhah as crystallized in recent centuries. From the halakhic point of view, the renewal of the independence of Israel is a veritable catastrophe—comparable to the destruction of the Temple, with all due regard for the vast difference between the two events. In effect, Judaism in the second commonwealth centered about the Temple and its service. Who could have imagined, on the tenth of the month of Av (the day following the destruction) in the year 70, that celebration of the Day of Atonement would persist among Jews? But we know that the Day of Atonement has continued to be observed and is still observed, and that our Day of Atonement, with all the differences in patterns of observance, is, for us, the legitimate form of the ancient Day of Atonement. In the same sense, the renewal of our independence also changes the complexion of the Halakhah. To reiterate things that I have written repeatedly, the presupposition underlying the crystallization of the Halakhah over hundreds of years has been the fact—the empirical datum–that the Jewish people was not independent and was bereft of any functions in the spheres of statehood, politics, security, diplomacy, and so on. The problems requiring halakhic decision have now changed drastically. This is the point of the new religious program, about which I have written extensively. But from the standpoint of faith the great question is different, and can be phrased in one sentence: do we conceive the essence of our Judaism to be the service of God, or do we conceive it as the fulfillment of the interests and needs of the people of Israel?

To this we must add now the dreadful question of our time: What is the "People of Israel"?

PART III

THE POLITICAL SCENE

CHAPTER 21

The Territories

(1968)

These comments were written and published several years before the
Yom Kippur war of 1973.

Should Israeli sovereignty be extended over the territories of Palestine (and Sinai) Israel conquered during the Six Day war? Should they be under Israeli rule or control in any other form? Should they be restored to Arab sovereignty?

These political options are the subject of a widespread public discussion, which suffers from confusion of pragmatic and ideological issues. On the one hand, political and economic interests and security requirements are invoked ("peace," "recognized and secure boundaries"); on the other, an appeal is made to feelings and values (the vision of messianic redemption, "the Undivided Land of Israel," "the sacredness of the land," "the inheritance of our forefathers," "the tradition of generations," "our dead who fell for the liberation of our land"). Each one of these arguments must be dealt with separately and on its own merits.

The crux of the political debate is "peace and security." If the term "peace" is used here in its true sense, as a condition of coexistence between the state of Israel and each of its neighbors on the basis of a peace treaty adhered to by both sides—then there is no prospect of such a peace today or in the foreseeable future. This is not the place for a probing examination of the historical question whether at any stage the Jewish-Arab conflict over the land might have been resolved by an agreement acceptable to both parties. It can, however, safely be said that if the twenty years since the establishment of the state included occasions in which a compromise might possibly have been reached, we neglected all of them.[1] In the present situation it is inconceivable that either side could freely propose terms of peace that would be freely accepted by the other. Only the pressure of the great powers prevents war in our region today and tomorrow. It may be that their power and pressure—if they agree among themselves—will bring about a counterfeit "peace" in the form of an imposed settlement which will be maintained as long as there is agreement between the powers. The clear-sighted—and there are clear-sighted people even in the government, though they seem to prefer to be silent—perceive that, without an agreement imposed from the outside, our situation will deteriorate to that of a second Vietnam, to a war in constant escalation without prospect of ultimate resolution. Tomorrow, perhaps, we will have to invade Amman or Damascus and nothing will be gained thereby.

"Security" is a reality only where there is true peace between neighbors, as in the case of Holland/Belgium, Sweden/Norway, the United States/Canada. In the absence of peace there is no security, and no geographic-strategic settlement on the land can change this. There is no direct link between security and the territories. There are no "secure boundaries." Positing defense on fortified lines—the Maginot Line mentality—always failed, from the time of the Chinese Wall and the Roman Lines through the Atlantic Wall of Hitler.[2] Our security problem is not a problem of specific boundaries nor solely a military problem, but rather one in which military, political and social factors are intertwined. So long as social organization and technology give us a qualitative advantage over the Arabs, and the American backing neutralizes the Russian involvement, we can repel the Arabs at any boundary. This was demonstrated by the outcome of the Six Day war, which we began with borders that touched Kalkilya and the wall of the Old City of Jerusalem. In the absence of any one of these factors, no border would avail us, not even if they were on the Suez Canal and the Jordan. This is the situation, realistically perceived. Now that we have gained borders that, according to the "experts," are "ideal from a security perspective," we are forced to dedicate a much greater portion of our national income and state budget to defense than in the years that preceded the Six Day war, before we got these "ideal borders." Our security has been diminished rather than enhanced as a result of the conquests in this war.

We are condemned to live in our country without peace and security, just as the Jewish people have existed for thousands of years. To safeguard this existence we will have to exert constant efforts and make great sacrifices. Hence it is incumbent upon us to understand the nature of the state for the sake of which we accept such an existence for ourselves and our children. Only in the light of such clarification may we adopt a position with regard to the problem of "the territories."

Our real problem is not the territory but rather the population of about a million and a half Arabs who live in it and over whom we must rule. Inclusion of these Arabs (in addition to the half a million who are citizens of the state) in the area under our rule will effect the liquidation of the state of Israel as the state of the Jewish people and bring about a catastrophe for the Jewish people as a whole; it will undermine the social structure that we have created in the state and cause the corruption of individuals, both Jew and Arab. All this will happen even if the Arabs did not become a majority in the state (as a result of their high natural increase) but remained a third or 40 percent of the population. The state would no longer be a Jewish state but a "Canaanite" state.[3] Its problems and needs would no longer be those of the Jewish people in Israel and the Diaspora. Its functions would no longer be geared to these needs. It would be concerned only with the specific problems of rule and administration of this state—the problems of ruling over both Jews and Arabs. Its situation would be much like that of the state of Lebanon, perplexed as it is with the relations between Maronite Christians, Moslems and Druzes. The state would be harassed by such problems. In a short time the spiritual and emotional links between it and world Jewry would be severed, as well as the cultural and sentimental ties to the historical tradition of the Jewish people and to Judaism. The only concern of the monstrosity called "the Undivided Land of Israel" would be the maintenance of its system of rule and administration.

Rule over the occupied territories would have social repercussions. After a few years there would be no Jewish workers or Jewish farmers. The Arabs would be the working people and the Jews the administrators, inspectors, officials, and police—mainly secret police. A state ruling a hostile population of 1.5 to 2 million foreigners would necessarily become a secret-police state, with all that this implies for education, free speech, and democratic institutions. The corruption characteristic of every colonial regime would also prevail in the state of Israel. The administration would have to suppress Arab insurgency on the one hand and acquire Arab Quislings on the other. There is also good reason to fear that the Israel Defense Force, which has been until now a people's army, would, as a result of being transformed into an army of occupation, degenerate, and its commanders, who will have become military governors, resemble their colleagues in other nations.

Out of concern for the Jewish people and its state we have no choice but to withdraw from the territories and their population of one and a half million Arabs; this action to be done without any connection with the problem of peace. I speak of *withdrawal* from the territories and not of "returning them," because we have no right to decide to whom to return them: to Jordan's King Hussein? to the PLO? to the Egyptians? to the local inhabitants? It is neither our concern nor our obligation nor our right to decide what the Arabs will do with the territories after we withdraw from them. We could continue to fortify ourselves in our Jewish state and to defend it. If we do not withdraw with honor—that is, of our free will and from an understanding of the true needs of the Jewish people and its state—the Americans and Russians will force us to withdraw shamefacedly.

As for the "religious" arguments for the annexation of the territories—these are only an expression, subconsciously or perhaps even overtly hypocritical, of the transformation of the Jewish religion into a camouflage for Israeli nationalism. Counterfeit religion identifies national interests with the service of God and imputes to the state—which is only an instrument serving human needs—supreme value from a religious standpoint. The "halakhic" reasons for remaining in control of the territories are ridiculous, since the state of Israel does not acknowledge the authority of the Torah and the majority of its Jewish inhabitants reject the imperative demands of its Mitzvoth. The conquest of the land by the army of the state of Israel is a great and impressive national achievement for every nationally conscious Jew, whether religious or secular. However, the conquest itself has no religious significance. Not every "return to Zion" is a religiously significant achievement: one sort of return which may be described in the words of the prophet: "When you entered you defiled my land and made my heritage an abomination" (Jer. 2:7). The mere fact of the restoration of Israeli rule over the Temple Mount has no religious significance: Jewish sovereignty over the territories of the land of Israel, as a purely political fact, is not the "tradition of generations" which the advocates of "the Undivided Land of Israel" constantly evoke. This is not the true meaning of the "historic tie" of the nation to the land. For its "religious" or pseudo-religious advocates today, "the Undivided Land of Israel" is only the ideal of a dominant sector in this generation; whereas "the generations" to which they refer aspired to the renewal of Jewish sovereignty on the land of Israel only in conjunction with the restoration of the sovereignty of Torah. Only in this context was there a historic tie between the people and its land.

The land of Israel is the Holy Land and the Temple Mount is a holy place only by virtue of the Mitzvoth linked to these locations.[4] These Mitzvoth were not associated with the land and the mountain because these are "holy." On the contrary, their "holiness" derives from the Mitzvoth associated with them. The idea that a specific country or location have an intrinsic "holiness" is an indubitably idolatrous idea. Consider what the prophet Jeremiah said about the "holiness" of the Temple when those who violated the Torah and Mitzvoth called it "the temple of God" (Jer. 7). Nationalism and patriotism as such are not religious values. The prophets of Israel in the period of the first commonwealth and the Jewish sages in the period of the second commonwealth were, for the most part, "traitors" from the perspective of secular nationalism and patriotism. The rabbis who argue today that we should keep the territories for "religious reasons" are not carrying on the tradition of Elijah and the prophets of God but rather of the 850 prophets of the Baal and Asherah, "who ate of the table of Jezebel."

We all understand the lament of many of our citizens: "Did our dear sons then fall in vain in the Six Day war? Will the land saturated with their blood be desecrated by returning it to the Gentiles?" To those who utter this cry we can only say: in all the wars of past and present, those who fell died a meaningful death—and at the same time, they fell in vain. There is meaning to their death, if they fell defending their nation and land. Yet they fell in vain because their death (even if they died in a victorious war) does not necessarily resolve the issues over which they fought and fell. Moreover, our brothers and sons who fell in the Six Day war saved the country from the imminent danger of the moment; but their victory and death did not end and did not even diminish the constant danger to the existence of the state of Israel. This danger continues and will continue irrespective of what will or will not be done with the territories. There is reason to fear that after all those who fell in the Six Day war, many more will yet fall for the defense of the homeland.

CHAPTER 22

Right, Law, and Reality

(1976)

O ur right–the right of the Jewish people to this land"; "our right as opposed to the right of the Palestinian Arabs"— these and similar slogans occupy much space in the current discourse of public relations and propaganda, and even in politics, domestic and international. The language gives rise to ideology, which is then transformed into a political program.

Such formulations are meaningless, based as they are on what the logicians call a "category mistake."

No nation has a right to any country. While a country is an objective datum, "right" and "nation" are constructions of the human mind. "Right" is a legal category, and the concept applies only within the context of institutions defined by law and statute, which in turn are determined by men. This notion is meaningless with respect to nature or with respect to a given historical situation.

What does it mean to say I have a right to the watch on my wrist? Why is it specifically my right and not somebody else's? There are several reasons, each of which constitutes a necessary conditions for the existence of this right. In the first place, I and other people—with whom I might have to deal in connection with this right—are members of a society that has established the legal institution of private property or personal possession, and which regulates the interpersonal relations pertaining to property or belongings. Furthermore, "I" am an entity which can be objectively distinguished as a "person," that is, as a defined unit within that legal system. My right to the watch as my property is based on criteria of ownership determined within the system. I bought it legally and paid for it with my own money, or received it as a gift, or inherited it. Finally, in the event that doubts arise concerning this right and it is contested, there is an instituted authority, accepted and recognized, that decides the issue: the *judge,* who rules according to his understanding of the positive law.

The factors grounding this *right* of mine are absent from the relations between one nation and another or between a nation and its country. A "nation" is not a natural entity amenable to objective definition. A "nation" is a being of the mind, which exists insofar as there is mental awareness of its existence. It has no existence apart from this awareness. Is there a British nation, or perhaps only an English nation, a Scottish nation, and a Welsh nation? Is there an objective answer to this question? Which is the German nation—the population of the two Germanies only, or perhaps one should include also 8 million Austrians and 4 million German-Swiss, who all speak the same language, have the same literature and cultural tradition, and for much of their history formed a single political unit? Are the Indians, who never had one language, a nation? Which is the Arab nation? Is it the population between the Atlantic Ocean and the Persian Gulf, or perhaps there is a Moroccan people, an Egyptian nation, a Syrian nation and so on? *Is there a Jewish people?* Consciousness of Jewish nationality has existed among Jews for some 3,500 years and persists to this day, yet in the view of many historians, social theorists, and political scientists of the nineteenth century and today, liberals as well as Marxists, its existence ended long ago. All these questions and similar ones have no objective answer. The answer is determined by the *consciousness* of those who feel that they constitute a national entity.

A mental entity has no rights in the legal sense. Its rights exist only in the minds of those involved. The link between a "nation" and a particular country is not a nexus created by law, and thus it differs fundamentally from the bond between a legal "person" and his property. Likewise, a connection between a nation and a particular country is not a natural datum. A particular country is the country of a particular people insofar as it is such in the collective consciousness of that people, not because of any objective facts. Fortunate is the people whose conception of its tie to its country is recognized by others, for should this connection be contested, no legal argument could establish it. Even the fact that at a particular historical moment a particular territory is populated by members of a certain nation does not constitute a valid legal claim. In Talmudic law there is a sound maxim pertaining to the law of presumptive title: "Without a claim, possession cannot confer presumptive life."[1] And there is almost no nation in history or in the present, whose claim to a right to a certain territory by virtue of its inhabiting that country could not be contested: "It is yours only by dint of robbery" (in the midrashic formulation). The attempt to justify the claim to such a right on historic rounds (occupation during generations) has neither legal nor moral validity. The historic past does not live in the present except as an act of consciousness. (It is in this sense that I raised the question "what is the source of the Swedish people's right to Sweden?"—a question that evoked reactions of surprise and even anger among the public.)

The connection between a nation and its country exists in the consciousness of that nation as mere fact. As such, it is incontestable, but it is still not defensible on legal grounds. For that nation, the connection is part of the *reality which it apprehends*. In this sense it is stronger than any legal bond. Nevertheless, the right of that nation to the country exists in the minds of members of other nations only insofar as they have become accustomed to the existing situation and none contests its rightfulness. This is the nature of the "right" of the Swedish people to Sweden.

This country, which is called *Eretz Israel* by us and *Falastin* by the Arabs, was the country of the people of Israel in the factual sense. With the destruction and the exile that followed, the Jewish people lost their country, but the nation continued to exist and its national consciousness endured to this day. For the Jews in whom this national consciousness is alive, this country is the country of their people, even without any claim to a "right," since no such counterclaim could deprive them of this consciousness. But in the perverse course of history, which is incorrigible, an analogous bond was created between the same country and *another* nation. In their consciousness this country is theirs, whether their "right" to it is recognized by others or not. In regard to this conflict claims of "right" by both sides, or the claim of the superiority of the "right" of one of the sides, are meaningless. Considerations of historical "justice" are irrelevant. The conflict is not one of imaginary "rights." Nor is it a clash "between Justice and Justice"— since the legal (or moral) category of justice does not apply in this case.

This conflict does not have a "just" solution based on legal considerations, or on weighing the relative "rights" of the contestants. From the impasse created by the distortion of history there is only one possible way out, given the present situation. The partition of this country between the two nations is the only feasible solution, even if neither of the two sides will recognize its justice and become inwardly reconciled to it. The alternative is war to the bitter end, which would amount to a catastrophe.

Perhaps the history of the Israeli-Arab relations in the last generation is an instance of the verse, "That which is crooked cannot be made straight" (Eccles. 1:15). It is certain that the conquest of the *whole* country by the Jews in the Six Day war makes it inconceivable that Jews and Arabs should *willingly agree* on the terms of the partition and their implementation. Consequently, the way out *for which we may hope* is the partition of the country *by a settlement imposed on both sides* by the superpowers.

CHAPTER 23

A Jewish State or an Unpartitioned
Eretz-Israel

(1968–1980)

This chapter consists of passages excerpted by the author from items published between 1968 and 1980. They all anteceded the current uprising of Palestinians in the occupied territories.

Shortly after the Six Day war, when most of the Israeli public (and a good part of Jewry in the Diaspora) were overcome by the intoxication of national pride, military arrogance, and fantasies of the glory of messianic deliverance, I expressed, both orally and in writing, my concern lest the great victory that led to the conquest (or "liberation") of the entire territory of the historical *Eretz Israel* (with the addition of the Sinai peninsula) prove in the course of history to have been the event initiating a process of decline and fall of the state of Israel. At the time these words evoked much anger. Today, after the 1973 (Yom Kippur) war and the ensuing developments, including the peace with Egypt, many people refer to those concerns, and many also remark that my fears are being justified.

If chances came up—prior to the Six Day war and after—for a genuine peace with the Arab world on the basis of an agreed compromise, we passed them all by. Moreover, already in the Sinai campaign of 1956, we led the Arab world to feel that Israel was not merely concerned with the security of the Jewish people inhabiting it, but with the expansion of its borders by conquest—a scheme that was foiled by the intervention of the superpowers. When in 1967 we launched a preventive war, we turned it into a war of conquest, whose "achievements" inevitably brought about the Yom Kippur war. The outcome of this war was not determined by our military capacity and prowess alone, but by the extent of the backing and support given to each side by one of the superpowers. International pressure brought about the cease-fire agreements and the partial retreats following this war. Fundamentally, this remains the situation even after the signing of the peace treaty with Egypt, which is a peace treaty in form, but a cease-fire agreement in actuality. It fails to remove the factor likely to cause renewal of hostilities, namely, Israel's rule over the Palestinian Arabs. The meaning of the Camp David accords, as these are construed not only by Egypt, but by the United States and by most of the world, is that Israeli rule over the occupied territories should be terminated within a reasonable period of time. However, since Israel construes the accord differently and impedes any step in this direction, Egypt's participation in the impending war is inevitable.

But in addition to endangering our security and foreign relations, "unpartitioned Eretz-Israel" is internally unstable. Even if the Arabs do not become the majority, the state will no longer be a Jewish state. Its problems, needs, and functions will no longer be those of the Jewish people in Israel and abroad, but those arising from the specific tasks of government and administration of this strange system of political domination. They would be the problems of ruling over two peoples that do not cohere as a single nation. To the intense national antagonism between them will be added the passionate hatred evoked by the rule of one people by the other. There would also be a deep social rift, similar to the one that existed in Rhodesia-Zimbabwe, with its constant fear and insecurity caused by the strained relations between whites and blacks. All that country's resources were consequently channeled into the one endeavor of maintaining white dominance over the blacks. The state of "unpartitioned Israel" is already beset by such problems, which are not problems of the Jewish people at all, but those of governing an Arab-Jewish "unpartitioned Eretz Israel."

The status quo has social consequences—we have already seen, in recent years, that all construction work stops during the Moslem holidays because most of the building workers are Arabs. On the same days hundreds of Jewish restaurants close down all over the country, since most of the kitchen workers are Arabs. There have even been instances of postponement of surgery in Jewish hospitals because the workers did not show up in the laundries serving the operating rooms. Our society is such that the normalcy of the life of Jews is dependent on the work of Arabs, tens of thousands of whom are driven every morning from their villages to work in the Jewish cities, and are returned there every evening. Jews no longer perform any of the more menial labor chores.

Furthermore, by obliterating the "green line" we have united the 400,000 Arab Israeli citizens with their million and a half brethren across the line; we are thus promoting their fusion into one Palestinian people ruled by the state of Israel.[1] The problem of the relation between the Jewish citizens, for whom Israel is their national state, and the Arab citizens who form a national minority is in itself a difficult and delicate problem, though peaceful coexistence between them is not an impossibility. That opportunity is eliminated by holding on to the territories, because an incurable hatred is developing between the state and 15 percent of its citizens—a condition sufficient in itself to corrode the foundations of its existence.

The state of Israel, within the borders that were determined as result of our War of Liberation in 1948, was recognized *de jure* by all the states of the West as well as by the Eastern bloc, and by most of the "third world" countries. For twenty years Israel had staunch friends among them. Not one state in the world today recognizes the 1967 boundaries, and the Israeli settlements in the occupied territories are generally considered illegal. Control over the territories and over the Arab people inhabiting them will end in a war to the bitter end between Israel and the entire Arab world, from Morocco to Kuwait, and in that war the entire world will support the Arab side.

Even without any connection with the problem of peace, but out of concern for the Jewish people and its state—we have no choice but to withdraw from the territories in which one and a half million Arabs live. If we do not withdraw with honor—that is, of our free will and from an understanding of the true needs of the Jewish people and its state—the Americans and Russians may force us to withdraw in shame. The repartition of the land by an arrangement imposed on both nations by the superpowers may be the only alternative to war. Such an intervention is desirable from the Jewish national point of view. A new partition would preserve Israel as the Jewish state, relieving it of the curse that clings to its body and soul: rule over a foreign nation. In the same way the French people were freed by a great patriot—Charles de Gaulle—from the bane of ruling over the Algerians.

The partition of the land between the two nations is an inescapable historical necessity. The history of the Jews and of this country for the last 2,000 years and of the Arab people for the last 1,400 years has created one land and two peoples, each of which feels most deeply that this land is his. In view of this inescapable fact, there is neither point nor sense to all the philosophical-historical and legalistic arguments assessing and weighing the respective "rights" of each side. In the given situation there is only the choice between two outcomes: war or partition. There is no third way out.

After all that has been said about the "religious" and pseudo-religious and even halakhic reasons for maintaining Jewish rule over the territories and their Arab inhabitants, and for the annexation of the territories to the state of Israel, I have nothing to add to what already appeared in the Scriptures, the same Scriptures to which the national religious fools appeal for support of their lust for conquest. Two thousand six hundred years ago the prophet Ezekiel foresaw Gush Emunim and the arguments of its rabbis and leaders. His words read as though he knew in advance the words and terms they would use, and he already gave them a reply which penetrates to the heart of the matter.

> Then the word of God came to me saying, Son of man, They that inhabit these waste places of the land of Israel speak, saying, Abraham was one man and yet he inherited the land, but we are many; the land is given us for inheritance. Therefore say to them, thus says the Lord God: You eat with the blood and lift up your eyes towards your idols, and shed blood; and shall you possess the land? You stand upon your sword, you carry out disgusting deeds, and you defile every man his neighbor's wife; and shall you possess the land?[2]

These words were not meant for Ezekiel's own generation only. He said them to all generations, and especially to the generation of the "liberators of the Holy Land" in our time. The Jewish people has legitimate claims to this country. But these claims have no "religious cover." To speak of the divine promise to Abraham and his issue as a gratuitous gift, to ignore the conditions of the promise, and to disregard the obligations it confers on the receivers is a degradation and desecration of the religious faith.

CHAPTER 24

Occupation and Terror

(1976)

I n our times of worldwide decolonization, a colonial regime necessarily gives birth to terrorism. Conditions and circumstances
today, both material and psychological, are no longer those of
earlier generations, when "primitive" (compared to the power centers
of Western civilization) populations accepted the rule of "developed"
states, or at any rate refrained from active, violent opposition to this
rule. The nature of colonial rule does not matter. Whether it treats the
subjects with a light or a heavy hand, whether it grants them material
or cultural benefits or exploits them to its own advantage—such rule
is not tolerated. The subjects rise up, or will rise up, against it and will
employ any means they consider effective. The type of "means" used
has also changed. Previously, when the material and military superiority of the Western world was clearly acknowledged, this recognition
was accompanied by the conscious or unconscious conviction that the
methods of political action prevalent in the Western world—or at least
recognized as the acceptable means of political struggle—were best.
Asian and African national liberation movements in the pre-World War II
era imposed great restraints upon themselves. They evinced tremendous patience, seeking to attain their goals by methods of persistent
political opposition, protracted and exhaustive negotiation, reliance on
accepted and agreed principles, and mobilization of public opinion.
Confusion and difficulties for colonial authorities were effected by passive resistance to its acts in the hope of finally reaching a recognized
agreement. To the extent the nationalists envisioned active rebellion, it
was in terms of an officially declared war conducted by regular armies,

as in the national liberation wars of Poland against the Russians in 1830–31, the Hungarians and Italians against the Habsburgs in 1848–49, Garibaldi's march against the Bourbons of Naples in 1860, and the like.

All this has completely changed. Not only has deference to the West's (or more accurately—the North's) power to rule over the East (more accurately—the South) been undermined, but the psychological factors making the colonial regimes possible have vanished, both for the former rulers, who call themselves "the developed world" or "the free world" (of which the state of Israel is also a part), and for the former colonial lands, called "the developing world" or "the third world." At the same time, the Western world itself, since 1914, has violated all accepted—or at least nominally accepted—restrictions on the means of violence in international conflict, as well as in struggles for liberation. Already in the years following the First World War the conditions for continued stability of colonial rule were being undermined. Light years separated the type of war fought by the Sinn Fein against the Black-and-Tans in the 1920s from the nineteenth-century version of national wars of liberation! After World War II the possibility of gradual, step-by-step progress toward independence disappeared. Patience and restraint were gone, and any delay necessarily led to terrorist activity, followed by counterterror in vicious sequence (Kenya, Algeria, and elsewhere).

In a world from which colonialism has been eliminated, Israel, since 1967, is endeavoring to impose colonial rule on the territory of a foreign people. Two aspects of Israeli rule over the West Bank and Gaza ought to be considered.

First is the question of the internal implications of including one and a quarter million Arabs of the West Bank and Gaza under the rule of the state of Israel. It will cease to be a state of the Jewish people, for whose history such a state cannot be a continuation. The colonizing situation will lead to the establishment of a political structure combining the horrors of Lebanon with those of Rhodesia—the state of a people possessing a common national heritage will turn into a system of imposed rule over two peoples, one ruling and the other ruled. In such circumstances, national conflicts become social conflicts. The Arabs will be the nation of workers and the Jews will be foremen, clerks, and police in a state dominated by security police. It is unlikely that human rights and civil freedoms can exist even in the Jewish sector.

The second problem involves the implications for Jewish-Arab relations. The occupation rule in the West Bank and Gaza will bring about solidarity of the half a million Israeli Arab citizens with their brothers in the occupied territories. This will lead to a radical change in their state of mind. Inevitably, they will no longer regard themselves as Arab citizens of the state of Israel, but rather as members of a people exploited by that state. In such a situation, one must expect the constant incidence of terror and counterterror.

Israeli policy in the occupied territories is one of self-destruction of the Jewish state, and of relations with the Arabs based on perpetual terror. There is no way out of this situation except withdrawal from the territories. "Withdrawal" is presented here as the antithesis to the slogan common among "dovish" circles in Israel: "territories in exchange for peace." This slogan means holding on to the territories indefinitely. There is no chance of "peace"—meaning an agreed solution—between us and the Arabs today or in the foreseeable future. It is a vision for the distant future. Only a solution imposed upon both sides by the superpowers, which will probably include withdrawal from the territories, offers an escape from a struggle threatening to escalate into an out-and-out war, which is likely to result in catastrophe for one side, perhaps for both. In any case, not only real peace (involving very extensive preliminaries), but any solution, including an imposed one, is conditioned on withdrawal. There is every reason for us to be prepared to accept such an imposed solution. We are obliged to strive toward this, though we do not know if peace or agreement will come, and if it comes—when.

The slogan "peace for territories" is a program for continuing the Israeli occupation "for the time being." But meanwhile, every day of continued occupation increases the tension and the hatred along with their inevitable consequences. New obstacles will impede the road to agreement. Corruption of state, society, and people is continually exacerbated. Neither decent treatment of the population by the occupying power (if the term "decency" can be used at all for colonial occupation), nor even the prospect of terminating the occupation upon achievement of an agreement, will relax the tension. They will not prevent terrorism, which inevitably flows from impatience and leads to repressive countermeasures. There is, moreover, no psychological possibility of preventing Jewish settlement in territories administered by Israeli rule. Such settlement will add fuel to the flames and make amelioration more and more difficult. Dialogue with the Palestinians is not likely to take place on the sole basis of the explicit intention to return the territories after reaching an agreement. Honest dialogue is not possible between rulers and ruled: it is possible only between equals.

Thus a program of "peace (or agreement) in return for territories" does not seem feasible. Evacuation of the territories necessarily precedes any serious effort toward peace (or any agreed arrangement). This is stated without illusions: while evacuation of the territories is a necessary condition for peace (or an agreement under pressure of the superpowers), it is not certain that it is also a sufficient condition. After withdrawal, a dialogue with the Arabs will perhaps become possible with the help of the superpowers. It is impossible before evacuation. Yet there is no guarantee that evacuation will bring us real peace, or even an agreement granting reasonable security. But "security" is not guaranteed even with an Israeli army of occupation on the Jordan River. If, as citizens of our Jewish state as it was, we were determined to maintain our political independence and defend it with all our resources, we—and the Jewish people and the whole world—would know what we were fighting for. The monstrosity known as "the undivided land of Israel" is ruinous from the human, Jewish, and Zionist perspectives. It could neither evoke the determination, dedication, and perseverance in ourselves, nor the understanding on the part of others, without which our independence will always be precarious.

CHAPTER 25

Forty Years After
(1988)

T
wo nations inhabit this country. In consequence of centuries
of history, members of each feel passionately that this is their
land. Such attachment goes well beyond any ideology, theory,
or faith. Recognition of it must serve as a point of departure for any
feasible political program. This deeply rooted feeling is the crux of the
matter; not the empty talk about the "right" of one of these peoples as
against the "right" or "lack of right" of the other. In this context, talk
of rights is pure nonsense. No nation has a "right" to any land. A
country is an objective datum. "Right" and "nation" are constructs of
human consciousness. "Right" is a legal term that designates a concept
which is inapplicable apart from an institutional framework defined in
terms of a legal system established by men. Its application to natural
reality is invalid, as is its application to any reality determined solely
by history and without reference to some given normative context.

Every society sets up the necessary conditions for establishing the
rights to given assets. The community maintains the legal institution
of property and orders relations between people in respect of property
and its transfer. Each claimant must be defined as a "person" within
the given legal system. Claims to rights must be based on criteria of
ownership recognized by that system. If doubts arise concerning someone's right, an accepted and recognized judicial authority adjudicates
the matter. None of these requisites for the constitution of rights are
present in the relations between nations or between a nation and a
country.

A "nation" is a being of the mind. It exists only insofar as there is consciousness of its existence. An entity of the mind has no legal rights. The nexus of a "nation" to a given territory is not established by law, and differs thereby from the bond which attaches a piece of property to the legal "person" who owns it. Even the fact that at some historical moment a territory is populated by members of a given nation does not validate a legal right to the territory. The claim of almost any nation to the territory it occupies can be countered by the claim: "it is yours only by dint of robbery" (a midrashic formulation).

In the consciousness of a people, the tie binding it to its country is unconditioned and not defeasible on legal grounds. By the same token, it is equally impossible to justify on such grounds. For the people in question it is part of their reality. As such, it is far more living and poignant than any legal bond or "right." Concerning rights one argues and negotiates; in matters involving national consciousness people may be ready to kill and be killed.[1]

But the practical policy which a nation requires the organs of its state to pursue cannot be determined by its subjective consciousness alone. Such decisions must take into account the objective circumstances in which the nation and the state exist.

The country we live in was in ancient times the land of the people of Israel. Even when, in the wake of destruction and exile, the people were physically severed from their country, the nation continued to exist and with it its national consciousness. Jews whose national consciousness is still alive continue to consider this country the "Land of Israel" even without regard to claims of right. No counterclaim can deprive them of this feeling. It is the same for the Arab inhabitants.

With respect to this conflict, claims to "rights" by both sides, or claims that the "rights" of one party have greater weight than those of the other are meaningless, and historically grounded considerations of "justice" irrelevant. The conflict is not one of "rights." These are non-existent. Neither is it a clash of "justice against justice," since neither the legal nor moral conception of justice applies here. This conflict has no "just" resolution grounded in considerations of law or the "rights" of the sides.

Only one way out of this historically created impasse is feasible in the present situation, even if neither side recognizes it as just or finds it really acceptable: partition of the country between the two peoples.

It is the only way to avoid a national and human catastrophe, perhaps for both parties, in any event for the Jewish side. Let us discuss the background necessitating such a resolution of the conflict and the chances of attaining it.

The state of Israel was projected as a framework of national-political independence for the Jewish people. It was a realization of the Zionist idea and came into being in accordance with the resolution of the United Nations. The same resolution left the Palestinians the option of achieving similar independence. Only by partition of the country could both these objectives be achieved. We accepted this proposal. The Palestinians and the Arabs states rejected it. The state of Israel emerged from the resulting war. Responsibility for that war rests with the Arab side.

By the Rhodes armistice agreements of 1949 the Arab states accepted the partition de facto. The state of Israel could exist as the state of the Jewish people—with an Arab minority—only in part of the land of Israel. The Palestinians retained the option of doing with the other part of the country what they would (or could). The inclusion of several hundred thousand Arabs as citizens of Israel (even if against their will) could not be regarded as subjection of the Palestinian people to a foreign rule.

The situation changed radically following the Six Day war of 1967. On the seventh day we had to decide—and we were free to decide—whether that war was one of defense or of conquest. Our decision turned it into a war of conquest, with all that this implied. Not only was the character of the state altered; the very foundation of its existence assumed a new aspect. The change was not simply of quantity but of substance. Its significance consists not in the increase of the number of Arabs subject to Israeli rule from half a million to two million, but in denial of the right to independence to the Palestinian people. Israel ceased to be the state of the Jewish people and became an apparatus of coercive rule of Jews over another people. What many call "the undivided Land of Israel" is not, and can never be, the state of the Jewish people, but only a Jewish regime of force. The state of Israel today is neither a democracy nor a state abiding by the rule of law, since it rules over a million and a half people deprived of civil and political rights.

That a subjugated people would fight for its freedom against the conquering ruler, with all the means at its disposal, without being squeamish about their legitimacy, was only to be expected. This has been true of the wars of liberation of all peoples. We call the acts of the Palestinians "terrorism" and their fighters "terrorists." But we are able to maintain our rule over the rebellious people only by actions regarded the world-over as criminal. We refer to this as "policy" rather than "terror" because it is conducted by a duly constituted government and its regular army. The "aberrant cases" of necessity became the rule, since they are not incidental to a conquering regime but essential to it.

We are creating—and have already created—a political atmosphere affecting the public as well as its individual members, in which a former Chief Justice of the Supreme Court legitimates the use of torture in the interrogation of Palestinian prisoners. The Israeli Defense Force, armed with up-to-date weaponry, kills within a span of weeks a hundred people who did not carry firearms, amongst them women and children; breaks the bones of men, women, and children by order of the Minister of Defense; forces its way into homes and humiliates their residents. In this same atmosphere one hears of cases of soldiers attempting to bury Arab boys alive; the Attorney General distinguishes between torture and "reasonable" torture; those in charge of the army distinguish "burial alive" from the burying alive of bodies without interring the heads. Similar tendencies characterize our foreign and defense policies. The vicious folly of the Lebanese war was an outcome of the intention to maintain and assure the continued rule over the occupied territories and their people. That war, initiated by the Begin government, was undertaken with the consent of the Alignment of workers' parties, which continues to this day to oppose negotiation with the PLO, the representative of the Palestinian people, over the repartitioning of the land.

Only by putting an end to our rule over the other people can we be saved from the dire consequences of persisting in the present policy.

If the present situation continues (and here the emphasis must be on "if"), the growing savagery of Israeli society will be as inevitable as the severance of the state from the Jews of the world. The policy of a government of Sharon, Raful, and Druckman (or their counterparts), which in such circumstances also seems unavoidable, will begin with suppression of reliable information, elimination of free speech, the set-ting up of concentration camps for "traitors" (like myself and perhaps like you), and end in mass expulsion and slaughter of the Arab popu-lation. All this will lead to a decisive war between Israel and the Arab world. In that war the sympathy and backing of the entire world will be for the Arabs. Already today, the state of Israel, to which most of the world's nations were once sympathetic, has earned contempt and hatred throughout the world. Its very existence has come to depend on a thin life-line stretching out to it from the White House. Above all, the state, which was to have been the pride and glory of the Jewish people, is rapidly becoming an embarrassment to it.

A government whose aim is the preservation of Israel as the inde-pendent state of the Jewish people, not Jewish rule over the conquered portions of the whole of the Land of Israel, would issue a call to the PLO to negotiate a permanent peace between the state of Israel and the Palestinian people, based on mutual recognition and the partition of the country between the two nations. All details would be negoti-able. Response to such a call will open the way to peace even though it will require considerable effort on the part of both sides to tread it. In any event, it will eliminate the imminent danger of total war. Should the other side fail to respond, we and the rest of the world will know that the feasible alternative to the present situation has been rejected, and, in case of war, it will be Israel who will have the sympathy and backing of the world.

Partition is the rational and moral resolution of the Israeli-Palestin-ian (or Jewish-Arab) conflict. It is also the only alternative to the destruction which will ensue in consequence of our continued pursuit of the policy of occupation. But partition is not just a necessity forced upon us. From our standpoint, it is the most desirable arrangement. True enough, in view of our deep attachment to the whole of this country as "the land of Israel," it is psychologically difficult for us to accept as final a scheme which involves relinquishing Shekhem, Hebron, and so on (just as the PLO will find it difficult to give up hopes of occupying Jaffa, Haifa, and so on). But partition will return Israel to us, in a portion of the land, as a Jewish state, in the true sense of these two terms:

"State"—in the sense of a democratic, well-ordered system of gov-ernance which deploys the means at its disposal to fulfill necessary functions which only the political organ of society is capable of performing;

"Jewish"—in the sense that the efforts of the state are directed primarily toward dealing with the problems of the Jewish people in the state and in the Diaspora. These comprise social, axiological, educational, and economic problems as well as issues of the relations of the state with the Diaspora and with the Jewish heritage.

In its present condition, as the political authority over "the Undivided Land of Israel," the state of Israel is incapable of functioning as a Jewish state in these terms, because all its efforts and resources are devoted to the maintenance of its rule over the occupied territories and their population, a goal foreign to its authentic ends. On this aim the state squanders all its physical and mental resources, while neglecting the functions incumbent upon it.

Some people oppose the withdrawal from the occupied territories on the grounds of security. Arab tanks will be stationed twenty-five kilometers from Tel-Aviv and fifteen kilometers from Natanyah. They ignore the fact that Israeli tanks would be stationed twenty-five kilometers from Shekhem and two kilometers from Gaza and overlook the fact that even a "security-boundary" along the Jordan River cannot guarantee that no missiles would be launched from Jordan to Tel-Aviv (one hundred kilometers as the crow flies), and that they could be launched against Amman from the coastal plain or the Negev. Both sides will have no alternative to coexistence.

Others believe that Israel's military fist will enable us to maintain the Jewish rule over the territories and their people indefinitely. They forget—or attempt to ignore—that the power of this fist derives from its being encased in a glove of American steel lined with dollars. Should it occur to the Americans to withdraw the glove with its lining—an eventuality which could materialize any day—the essential weakness of that fist will be revealed.

No conditions, no strategic boundaries, could assure Israel's security with absolute certainty. When we established our state in this country, we undertook to pay a price for our national independence: namely, a precarious existence. We shall always have to exert considerable effort to survive. The dangers can only be minimized through our political sagacity. Without it, our power alone will not suffice.

Wherever Jews in the Diaspora are socially and politically integrated with the national community within which they live, their physical existence is secure. We who chose independence must provide for our own defense.

Any discussion of what the future ought to be, given the possibilities inherent in the present, requires us to lay bare the roots of this dreadful present. We must trace out the path that led to the atrocities committed in the past months [early in 1988] in the occupied territories, atrocities which we attempt to obscure by preventing the dissemination of reliable information. A most penetrating formulation of the nature of the drives that culminate in such brutality may be found in the words of Franz Grillparzer, who witnessed the "Spring of Nations" in 1848. He warned his contemporaries against following the path which led "from humanity through nationality to bestiality." But this is precisely the direction toward which the youth of today and an entire generation is being educated in our world, a world of Jews bereft of the values of Judaism, who can express their Jewishness only in mundane political nationalism, whether in a humanistic-secular or a fideistic-religious style.

The two styles have one thing in common. The humanism of our "enlightened" circles and the national religiosity of official Jewish religion in Israel carry as little weight as did elsewhere the socialism of national socialism. When nation, country, and state are presented as absolute values, anything goes. For their sake anything may even become one's duty. It is therefore incumbent upon every teacher, educator, counsellor, and every intellectual who is not a fascist to reiterate insistently that nation, country, and state are not absolute values. They are subject to criticism.

Even a person who is strongly attached to his people and its land and is loyal to his state must recognize and understand that the legitimate government and the military command are not supreme normative authorities. In some situations the loyal citizen and good soldier will disobey instructions and orders, as will the man of religious faith out of his awareness of his position before God, and the genuine humanist because he is conscious of his relation to fellow men. In extreme situations, none of them will agree to recognize his allegiance to nation and state as the relevant criterion.

As Emerson stated, "Good men must not obey the law too well." In this spirit, there is good reason to encourage those who refuse to serve in the occupied territories lest, against their will and judgment, they become murderers. In the language of the gloss on the opening section of the *Shulhan Arukh*, they may be told "not to fear those who ridicule them." The initial instances of conscientious objection must be developed into a mass movement.

Even if the ruling establishment in Israel fails to appreciate the necessity of disengaging from the occupied territories, and even without a mass movement to force the government into taking such steps, it is plausible to assume that the country will eventually be repartitioned, however difficult it is to imagine that this will be done with the willing consent of Israel and the PLO (whose position in the matter remains vague). It is most probable that both we and the Palestinians will be coerced into such an arrangement by the world powers; by the United States, perhaps in conjunction with the Soviet Union and the United Nations. If we do not withdraw from the territories of our own free will, we may be compelled to relinquish them and thus be saved from corruption by fascism and from all-out war. It may well be the irony of history that the Gentiles will save the state of Israel from the Jews who are bent on its destruction.

PART IV

JUDAISM
AND
CHRISTIANITY

CHAPTER 26

Hochhut's Error

(1964)

R olf Hochhut's play *The Deputy* (1963) stirred up debate in both Jewish and Christian circles. It has been translated into many languages, including Hebrew, and has been presented on the stage in many countries, including Israel. The point of this impressive work of the German author is a confrontation between "noumenal" Christianity and "phenomenal" Christianity, between Christianity as Hochhut understands it and Christianity in practice. This intention, implicit in the play, was made explicit in a lecture he delivered in answer to the stormy debate aroused by the work, "Durfte der Papst schweigen? Pius XII und die Juden" (1963).

Hochhut has no doubts about the essence of Christianity and the Christian god; his conception permeates the whole play. It is realized in the figure of the "true Christian," whose function in the play is to give greater prominence to the contrast between genuine Christianity and its official representative, betrayer of the Christian savior, whose deputy he is supposed to be. Hochhut is not a Catholic, and it is questionable whether he is a Christian in faith. However, he accepts as axiomatic a certain concept of Christianity together with its corollaries, which are impossible to reconcile with the participation—passive, bordering on active—of the deputy of the Christian god in the mass murder of human beings. In the religious-moral equation containing the magnitudes "Christianity" and "the Pope," the constant magnitude is "Christianity," whereas the value of the "unknown," Pius XII, is determined by reference to the value of the constant.

Hochhut's conception of the obligations entailed by the "true essence" of Christianity is common to most intellectuals of the Western world, including Gentiles who have rejected the Christian faith and Jews who have adopted this concept of Christianity and its concurrent evaluation from the Gentiles.

In the debate over the significance and truth of Hochhut's play, most of the participants proceed from the author's own assumptions. All of them, including the Jewish critics, take it for granted that the principles attributed explicitly or implicitly by Hochhut to Christianity are indeed its very essence. The criterion by which Pius XII is judged is that of the conformity of his actions or inactions with this notion of Christianity.

Those who concur with Hochhut's criterion regard Pius XII as having been false to his vocation and having betrayed the Christian god. The Pope's defenders accept the standard of evaluation but deny Hochhut's factual allegations. According to them, the Pope did not act, or did not refrain from action, in the manner described by the playwright. His description and, consequently, his evaluation are libelous and defamatory. This implies that were the defenders convinced of the truth of the allegations on which Hochhut bases his case, they too would have to join in the condemnation of the man who served as the deputy of the Christian god.

There are good grounds for challenging the assumptions common to both sides in this debate. This demurrer is addressed primarily to Jews and is a rejection of the frequent and distorting juxtaposition of Judaism-Christianity, which many of them make.

To understand the antagonistic confrontation involved in this juxtaposition it is not necessary to clarify the Pope's behavior or the principles proclaimed by the Church, which may change in accordance with the spirit of the age. The character of this confrontation is determined by the nature of the relationship of Christianity to Judaism, which is of the very essence of Christianity and not amenable to change. Given this relationship, it would appear that Hochhut was guilty of an abysmal error. If the facts are such as described in the play—and everything that has been uncovered and published in recent years tends to corroborate and even add to this description—there is no justification for criticizing the Pope from a Christian standpoint and accusing him of betraying the Christian god. On the contrary, precisely because Pius XII was a good Christian (and there is no reason to doubt his faith), and because he regarded himself as the deputy of Jesus (and there are no grounds for doubting that he viewed himself and his office in this light), he might have been expected to act as he did. His action (or failure to act) only put into practice what was implicit in Christianity from the days of its founder.

For the issue Hochhut poses is not the attitude of the Pope to the mass-murder of human beings, which the Church does not condone— or even the mass-murder of Jews, to which the Church would also take exception—but rather the murder of masses of Jews with the intent of annihilating the entire Jewish people in order to bring about the extinction of Judaism. The call for obliteration of Judaism was not something grafted upon Christianity as a result of some historical development, something which Christianity is capable of overcoming and even of rejecting. It is of the very essence of Christianity since the day on which the Christian god appeared on earth. It is nothing but the denial of the right of Judaism to exist; in a sense, a denial of its very existence. The relationship of Christianity to Judaism is unlike that of other religions or faiths, whether pagan or Islamic, which deny the Torah of Israel and would nullify it. Christianity does neither, but claims that *it* is Judaism and there is no Judaism apart from it. On this claim it bases its very legitimacy, and therefore can never concede this point. From the standpoint of Christianity, the existence of Judaism apart from Christianity has ceased to be legitimate. Its continued existence can only be interpreted as a deviation from the proper divine order of the world. The Church could be reconciled to the continued existence of the Jewish people only to the extent that this existence was severed from the proper existence of mankind, that of the Christian world, whose members are the "true Jews." The Jewish people could be permitted to exist only if their existence were disfigured, cursed, and degraded. The entry of Jews into the mainstream of the life of Christian society while still remaining Jewish, a process which began with the emancipation, must appear in the eyes of the Church as a challenge to the very root of Christianity. Christianity regards itself as the legitimate heir of Judaism, and the heir cannot take possession of his inheritance while the testator is still alive. The Church did not desire the physical annihilation of Jews. It was interested in the liquidation of Judaism, and every Jewish convert was precious as testimony to its truth. The Church desired the repentance of Jews and not their death. However, the experience of scores of generations clearly indicated that there was no prospect of a total conversion of the Jewish people, and only "with the last of the Jews would there be an end to Judaism." In effect, the extinction of Judaism could only be attained by the annihilation of the Jews.

Here the Church was impaled on the horns of a cruel dilemma: on the one hand, the need for annihilation of the Jewish people, on the other hand, the inability of the Church to accomplish this by itself or even to demand it explicitly, since according to its principles "it does not shed blood"—not even the blood of heretics, let alone Jews. The coming of Hitler resolved this dilemma. The task which the Church itself was not permitted to carry out was undertaken by another agent. The Pope, as a faithful Christian entrusted with upholding Christianity, could not help but see the finger of the divine agency in the appearance of Hitler, proponent of "the final solution" of the Jewish problem, a solution which concurrently achieves a goal of Christianity since its inception, that is, the obliteration of the Torah of Israel. The Pope was not motivated by any love of Hitler or of Nazism. One can readily imagine what the learned aristocrat Pacelli must have felt in the face of the mob spirit, rowdiness, and boorishness of the gang of German rulers. But he must also have felt that he was not at liberty to oppose the providential design which brought this gang to power in order to carry out the divine judgment against the Jews and grant Christianity its historic victory. On this account, he could not pay attention to those few among his priests who, out of humanitarian feelings and pity—feelings they shared with humanistic secularists—wanted to protect the Jews against the will of the Christian god and against the interest of the Church. Neither personal timidity, nor political-historical considerations (fear of atheistic communism), nor concern for the property of the Church and its legal position in Nazi-occupied lands motivated the Pope, as Hochhut believes and hints. Pius XII acted with a Christian religious interest in view.

This perspective on the position of Christianity *vis-à-vis* Judaism is not refuted by the "Jewish document" which was adopted by Vatican II and the heirs of Pius XII twenty years after the extinction of the major portion of European Jewry. The myth of the life of Jesus and his crucifixion by the Jews is not the root cause of the Christian hatred of Judaism; it stems from the fact that Judaism continues to exist despite its rejection of Jesus, thus contradicting the Christian message. The story of the crucifixion can be presented and interpreted in various ways, in accordance with the changing circumstances and attitudes current at different times. Today the Church finds it convenient to blur the concept of Jewish guilt of deicide, which is unacceptable to the faithful in the "enlightened" Western lands. They had been influenced by liberal humanitarian attitudes derived from secular sources and were shocked by the horror of the "final solution." This does not in the least affect the denial by Christianity of the legitimate independent existence of Judaism and the hope that Judaism will cease to exist.

This perennial hatred of Judaism by Christianity is felt even among intellectuals of the Western world who have cast aside the Christian faith, after having been raised and educated in cultures which have been molded by the concepts and values of Christianity. If these intellectuals have succeeded in overcoming their conscious hatred of Jews, they still feel—unconsciously, and sometimes even consciously—a deep antagonism to Judaism. At the very least, they perceive Jews as foreigners in a way quite different from the way they regard other strangers. This was the attitude current in the age of enlightenment. It may be discerned in the evaluation of Judaism by Voltaire, Gibbon, Kant, Goethe, and Hegel, and consequently in their attitudes toward Jews. It is prevalent even today. Without the assumption that in their collective unconscious Westerners felt the Jews to be "strangers," creatures set apart from normal human beings, how can one account for the indifference of the enlightened liberal Western world to the extermination of the Jews by the Germans, or the stand of men like Roosevelt and Churchill who made no effort to save the Jews?

There cannot be an honest exchange of ideas between Judaism and Christianity or a sincere "Jewish-Christian dialogue." A dialogue between Judaism and Christianity (as distinct from a dialogue between Jews and Christians)—to which certain liberal Jewish circles aspire—is possible only for Jews who have lost any appreciation of what abrogation of the Torah and it Mitzvoth signifies and for Christians who are no longer sensitive to what the image of Jesus connotes.

CHAPTER 27

"The Common Judeo-Christian Heritage"

(1968)

I n certain circles of the Jewish community, discussion of the relations of Christianity and Judaism has recently become the vogue. Questions of essential nature as well as of historical fact are brought up. The point of the discussion is the improvement of these relations: the possibility, prospects, need, even the obligation to promote such an improvement. A variety of factors animates this new interest: events which are interpreted as melioration of the traditional Christian animosity against Judaism; pronouncements of Christian personalities and Church institutions in reconsideration of the past, which appear as expressions of a tendency to revise the traditional evaluation of Judaism and its significance for Christian religious thought; the "Jewish document" of Vatican II, which left some impression in the Christian world and caused considerable excitement in certain Jewish groups; the reestablishment of Jewish rule over Jerusalem, regarded, according to a common cliché, as "the cradle of the three monotheistic religions" and sacred to all three; attitudes current within circles of liberal and Reform Jewry—consciously or unconsciously assimilated—aware of their alienation from the Jewish tradition and affinity for the world of "Western-Christian civilization"; even problems raised and incidents induced by increased missionary activity in Israel. There is already a considerable literature as well as a number of "interdenominational" organizations of Jews and Christians (in the United States and Israel) which aim at effecting a Jewish-Christian rapprochement, with slogans such as "worldwide Judeo-Christian alignment" and "the common Judeo-Christian heritage." The flood of

articles and letters to the editor on this theme includes explicit explanations that Judaism is part of "Western Christian civilization" because
Judaism was the "progenitor of Christianity, and Christianity was born
into the world out of the rib of Judaism" and today "only subtle
nuances distinguish Judaism from Christianity." The difference is said
to be so slight that representatives of the non-Western world at international conferences of intellectuals (Africans, Indians, Japanese, del-
egates from South-East Asia, and so on) seem to find it difficult to
understand what distinguishes Jews from Christians.

Now, if any one person in the modern age reflected the characteristic
values and main currents of Western civilization from antiquity until
recent time, and incorporated them in classical fashion in his life and
work, that person would be Goethe. Goethe devoted much thought
to the foundations of his civilization and its roots in Christianity. In
this context he considered Judaism as well (see, for example, *Wilhelm
Meisters Wanderjahre*). In this matter, Goethe cannot be suspected of
partiality; he rejected both Judaism and Christianity. He recognized
the great truth which is ignored by the naïve or pseudo-naïve liberals,
Christian and Jewish, who prate about "the common values of Judaism
and Christianity" or "the common Judeo-Christian heritage." His
thoughts on this subject were summarized in the sentence: "Christianity stands in far greater opposition to Judaism than to paganism."[1]
With his penetrating insight Goethe apprehended the pagan and anti-
Judaic essence of Christianity and drew the conclusions. Goethe
detested Christianity to the point of loathing its basic dogmas, symbols, and rites. Nevertheless, like most European intellectuals, he
believed that, with all its shortcomings, Christianity was the repository
of human values and the one and only necessary and legitimate framework within which European culture could develop. The enlightened
personality progressing toward the humanistic ideal appeared to
Goethe's imagination not, indeed, as a Christian, but as one who had
been molded in the workshop of Christianity. This was why Goethe
regarded Judaism and the Jews as outside the pale of European culture
and barred from participation in the community of civilized Europe-
ans; hence his vigorous opposition to emancipation of the Jews.

Goethe's contemporary Edward Gibbon, a typical representative of
eighteenth-century Enlightenment, assessed Judaism in similar fashion. He hated Judaism for two reasons which were only *prima facie*

contradictory: Christianity, which he detested, grew out of Judaism. But also, the Jews refused to accept Christianity. Something of the same attitude is discernible in Kant.

Against the testimony of Goethe, supported by Gibbon, Kant, and even Hegel, we are now offered the testimony of Africans and Asians to the affinity of Christianity and Judaism—the testimony of members of distant cultures whose knowledge of Christianity (and of Western civilization) is derived from secondary or tertiary sources and whose knowledge of Judaism is based on what they heard from Christian missionaries and other "reliable" Christian sources, or from assimilated Jews.

This common "Judeo-Christian heritage," which Reform or assimilated Jews, especially in the United States, hope will advance recognition of their Judaism by the Christian world as the Judaic branch of Christianity, has never existed. The very concept is absurd, no less so than that of a square circle. Christianity, as we know it, was not an outgrowth of Judaism. Insofar as Judaism is the religion of Torah and *Mitzvoth,* Christianity is its negation. Whatever may have been its origin, the Christianity which spread throughout the Roman Empire was a child of Hellenism and the religious syncretism which was being propagated at the time in the Mediterranean basin. It would not be amiss to consider it the "sixth stage of Greek religion," according to Gilbert Murray's scheme in his *Five Stages of Greek Religion.* This claim is not invalidated by the fact that hellenizing Jews contributed to the shaping of Christianity, that Christianity draws upon the literary sources of Judaism and their characteristic terminology for its own purposes, and borrows the authority of these texts as well as of historic Jewish figures.

The real connection of Christianity to Judaism is like that of *Hamlet* to the history and culture of Denmark. In ideational content and meaning, *Hamlet* is a product of the late Renaissance in Elizabethan England and the spiritual creation of William Shakespeare. Shakespeare's *Hamlet* does not belong to the culture or actual history of the Danish people. It did not grow from Danish roots, was not influenced by Danish culture, and was not expressive of it, even though Shakespeare set the scene of action in Denmark and made use of a story borrowed from a Danish chronicle. In like manner, a Greek-Oriental syncretism associated its spiritual product, Christianity, with elements borrowed from

Judaism but totally divorced from their original meaning. It may plausibly be asserted that Christianity, or something resembling it, would have arisen from decadent Hellenism even without contact with Judaism.

While writing these words in the month of Tishrei [usually September], a few days after the Days of Awe, it is only fitting to contrast the highest symbol of faith in Judaism with that of Christianity: the Aqedah versus the Crucifixion. Thus Abraham is told: "Take now your son, your only one that you love . . . and offer him there for a burnt offering on one of the mountains that I shall tell you." It is a test in which human values and even divine promises ("for through Isaac shall you have descendants") are shunted aside before reverence for God ("Now I know that you truly fear God") and love of God ("Abraham who loves me"). The Christian symbol is that of the deity who sacrifices his only son for man. This is the great contrast between theocentric religion, in which man strives to serve God, and anthropocentric religion, in which God fulfills man's need for salvation. The actual manifestation of Jewish faith in daily living was, historically, the system of Mitzvoth, the Halakhah, the organization of man's life as a program of service to God in day-to-day existence. In contrast, the program of Christianity from its inception to this very day emphasized the abrogation of the "Law." This is the "subtle nuance" which distinguishes Judaism from Christianity. Only Jews who have cast aside the yoke of Torah and have emptied Judaism of all specifically Jewish content can overlook this nuance, as can Christians who have lost their faith in man's salvation through the sacrifice of Jesus. Such "Jews" really do belong to the same world of Western civilization as such "Christians." But after the elimination of this nuance, there is no serious reason for the continued existence of Judaism as a separate entity. If the Jewish nation is defined by its Judaism, then, on this view, the continued existence of the Jewish people has also lost its rationale.

However, if this nuance still obtains, no Judeo-Christian synthesis or even symbiosis is possible, and, to the extent that Western civilization has been molded by Christianity, Judaism does not quite cohere with it. This is what Goethe had in mind when he noted the affinity of Christianity with paganism and their mutual antagonism to Judaism. The poet Goethe dovetailed Greek and Christian mythology in his work because of their affinity, whereas the great humanist Goethe opposed the civil emancipation of the Jews because, in his eyes, they were alien to European culture. Only one who had passed through the crucible of Christianity could belong to this culture. This was the deep conviction of the man who himself rejected Christianity, but viewed it as a necessary stratum in the structure of the culture which he advocated. An attitude toward Judaism as something so alien that it arouses psychological and even physical revulsion can be discerned to this very day among intellectuals of the Western world, even among those who have completely rejected the Christian faith, but had been raised and educated in the civilization molded by the concepts and values of Christianity. If these intellectuals succeeded in overcoming any conscious dislike of Jews, they continue, unconsciously but sometimes even consciously, to feel deeply antagonistic to Judaism. Toward Jews they retain a feeling of strangeness quite different from that which they feel toward foreigners of other nations.

Let us now turn from what the "pagan" Goethe and other non-Christians among the outstanding representatives of Western civilization thought about Judaism and Christianity to Christianity itself and its great representatives. The Christian religion has never recognized and will never be able to recognize de jure the right of Judaism to subsist, even if it is forced to recognize this existence de facto; for the relationship to Judaism of Christianity is unlike the relationship of other faiths. The others deny the Torah of Israel and discredit it, whereas Christianity claims that it is the true Judaism and that there is no legitimate Judaism other than Christianity. Many centuries ago, our Sages already recognized the character of this attitude of Christianity toward Judaism. "God foresaw that the Gentiles are going to translate the Torah and read it in Greek, and they will say 'we are Israel.'"[2] The Midrash also states that within this context, taken in itself, it is not possible to decide in favor of either Jews or Gentiles ("till now the scales are balanced"), but "the Mishnah and the Talmud distinguish Israel from the nations." With the abrogation of the Halakhah, the specific individuating attribute of the Jewish people would be cancelled and no other factor can prevent its disappearance among the nations.

From the Christian point of view, the legitimate existence of a Judaism outside Christianity ceased long ago, and that community which has continued nominally to exist for more than 1,900 years in the form of a Jewish people that is not Christian is not a genuine religious community but a ghost, a mirage, or an act of Satan intended to mock Christianity and enrage it. The very admission of the right of Judaism to exist is equivalent to admission that Christianity is false and counterfeit, rather than the legitimate heir of Judaism.

This idea was well understood and expounded not only by the Church Fathers in the early centuries of Christianity, but also by outstanding exponents of Christian thought in modern times, such as Pascal in the seventeenth century and Dostoevski in the nineteenth. The Russian's profound hatred of Jews was rooted in his feeling that the continued existence of Jews after the year 33 C.E. constituted a factual refutation of the truth of Christianity. Basically, the atheistic-humanistic anti-Semitism of Kant and Goethe is no different from the Christian-Russian anti-Semitism of Dostoevski. Among contemporary Christian theologians none is greater than Karl Barth; moreover, by his vigorous struggle against Nazism, he proved that he cannot be suspected of anti-Semitism in the sense of political-ethnic hatred of Jews. Yet Barth testifies that Judaism (that is, after Jesus, which continues to exist without Jesus) is "the synagogue of death," "a tragic figure which arouses horror by its pain and blindness," "a monstrous figure from the world of the dead," "a pretentious lie" (*hochmütige Lüge*). "The God of whom the Christian conception of Providence teaches, the God who can be known through Jesus the Christ, whose will is therefore not hidden but known (to man) . . . this God is different from the God of Judaism and Islam." In contrast to these vigorous words, how vapid are Martin Buber's "two modes of faith" (*zwei Glaubensweisen*) or Franz Rosenzweig's "two ways of faith" (*zwei Glaubenswege*), both of which lead to God! Barth is fully cognizant that Christianity cannot admit the right of Judaism to subsist as another "mode" or "way" of faith: "The existence of the synagogue alongside the Church is of the nature of an ontological impossibility, a wound, an ulcer in the body of Christ himself, an unbearable pain."[3]

For the Jew who regards Judaism as embodied in Torah and Mitzvoth, there can be no coexistence of ideas (in contradistinction to a factual coexistence) between Judaism and Christianity and no place for the "Judeo-Christian dialogue." It is possible for Judaism to engage in dialogue with every faith and religion that denies the Torah of Israel and opposes its own teaching to it, which denies the God of Israel and sets up against Him its own version of divinity. With such religions it is possible to enter into debate. To all of them one can apply the biblical verse, "For let every people walk everyone in the name of his god and we will walk in the name of the Lord our God forever" (Mic. 4:5). As for Christianity, Judaism can maintain such a coexistence only with the Marcionites who explicitly repudiated the identification of the Christian god with the God of Israel and did not accept the Hebrew Bible as part of the Christian Scripture, but interpreted the New Testament as directed against the Hebrew Bible. There is no possibility of maintaining a dialogue with official Christianity, which claims, blasphemously from the point of view of Judaism, that the Torah has a Christian meaning and that He who once gave the Torah then abrogated the Mitzvoth.

This explains the repugnance Judaism has for Christianity. This feeling is an integral aspect of the living Jewish awareness and is very different from the Jewish attitude to other forms of worship of strange gods, and, needless to say, to Islam. This negative position is still discernible among outstanding liberal and Reform personalities in the nineteenth century, from Abraham Geiger to Herman Cohen, who imbibed the living tradition of Judaism. It is no longer to be found in Franz Rosenzweig, Martin Buber, or Samuel Hugo Bergmann. It has ceased to exist among those Jews who rejoice at the absolution of Judaism by the Vatican Church Council and attribute importance to its statement concerning the "guilt of the Jews." It is hardly characteristic of modern Reform Judaism in the United States and is completely absent from the secular state of Israel. It can hardly be eradicated from the hearts of Jews who accept the yoke of Torah and Mitzvoth.

Notes

Sources and Translations

Index

Notes

Editor's Introduction

1. A Hebrew translation of Sir Isaiah's tribute appeared in *Ha'aretz*, March 4, 1983.
2. *Ha'aretz*, April 15, 1983.
3. Yeshayahu Leibowitz, with student-colleagues, *Conversations about the "Eight Chapters" of Maimonides* (Jerusalem: Keter Publishing House, 1986) (Heb.).
4. The Halakhah is the body of Jewish religious law as set forth in the talmudic sources, elaborated over the centuries in the rabbinic literature, and exemplified in the practice of the Jewish communities.
5. The Histadruth, to this day, is a trade union organization on the one hand and a conglomerate of cooperatives, agricultural settlements, banking and business concerns on the other.
6. For a brief description of the incident see the prefatory remarks to chapter 17.
7. See chapter 22 of this book.
8. The belief of some critics that Leibowitz is inconsistent in this respect stems from their taking it for granted that autonomy must be valuable in itself. Certainly nothing in Leibowitz's views is inconsistent with regard for freedom from external coercion (Isaiah Berlin's negative freedom) as a most important instrumental value—a basic condition for the possibility of men's striving to realize any value whatsoever.
9. Leibowitz's failure to make this point in more than one or two explicit statements has misled some critics as well as some followers into attributing to him a total rejection of the inner religious experience. It should have been clear that his conception of worshipful motivation of religious praxis (*lishmah*) necessarily involves an inner dimension. But the specific content of such an inner experience is unique to each individual and cannot be socially shared.
10. The relevant clause of the King's Order in Council of 1922 read: "the rabbinical courts of the Jewish community shall have exclusive jurisdiction in matters of marriage and divorce, alimony and confirmation of wills, of members of their community other than foreigners."

11. It is worth noting that the Kadi Act of 1961 granted the Moslem courts a status similar to that of the rabbinical courts.

12. For a concise description and analysis of the Knesseth debates over the proposed constitution see: Eliezer Goldman *Religious Issues in Israel's Political Life* (Jerusalem: World Zionist Organization, 1964), pp. 47–66.

13. See note 4 above.

14. This does not exclude moral considerations, corresponding to what are usually called "human rights." But in the present context the terminology of legal discourse is more confusing than enlightening.

1. Religious Praxis

1. The term Mitzvoth is usually translated as "commandments." The connotations of the Hebrew word, however, are far richer. They include halakhic precepts as developed in the orah Torah—Ed.

2. The phrase in quotes is an allusion to an aggadic narrative in the Talmud concerning the controversies of Beth Hillel and Beth Shamai. The story is that a voice called out from heaven: "Both these and these [opinions] are the words of the living God, but the binding halakhic opinion is that of Beth Hillel" (B. T. *Erubin* 13b)—Ed.

3. The term "Torah" must be understood as referring to the written Torah together with oral teaching. "Torah" in its traditional usage, and not in its formal meaning referring to the Pentateuch or the Hebrew Bible.

4. The phrase is taken from a Jewish Credo of the fourteenth century, which is a popularized and concise version of Maimonides' thirteen articles of the Jewish faith expounded in his commentary to the Mishnah, Tractate *Sanhedrin*. It correctly renders Maimonides' absolute rejection of divine attributes, including ones imputed by way of analogy—Ed.

5. Community of the believers, or community of those recognizing the uniqueness and unity of God and its logical implications—Ed.

6. Samuel David Luzzatto (1800–1865) was a biblical scholar, philosopher, and literary critic. He opposed the rationalistic stream in Jewish thought as well as the modern critical endeavor to separate morality from religion.

   Ahad Ha'am, pen-name of Asher Ginsberg (1865–1927), was a Hebrew writer and a major contributor to Zionist thought. He attempted to develop a conception of secular Jewish nationalism which would do justice to the Jewish historic tradition. One of his central conceptions was that of Judaism as the bearer of an absolute morality.

   Hermann Cohen (1842–1918), was the founder of the Marburg school of neo-Kantian philosophy. Throughout most of his career he entertained a Kantian conception of the relation of morality and religion. His last works were devoted to a philosophy of Judaism. It is questionable whether his inclusion with Luzzatto and Ahad Ha'am does justice to the shift in his later thought on Judaism—Ed.

7. Bahya ibn Paquda (eleventh-century, Spain). His book, *The Duties of the*

Heart, is one of the most important Jewish ethical treatises. It reflects both rationalistic philosophic influences and Sufi mysticism.

Moshe Hayyim Luzzatto (1707–1746) was a Kabbalist and poet. His book of ethical guidance, *The Path of the Upright,* was perhaps the most studied work of its kind in the circles of the Mussar movement, which influenced the Lithuanian yeshivoth late in the nineteenth century—Ed.

8. See note 5.
9. Isaac Luria (1534–1572), a central figure among the Safed Kabbalists of the sixteenth century, whose original system profoundly influenced subsequent kabbalistic thought—Ed.
10. This is an allusion to Maimonides, who at the end of the *Guide of the Perplexed* places this construction upon Prov. 5:17, in arguing that the *Summum Bonum* is a state of pure intellection. Any other good is not fully one's own—Ed.
11. Moses Maimonides, *Guide of the Perplexed,* trans. S. Pines (Chicago: University of Chicago Press, 1963), III 27, pp 510–512, III 51, pp. 618–622.
12. Ibid., III 34, pp. 534–535.
13. For a change in the author's position on this question, see chapter 8—Ed.
14. The author here alludes to talmudic sources from which we learn that the Sages considered the books of Ezekiel, Ecclesiastes, and Proverbs as candidates for apocryphal status. Only by dint of interpretation were they retained in the canon. See B. T. *Sabbath* 13b and 30b; *Haggigah* 13a; *Menahot* 46a. There is also a mishnaic source which appears to imply that as late as the second century the Sages disputed the admissibility of the books of Ecclesiastes and the Song of Songs to the canon. The decision to admit them was made only after the question was put to a vote. *Yadayim* 5, 6—Ed.
15. B. T. *Kiddushin* 31a, and elsewhere.
16. The Hebrew word *lishmah* which recurs constantly in these essays, signifies "for its own sake," meaning "to the exclusion of ulterior motives"—Ed.
17. Aqedah (literally the binding) refers to the binding of Isaac on the altar—Ed.
18. Don Isaac Abravanel (1437–1508) was a statesman in the courts of Portugal and Spain, a philosopher, and biblical exegete—Ed.
19. Rabbinic usage refers to the *Yetzer Hatov* (the good inclination) and the *Yetzer Hara* (the evil inclination), meaning the drives ordinarily directed toward the good conduct and those usually leading to violation of one's duties—Ed.
20. The Ne'ilah service, begun before sundown at the culmination of a day of fasting and prayer and ending with the onset of darkness, is, for most observers of Yom Kippur, the most solemn moment of the day. It ends with the proclamation of Shema (Deut. 6:4) by the congregation. Immediately afterwards the weekday evening service begins.
21. Moses Maimonides, *Mishneh Torah: Book of Knowledge,* English translation by Moses Hyamson (Jerusalem: Boystown Press, 1962), "Laws Concerning the Study of the Torah," 1. 10, p. 58a.
22. Mishnah *Aboth* 2, 13.
23. In like manner, Hans Sachs (in Wagner's *Meistersinger*) explains to Walther the difference between a pretty song (*ein schoenes Lied*) a youth may sing on

a fair day when the sun shines and the flowers bloom, and the artistic achievement of real poetry (*ein Meisterlied*) a man may create against the damping forces of the autumn of life and the autumn of nature.

24. Rabbi Kook was the first Chief Rabbi of Palestine under the mandatory rule; one of the few original thinkers in rabbinical circles in this century—Ed.
25. B. T. *Berakhoth* 28b.
26. This is the mishnaic description of the content of Shema. The phrase recurs in the liturgy—Ed.
27. *Olam keminhago noheg;* literally, "the world conducts itself in accordance with its habit"—Ed.
28. The metaphysical distinction between body and soul is irrelevant and unnecessary from the standpoint of religious faith. From a religious point of view the dividing line does not pass between "matter" and "spirit" but between Creator and creature, between God and the world.
29. B. T. *Sanhedrin* 98b.
30. The cardinal trespasses a Jew is required to avoid even at the cost of his life—Ed.
31. An Arab village in the Sharon plain, within the borders of Israel. When the Sinai campaign began in October 1956, a curfew was imposed on all the villages of the Arab "triangle" starting at six in the evening. Residents of Kafr Kasm who were in the fields or elsewhere outside the village and returned after the curfew were stopped by a unit of the "border-guard" and shot without warning and without a hearing. Fifty-one residents of the village were killed, among them women and children (October 29, 1956). The incident came as a shock to the public and those responsible faced trial. Superior officers were found guilty of issuing the curfew order improperly; they received symbolic punishment. The commander of the unit and several of his subordinates were found guilty of illegal execution of a command, sentenced to relatively short terms of imprisonment, and released soon after. The government compensated the families of the victims and arranged for a traditional *Sulha* (the traditional Arab ceremony for settling a blood feud).
32. This is a slight variant of a phrase occurring in Jewish mystical writings—Ed.
33. *Guide* III 27, p. 511.
34. *Guide* III 51, p. 622.
35. Rabbi Abraham Isaac Hacohen Kook, *Oroth Hateshuvah* (Jerusalem: 1925), chap. 5.
36. Rabbi Jacob Meir Harlap, *Mei Merom,* a commentary on Maimonides' "Eight Chapters" (Jerusalem, 1935).
37. Ibid., chap. 8.

2. Of Prayer

1. The *Shulhan Arukh* is a halakhic code compiled by Rabbi Joseph Caro (1488–1578) and, together with its glosses, is regarded as authoritative. The citation is from *Orah Hayyim* (the first part of the code) A.a—Ed.

2. What in halakhic sources is technically called *Tefilah* or prayer, is a set of eighteen benedictions, later extended to nineteen—Ed.
3. *Tefilah bekhavanah* is prayer recited with awareness—Ed.
4. *Iyyun Tefilah* means careful examination of what one is saying while praying—Ed.
5. See *Jerusalem Talmud Berakhoth*, chap. 2 Halakhoth 4, 5; B. T. *Berakhoth* 31a, 32b, 54b; *Sabbath* 118b, 127a; *Rosh Hashanah* 16b and elsewhere. See also Rashi and the Tossafists at these locations.
6. Responsum 344
7. *Midrash Tanhuma* to Gen. 43; 14.
8. Rosh Hashanah and Yom Kippur—Ed.
9. A *Piyyut* (hymn) included in the Ashkenazic and Italian liturgies for the Days of Awe and describing the divine judgment on Rosh Hashanah—Ed.
10. Rabbi Naphtali Zvi Yehudah Berlin (1817–1893) was head of the Volozhin Yeshivah from 1852 to his death. The statement in the text is from his gloss on Deut. 26:15 in his commentary to the Pentateuch, *Ha'amek Davar* (Jerusalem: El Hamekoroth), p. 213. The word *Ar'ar*, usually translated "the destitute," is here interpreted as stemming from a root meaning "to awaken"—Ed.

3. The Reading of Shema

1. The opening words of Tractate *Berakhoth*, the first tractate of the Mishnah—Ed.
2. Moshe Hayyim Luzzatto, *Mesillat Yesharim, The Path of the Upright*, critical edition and translation by Mordecai M. Kaplan (Philadelphia: Jewish Publication Society).
3. The Shema consists of three portions: Deut. 6:4–9; Deut. 11:13–21; Num. 15:37–41—Ed.
4. B. T. *Berakhoth* 61b.
5. *Aher*, meaning "other" or "another," was the appellation given Elisha ben Abuyah after he ceased observing the *Mitzvoth*—Ed.
6. The following works of Maimonides are used as the main sources: Commentary on the *Mishnah*, introduction to the tenth (in some editions the eleventh) chapter of Tractate *Sanhedrin; Mishneh Torah: Book of Knowledge*, "Laws of Repentance," chap. 10; *Guide of the Perplexed*, III 23 (Job!), 27–28, and above all chapters 51 ("remark") and 52.
7. These citations are taken from Maimonides, *Guide* III 52, p. 630.
8. The reference to Abraham's faith and the statement that one must aspire to attain this way of serving God appear in Maimonides' introduction to the tenth chapter of *Sanhedrin*—Ed.
9. Ibid.
10. Maimonides, *Guide* III 51, p. 622.
11. Maimonides, *Mishneh Torah: Book of Knowledge*, English translation by Moses Hyamson (Jerusalem: Boystown Press, 1962), "Laws of Repentance," X, 5.

The passage, in its entirety, places the quotation in proper perspective from Maimonides' stand-point: "Whoever engages in the study of Torah in order that he may receive an award or avoid calamities is not studying the Torah for its own sake. Whoever occupies himself with the Torah neither out of fear nor for the sake of recompense, but solely out of love for the Lord of the whole Earth, who enjoined us to do so, is occupied with the Torah for its own sake [*lishmah*]. The Sages, however, said 'one should always engage in the study of the Torah, even if not for its own sake; for he who begins thus will end by studying it for its own sake'." The statement, as phrased in the author's text, is the wording of the current versions of B. T. *Pesahim* 50b, which Maimonides is quoting—Ed.

12. B. T. *Pesahim* 7a.
13. B. T. *Ta'anith* 7a.
14. B. T. *Berakhoth* 31b; literally: "the Torah spoke in the language of human-kind"—Ed.
15. Rabbi Meir Simhah Cohen (1842–1926) was rabbi of Dwinsk (Dinabourg in Latvia) from 1886 to his death. *Meshekh Hokhmah* is a book of homiletical and halakhic comments on the Pentateuch. The statements cited occur at various points in this work. Most of them are to be found in the glosses on Exodus 19 and 32—Ed.

4. Fear of God in the Book of Job

1. An Amoraic opinion. See B. T. *Baba Bathra* 15a.
2. *Midrash Tanhuma* to Gen. 18:23.
3. B. T. *Sotah* 31b.
4. Maimonides, *Guide* III 25, p. 496.
5. Ibid. III 23, pp. 492–493.
6. Ibid. pp. 496–497.

5. Divine Governance

1. B. T. *Berakhoth* 33b, and elsewhere—Ed.
2. Maimonides, *Guide* III 17–18 and 23–24—Ed.
3. The references are to *Guide* III 51–54 and Maimonides, *Mishneh Torah: Book of Knowledge*, "Laws of Repentance," X—Ed.
4. In the opening of "Eight Chapters" the opinion of the physicians (Galen) regarding the multiplicity of souls in man is juxtaposed with the view of the philosophers (Aristotle) on the unity of the soul as the form of man. Maimonides rejects the former and adopts the latter. Undoubtedly, among his reasons for this decision were the anthropological-philosophical grounds for ruling out any segregation of the "true opinions in Torah" and the practical *Mitzvoth*. Here Maimonides reveals himself in all his greatness as the "right-corner pillar" of halakhic Judaism!

5. The expressions in inverted commas occur in the first chapter of *Mishneh Torah*—Ed.

6. For Maimonides' discussion of these three concepts, see *Guide,* III 53, pp. 630–632.

7. Diametrically opposed to Maimonides' conception of providence is the view of Nahmanides: "no one can have a part in the Torah of Moses our teacher unless he believes that all our words and our events are miraculous in scope, there being no natural or customary course of the world in them" (Nahmanides, *Commentary on the Torah,* translated and annotated by Charles B. Chavel, (New York: Shilo Publishing House, 1973), vol. 2, p. 174.

8. Maimonides, *Guide* III, p. 629.

9. Maimonides' intention here was ably expounded and clarified by Moshe Narboni in his commentary on *Guide* III 51, where he points out his predecessors' error. See Moshe Narboni, *Glosses to the Guide of the Perplexed* (Vienna: 1852), p. 59 (Heb.).

10. See chapter 4 above.

11. Hassidic doctrine adopts a similar position (in the name of the Maggid of Mezrich) in a remark on the prayer verse, "and inscribe us in the book of life": *"The inscription in the book of life is to be construed as an engraving in the thought of man."*

6. *Lishmah* and Not-*Lishmah*

1. These were the first words in the series of articles by M. S.—Ed.

2. Gush Emunim is an organization for promoting Jewish settlement of the occupied territories. Its core membership is highly motivated by a chauvinistic religious ideology characterized by a racist conception of the election of Israel, a fetishistic account of the sanctity of the Holy Land, and a messianic interpretation of the founding of the state of Israel—Ed.

3. B. T. *Pesahim* 50b.

4. B. T. *Ta'anith* 7a.

5. For Maimonides "truth" is none other than the truth of the faith in God. See his Code, "Laws Pertaining to the Foundations of the Torah," chap. 1, end of clause 1, end of clause 3, and all of clause 4.

6. Commentary on the Mishnah, introduction to chap. 10 of Tractate *Sanhedrin.*

7. *Guide* III 51 p. 622.

8. Rabbi Hayyim of Volozhin, *Ruah Hayyim: A Commentary on Tractate Aboth* (Vilna: 1859) p. 1a. (Heb.) Rabbi Hayyim founded the great Yeshivah in Volozhin and was the disciple of Rabbi Eliyahu, the Gaon of Vilna—Ed.

9. *Guide,* introduction, p. 18.

10. Ibid., p. 20.

11. Rabbi Aqiba was an enthusiastic supporter of Bar Kokhba's revolt against the Romans in the years 132–135 and regarded Bar Kokhba as a messianic figure. The revolt resulted in the decimation of the Jewish population of Judaea—Ed.

7. The Uniqueness of the Jewish People

1. Judah Halevi attributed to the Jewish people a unique native faculty for the intuitive perception of divine matters. Since this was a faculty above reason, he went so far as to maintain that, in that sense, Israel was a species apart. Rabbi Kook, who embraced the idea of the *Volksgeist,* adapted it to a conception of a world-soul which, at the level of humanity, becomes individuated into collective national souls, each with its specific characteristics. The Jewish national soul, on his view, differs from the others not by a specific characteristic, but by embracing the partial truths of the other national souls into a universal synthesis—Ed.
2. The term *Taharath Hamishpahah,* which is here literally translated, refers to the separation of man and wife during the menstrual period until after a ritual immersion—Ed.
3. This was not true in the legal-halakhic sense whereby the son of a Jewish mother is a Jew and is considered to be subject to halakhic jurisdiction. From a sociological point of view, however, deliberate detachment from the halakhic way of life, as distinct from mere violation of Mitzvoth, was also detachment from the body of Israel—Ed.
4. The Hebrew word *Umah,* here translated as "nation," is peculiarly apt to perpetuate confusion. In medieval Arabic the same word was used to denote the world brotherhood of Islam. Jewish writers used it to refer to the communities of Judaism, Christianity, and Islam. Contemporary Jewish religious circles use the term for the "nation" in the contemporary setting, while retaining the connotations of its medieval usage—Ed.
5. The Hebrew expression *Netzah Israel* had to be translated in a manner which distorts its meaning in the original context. The King James version of the Bible has "the Strength of Israel" in the reference to God who is the source of Israel's victories. This accords with the Targum (the Aramaic translation of the Bible). An alternative English translation is "the Eternal of Israel"—Ed.
6. Rabbi Judah Loew ben Bezalel (called Maharal) of Prague (c. 1525–1609) considered Israel to be inherently different from any other people by virtue of the pure spirituality of its nature as contrasted with the materiality of others.
7. From the benediction recited prior to reading or studying the Torah—Ed.
8. Mishnah *Kelim,* I, 7–8, p. 5a. The *Omer* is the sheaves of barley cut on the second day of Passover and "waved before God" in the Temple (Lev. 23:10). The first fruit and the two loaves of bread were brought to the Temple on the Feast of Shavuoth, the fiftieth day after the bringing of the Omer. Ibid. 23:17—Ed.
9. Rabbi Meir Simhah Cohen, *Meshekh Hokhmah.* See chapter 3 n. 15.

8. The Individual and Society in Judaism

1. Abravanel's antimonarchical views reflect his experience in the service of the kings of Portugal and Spain compared to the political order of Venice, which he came to know toward the end of his life—Ed.

2. These remarks by Rabbi Naphtali Zvi Yehudah Berlin are to be found in his commentary on the Pentateuch at the verse in question—Ed.
3. Mishnah *Sanhedrin* 4, 5
4. Alenu Leshabe'ah, the prayer which accompanies the blowing of the Shofar and has been included in each of the three daily prayers, has two paragraphs. The first describes God's cosmic reign and ontological uniqueness. The second expresses hope for the establishment of God's kingdom on earth—Ed.
5. See also chapter 2 above—Ed.
6. Both books set before the reader a systematic ascent on the rungs of piety. The first was written by R. Bahya ibn Pakuda; the second by Moses Hayyim Luzzatto. See chapter 1 n. 7—Ed.
7. Maimonides, *Guide* III 34, pp. 534–535.
8. Ibid. II 36, p. 372. In context, Maimonides is explaining that people of great intellectual achievement may not attain prophecy because of their wish "to dominate or to be held great by the common people and to obtain from them honor and obedience for its own sake."
9. Ibid. III 51, p. 622.

9. A-historical Thinkers in Judaism

1. Levi ben Gerson (called Gersonides) (1288–1344) was a mathematician, philosopher, and biblical exegete. Hasdai Crescas (second half of the fourteenth century to the early years of the fifteenth, was a rabbinic scholar, communal leader of Aragonese Jewry, important theologian, and innovative philosopher—Ed.
2. B. T. *Berakhoth* 33b. The phrase in question is included in the opening benediction of the Amidah prayer. It occurs in Deuteronomy 10:17 and in Nehemiah 9:32, as part of a Levitical prayer. The subject is discussed in Maimonides' *Guide* I 59, pp. 140–141—Ed.
3. Maimonides, *Mishneh Torah: Book of Judges* (New Haven: Yale University Press, 1949), "Laws of Kings," XIII.
4. *Zera'im* is the first order of tractates of the Mishnah, those dealing with halakhic practices applying to agriculture. The Tractate *Berakhoth* dealing with prayer and benedictions was included. *Kodashim* deals with the Temple service, but includes *Hulin* which deals with laws applying to nonsacrificial consumption of meats. *Tahoroth* contains tractates dealing with laws of ritual purity. *Nezikim* encompasses the civil law. It includes the Tractate *Sanhedrin*, which, as the name implies, is concerned with the powers, composition, and procedures of the Sanhedrin (the highest judicial and religious council)—Ed.

10. The Religious and Moral Significance of the Redemption

1. Rabbi Se'adiah ben Joseph (892–942) was a rabbinic scholar and head of the Yeshiva of Sura, philosopher, biblical exegete, grammarian, and poet—Ed.
2. The reference is to Isa. 49:6: "It is too slight a thing that you should be my

servant to raise up the tribe of Jacob, and to restore the preserved of Israel. I will also give you for a light to the nations"—Ed.

3. The Tossafists were Ashkenazic scholars of the twelfth and thirteenth centuries. Many of their opinions were collected in the *Tossafoth*, or comments additional to Rashi's commentary on the Babylonian Talmud. These are printed in the standard editions of the Talmud alongside the text—Ed.

4. The statement occurs in a Tossafist comment to *Yevamoth* 50a and refers to the prophecy in 1 Kings 13:2 concerning the birth of Josiah. The Tossafist points out the contingency of this prophecy, which might have remained unfulfilled had not Hezekiah repented, been granted additional years of life, and subsequently begat Menasseh, Josiah's father. He answers that the prophet prophesied what ought to have happened had Hezekiah not sinned and been punished with illness—Ed.

5. The Frankists were a Sabbatean sect among Polish and Moravian Jews led by Jacob Frank (1726–1791). In the sixties of the eighteenth century many of them, including Frank himself, converted to Christianity, even as Sabbatai Zevi converted to Islam—Ed.

6. For several centuries Yemenite Jewry was strongly influenced by Maimonides. His halakhic rulings were generally accepted and his theological outlook dominated learned circles. The efflorescence of Palestinian Kabbalah in the sixteenth century left its mark on the practice and thought of Yemenite Jewry, as it did all over the Diaspora. Rabbi Yahieh Qafah led a religious movement in the early years of this century, which might be described as a return to Maimonides. The terms "long-nosed" and "short-nosed" are ultra-literal renditions of widespread appellations for two groups of *Sefiroth* (emanations). "Decemy," referring to the system of Sefiroth in its entirety, was intended to suggest a parallel to the Christian Trinity—Ed.

7. The epithets "great eagle" and others occur frequently in references to Maimonides in the rabbinic literature—Ed.

8. Kabbalists who reacted in this manner include Rabbi Joseph Karo, in *Maggid Mesharim*, R. Meir ibn Gabbai in *Avodath ha-Kodesh*, the Vilna Gaon, and others.

9. B. T. *Sukkah* 52a.

10. Maimonides, *Mishneh Torah: Book of Knowledge*, "Laws Concerning the Basic Principles of the Torah," I, 1.

11. The sentences in quotes are taken from passages recited before the morning prayer. The reference to Maimonides' Code is to the third clause of the opening chapter—Ed.

12. The quoted phrases are taken respectively from the benediction before reading or studying the Torah and from the Qiddush of the holidays—Ed.

13. Maimonides' responsa.

14. *Mishneh Torah: Book of Knowledge*, "Laws Concerning the Basic Principles of the Torah," VII.

15. For additional details see note 8 of chapter 7.

16. R. Meir Simhah Cohen, *Meshekh Hokhmah* to Exodus 32:19.

11. Redemption and the Dawn of Redemption

1. Compare the version of the Sabbath commandment in Deut. 14 with that of Exod. 20.
2. Maimonides, *Guide* III 50, pp. 615–616.
3. Maimonides, *Mishneh Torah: Book of Knowledge,* "Laws Concerning the Foundations of the Torah", VIII, 1.
4. Ps. 113–118. The recitation of the so-called "half-Hallel" on Passover in the morning prayers after the first day, which omits portions of psalms 115 and 116, is a usage rather than a halakhic precept.
5. *Yevamoth* 49a.
6. Maimonides, *Mishneh Torah: Book of Judges,* "Laws Concerning Kings and Wars," XII, 2.
7. *Reshith tsemihath ge'ulateinu* (the dawn of our redemption) is a catch-phrase current in national-religious circles, which has even been incorporated in a prayer for the welfare of the state—Ed.

12. The Status of Women

1. Women are required to observe all halakhic prohibitions. They are exempt from positive duties, observance of which is restricted to certain occasions. For example, they are not required to eat in the *Sukkah* (booth) during the feast of Sukkoth. They are exempt from wearing *Tsitsith* and *Tefilin* (phylacteries), as these *Mitzvoth* are performed in the daytime—Ed.
2. The implausibility of barring women from any study of Torah troubled most of the halakhists. The exclusion is usually taken to refer only to the Oral Torah and, even then, not to such study as is necessary to acquaint a woman with her halakhic duties—Ed.
3. See Mishnah *Aboth,* 3, 6
4. A considerable body of halakhic opinion in recent years, which has been ignored by the religious establishment in Israel, seeks to improve the religious and practical standing of women. For an important summary of recent halakhic discussion over the rights of women to active and passive participation in elections to public office, see the opinion of Justice Elon in the decision of the Supreme Court of Israel sitting as a High Court of Justice in the case of Leah Shakdiel vs the Ministry of Religious Affairs, 151/17—Ed.

13. Religion and Science

1. This is, of course, a reference to the great geometric ingenuity Ptolemaic astronomy deployed in reducing the visible motion of the planets, which is neither circular nor uniform, to complex sets of uniform circular motions on epicycles, about eccentrics, and so on—Ed.
2. The first word of the Torah, *Bereshith,* "in the beginning," already involves us in problems concerning time, if taken literally—Ed.

3. The second word, *Bara,* "created," is ordinarily taken to denote something which is beyond any possible human experience: the coming into being of all experiencing—Ed.

4. Abraham ibn Ezra (1089–1164) was a biblical exegete, grammarian, poet, astronomer, and philosopher—Ed.

5. Maimonides, *Guide,* III 23, p. 496.

6. Ibid.

14. The Social Order as a Religious Problem

1. The *Yishuv* was the term used to designate the Palestinian Jewish community prior to the foundation of the state of Israel. When this chapter was written, the labor movement set the tone for both the social and cultural complexion of the Jewish community in mandatory Palestine—Ed.

2. See chapter 1, n. 7.

3. *Hoshen Mishpat* is the part of the *Shulhan Arukh* devoted to civil law.

4. *Urim* and *Tumim* were the jewels on the high-priest's breast plate which were consulted as oracles. See Num. 27:17 and 1 Sam. 28:8. *Lishkath Hagazith* was a chamber on the Temple Mount where sessions of the Sanhedrin were held until several decades prior to the destruction of the Temple—Ed.

5. The annotations to the *Shulhan Arukh* by Rabbi Moses Isserles (1525?–1572) represent the accepted halakhic practice of the Ashkenazic community.

6. This was the motto of the Mizrahi, the religious party within the Zionist movement.

15. The Crisis of Religion in the State of Israel

1. See Deut. 21:18–21 and 13:13–19. and B. T. *Sanhedrin* 71a—Ed.

2. For proof of this see Maimonides' Code, *Book of Judges,* "Laws Concerning Kings and Judges" III 14, where, after an exact and detailed enumeration of the laws of capital punishment, the following principle is set down: "The king has authority to execute, without proof positive, or on the testimony of one witness . . . for he may order the public welfare in accordance with the needs of the hour. He may execute many on one day and leave them hanging for many days, if he deems it necessary to deter criminals and to break the power of the wicked . . . for the king is appointed, in the first place, to administer justice and lead in war"—Ed.

3. B. T. *Sanhedrin* 19b—Ed.

4. I Maccabees 2.

5. B. T. *Erubim* 45a.

6. Mishnah *Makkoth* 1. 10—Ed.

7. Neturei Karta are a small group of Orthodox extremists who dissociate themselves completely from the state of Israel—Ed.

8. On the restrictions imposed on agricultural production during the Sabbatical year, see Leviticus 25. The author's contention is that although individual

farmers could find ways of subsisting and yet observe all these restrictions, their observance by the entire agricultural community would be disastrous for the nation as a whole—Ed.

16. A Call for the Separation of Religion and State

1. *Hillul Hashem*, an expression derived from a locution used by the prophet Ezekiel and meaning desecration of God's name, is used as a derisive designation for the actions of pious Jews which disgrace their religion—Ed.
2. "Israel is a state ruled by law, not by Halakhah" was a favorite dictum of Ben Gurion.—Ed.
3. The allusion is to the rabbis appointed by the Czarist government to further its policy with respect to the Jews.—Ed.
4. The reference is chiefly to the period of mass immigration in the early fifties, when many immigrant children from religious homes were arbitrarily assigned to secular educational institutions rather than to schools of the religious stream within the state educational system—Ed.
5. The Ministry of Religions maintains most of the religious facilities and pays the salaries of the duly constituted religious functionaries of the Moslem and Druse communities. It participates in the maintenance and construction of buildings serving the religious purposes of Moslems and Christians—Ed.
6. Such a situation obtained in the Hagganah, the Jewish defense force which operated under the conditions of mandatory rule. Religious members were organized in separate units in which they were able to avoid unnecessary desecration of the Sabbath—Ed.
7. The Halakhah does not recognize a status of bastardy. A child of an unmarried mother is legitimate in every respect. However, a child born of an incestuous or adulterous relation, called "mamzer," can only marry a person of like status—Ed.
8. The question whether, from a halakhic standpoint, a couple wed by civil marriage requires a halakhically valid divorce in order that the wife may remarry has been the subject of controversy among rabbis. Because of the doubt concerning the status of such a couple, the tendency has been to require halakhic divorce in such cases. The point made in the text is that the explicit refusal of the couple to be halakhically wedded may make it unnecessary to require a halakhic divorce. It eliminates the chief ground for its need—Ed.

17. After Kibiyeh

1. American citizens Julius and Ethel Rosenberg were found guilty of nuclear espionage for the U.S.S.R. They were condemned to death and executed on June 15, 1953.
2. *Pesikta* 2.
3. Gen. 34.
4. See Gen. 49:5–7—Ed.

18. Jewish Identity and Israeli Silence

1. A. D. Gordon, one of the ideologists of the kibbutz movement, advocated the benefits of physical labor in communion with nature. He favored a small collective community based on intensive interpersonal ties. Shlomoh Lavi's preference was for the large kibbutz capable of attracting a massive membership and gaining a dominant influence on the general economy and the rest of society—Ed.

2. The Canaanites were a literary-ideological circle which advocated severance of the Israelis from contemporary Jewish culture and from Jewish history in the exilic period, and argued for their self-definition as Israelis defined by the territorial environment rather than as Jews—Ed.

3. Hayyim Weizmann was instrumental in obtaining the Balfour Declaration, which announced the British government's support for the creation of a Jewish national home in Palestine. He headed the Zionist organization in the 1920s and 1930s and became the first president of Israel.

   Louis D. Brandeis, American jurist who eventually became a justice of the Supreme Court, was an active Zionist during and immediately following World War I. His stand on some central issues of Zionist policy, both political and economic, was opposed to that of Weizmann—Ed.

4. See chapter 1 n. 31.

5. During the fifties and most of the sixties, the Arabs of Israel were subject to a military control which curtailed their freedom of movement and subjected them to discriminatory regulations—Ed.

6. In 1960, Yossele Schuchmacher, age 8, was hidden from his parents by his maternal grandfather and his ultra-orthodox friends to assure his religious upbringing.

7. These terms designate the established old-timers and affluent immigrants on the one hand, and the penurious immigrants from the underdeveloped countries on the other—Ed.

20. The Religious Significance of the State

1. "Rabbi Yohanan said: How did Yarov'am son of Joash king of Israel merit to be counted among the kings of Judah? Because he did not accept slander against Amos" (B. T. *Pesahim* 87b). The inclusion among the kings of Judah refers to the first verse of the Book of Hosea—Ed.

2. In 1096 the Jews of northern France and the Rhineland were massacred by the Crusaders, although they could have saved their lives by converting to Christianity. In 1648 the Jewish population of Poland and Ukraine were decimated by the followers of Bogdan Chmielnicki—Ed.

3. The Hasmonaean monarch who extended the territory under Judaean rule to the north and to the east of the Jordan—Ed.

4. Mishnah *Aboth* 3.2.

5. This is an allusion to the kabbalistic notion of our world being directed by the divine overflow descending through the world of the Sefiroth to the lower worlds—Ed.

21. The Territories

1. Such opportunities existed, perhaps (!), immediately after the signing of the Rhodes agreements, on the eve of the Suez war, and immediately after the Six Day war.
2. And now we can add the Bar-Lev Line.
3. See chapter 18 n. 2.
4. See Mishnah *Kelim* I.6.

22. Right, Law, and Reality

1. B. T. *Baba Bathra* 41a.

23. A Jewish State

1. In maps of Israel prior to the war of 1967, the border between Israel and the parts of Palestine under Jordanian rule was marked by a green line—Ed.
2. Ezekiel 33:23–26.

25. Forty Years After

1. For an elaboration of these points see chapter 22.

27. "The Common Judeo-Christian Heritage"

1. "Die Christentum steht mit dem Judentum in einem viel stärkerem Gegensatz als mit dem Heidentum" (*Nachlass*).
2. Midrash *Tanhuma* to Exod. 34:27.
3. "Die Existenz der Synagoge neben der Kirche [ist] . . . so etwas wie eine ontologische Unmöglichkeit, eine Wunde, ja eine Lücke im Leib Christi selber, die schlechterdings unerträglich ist" (*Kirchliche Dogmatik*, IV/1, p. 749).

Sources and Translations

All the chapters in this book, with the exception of chapters 24 and 25, were taken from two Hebrew collections: *Judaism, Jewish People, and the State of Israel* (Jerusalem and Tel-Aviv: Schocken Publishers, 1975), hereinafter *Judaism;* and *Faith, History and Values* (Jerusalem: Academon, 1982), hereinafter *Faith*. Transliterated Hebrew titles of the chapters are given below wherever they have not been literally translated in this collection.

All the translations from *Faith* are by Yoram Navon. Chapters 1, 2, 14, 16, 17, 21, and 25 were translated by the editor. The first part of chapter 13 was translated by Zvi Jacobson, the rest by the editor. Chapter 15 is an abridged translation by Rabbi Gershon Levi, to which several passages translated by the editor have been added. Chapter 18 is essentially as translated in Ehud ben Ezer's *Unease in Zion*. Chapter 19 is from the English protocol of the session. Chapters 8, 11, 26, and 27 are from Raphael Levy's translation of *Judaism*. All translations were to some extent revised by the editor.

The sources of the chapters in this book are as follows:

Chapter 1. *Judaism,* 13–36. An expanded version of a lecture originally delivered at a seminar on Jewish Studies, Haifa (1953). Hebrew: "Mitzvoth Ma'asiyoth" (Prescriptions of Practice).

Chapter 2. *Judaism,* 385–390. Originally published in *Deoth,* 11 (1960) 35–37.

Chapter 3. *Faith,* 11–19. Originally published in *Ways to Faith in Judaism: Proceedings of the Annual Conference on Jewish Thought,* 23 (1981), 41–51. Published by the Ministry of Education and Culture, Department of Torah-Culture.

Chapter 4. *Faith,* 20–24. From a series of radio broadcasts on the daily Bible chapter.

Chapter 5. *Faith,* 51–54. Originally published in *Turei Yeshurun,* 33 (September 1973), 7–10. Published by Yeshurun Synagogue, Jerusalem.

Chapter 6. *Faith,* 25–45. Originally published serially in *Ha'aretz* (January

1977) in rebuttal of a lengthy criticism. Abridged by omission of passages which were relevant only at the time this debate was conducted.

Chapter 7. *Faith*, 112–119. Originally in *Petahim* C (33) (June 1975), 21–24.

Chapter 8. *Judaism*, 314–321. Originally in *The Education and Vocation of Man: Proceedings of the Annual Conference on Jewish Thought*, 11 (Jerusalem: 1966), 25–27. Published by the Ministry of Education and Culture, Department of Torah Culture.

Chapter 9. *Faith*, 156–164. From *Society and History: Proceedings of the Annual Conference on Jewish Thought* (Jerusalem: 1980), 685–690. Published by the Ministry of Education and Culture, Department of Torah Culture.

Chapter 10. *Faith*, 120–133. From a symposium, "Between Israel and the Nations," Jerusalem, 1977.

Chapter 11. *Judaism*, 415–418. Originally in *Turei Yeshurun* 19 (1971), 5–6. Published by Yeshurun Synagogue. Jerusalem. Hebrew: "Al Geulah ve'al Athalta De'geulah."

Chapter 12. *Faith*, 71–74. From a symposium on "The Status of Women in Judiasm" held in Jerusalem, March 1980.

Chapter 13. *Judaism*, 376–384. Lecture at the Annual Conference on Jewish Philosophy entitled "Revelation, Faith and Reason," held at Bar-Ilan University, 1973. An English translation of the first part of the lecture appeared in *Immanuel*, A Bulletin of Religious Thought and Research in Israel, 8 (Spring 1978), 106–111.

Chapter 14. *Judaism*, 98–108. *Haoved Hadati*, 4 (1947).

Chapter 15. *Judaism*, 121–145. "Hadath Bamedinah Ve'hamedinah Badath" (Religion in the State and the State in Religion). Originally published in *Beterem*, 148/149 (1952). The essay in its present form is based upon an abridged English translation which appeared in the journal *Judaism*, 2: (July 1953), 214–254.

Chapter 16. *Judaism*, 155–164. Originally published in *Beterem*, 259/260 (1959).

Chapter 17. *Judaism*, 229–234. Originally published in *Beterem*. 189/191 (1953/1954).

Chapter 18. *Judaism*, 247–259. An interview by Ehud ben Ezer. Originally in *Moznayim*, 22:263 (1966), 237–245. Published by the Association of Hebrew Writers. An updated English translation appeared in Ehud ben Ezer, *Unease in Zion*, 177–200. Published by New York Times Book, 1974. Passages dealing with matters which have been dealt with at length elsewhere in these papers or refer to events specific to the time have been omitted.

Chapter 19. *Judaism*, 291–302. From discussion of "Judaism and Jewishness" at The Sixth Annual American-Israeli Dialogue, 1968: "The Future of a Relationship." Originally published in English in *Congress*, 36:3 (1969), published by the American Jewish Congress.

Chapter 20. *Faith*, 134–139. From discussion at a meeting of "The Movement for Torah-Judaism". First published in *Mahalakhim*, 8–9 (May 1975).

Chapter 21. *Judaism*, 418–422. Originally published in *Dorban*, a student publication at the Hebrew University in Jerusalem; thereafter in various newspapers in 1968, 1969, 1970.

Chapter 22. *Faith,* 196–198. Published in *Ha'aretz* of Nov. 3, 1976.

Chapter 23. *Faith,* 214–217.

Chapter 24. *New Outlook,* 19:6 (September–October 1976).

Chapter 25. *Politika,* 20 (April 1986), 16–19.

Chapter 26. *Judaism,* 322–325. First published in *Deoth,* 28 (1964), 103–106.

Chapter 27. *Judaism,* 327–333. First published in *Ha'aretz* (1968).

Index

on Sabbath, 166, 180; justification of, 187–188, 211, 227–228. *See also* Peace
Wars: Six Day War (1967), xxix, 203, 211, 219, 223, 224, 227–228, 232, 233, 243; Yom Kippur War (1973), 233; War of Liberation (1948), 235, 243
Weber, Max, xiv
Weizmann, Chaim (or Hayyim), 117, 195
Welfare: of the body, 68; of the mind, 68
Welfare state, xxvi
West Bank, xii–xiii, xxix–xxxi, 238–239. *See also* Israel, occupation of territories conquered in 1967
Wigner, Eugene P., 62, 63, 69
Withdrawal from occupied territories. *See* Israel, occupation of territories conquered in 1967
Women, status in Judaism, 128–131, 170
Women's *Beth Midrash*, 130

Yahieh Qafah (rabbi), 112
Yarov'am, 175, 210, 216, 217
Yetzer: Yetzer Hara (the evil inclination), 14, 25, 267n19; *Yetzer Hatov* (the good inclination), 14, 267n19
Yishuv, xxiii, xxv–xxvi, 146, 186
Yoke of the Kingdom of Heaven, 74, 131
Yom Kippur, 15, 28, 31, 35, 43, 48, 91–92, 137–138. *See also* Day of Atonement
Yom Kippur War (1973), 233

Zakai, Rabbi Yohanan ben, 19, 33, 158
Zionism: and halakhic Judaism, x–xi; military activity of, x–xi; secularism of, xii, xx, 76–77, 115–118; rabbis' opposition to, xxiv; political aspirations of, 116–117, 118, 214; definition of, 191; and Arab-Jewish relations, 195–198
Zionist Organization, xxv, xxvi